Janelle Palmer
1457 Edgewood Circle
Jacksonville, Florida
32205

3871987

13 50

AD01

THE COMPLETE BOOK OF DOLL COLLECTING

The Complete Book of DOLL COLLECTING

By HELEN YOUNG

G. P. PUTNAM'S SONS NEW YORK

Library of Congress Catalog

Card Number: 67–21216

PRINTED IN THE UNITED STATES OF AMERICA

FOR MY CHILDREN
BARBARA, JANET, MALCOLM

ACKNOWLEDGMENTS

The author wishes to express her gratitude to the following individuals and organizations for their generous assistance and for the photographs they have contributed for use in this book, and to Ruby Short McKim of Kimport Dolls for her careful research of source material:

Covina Public Library
Dennison Mfg. Co.
Miriam Denton
Mrs. Hugh Dyer
Mrs. William Foster
Franks Antiques and Doll Museum
Mrs. Luella Hart
Mrs. Elizabeth Holloway
Mrs. Bernice Large
Dr. Byron P. Merrick
Movieland Wax Museum
National Institute of Doll Artists
The Newark Museum
San Diego City School District
Santons de Provence
Mrs. Mable Scheele
Lori Silverwood
Richard Simonds
State Historical Society of Wisconsin
Traphagen School of Fashion
Marie and Grace Turner
Mrs. Walter Wagner
Robert L. Walker, Jr.

CONTENTS

THE COMPLETE BOOK OF DOLL COLLECTING

1

DOLL COLLECTING

WITH DOLLS, as with other pleasures of this world, one thing often leads to another. You are a child. Someone gives you a doll. You play with it for a time. Growing older, you put the doll away, yet you keep it. One day you find it again, and you look at it a second time because you have heard that some people collect dolls. What a good idea! You decide to do it yourself. And that's it—you're a doll collector.

Little girls treasure dolls for their own secret reasons, which are sometimes hard for them to express. Older girls like dolls for the same reasons, but in addition they have found that dolls are fun to dress and to share with their friends. As the years move on, older girls become young women "too old for dolls," but they never quite forget the past. Yesterday's girls are today's mothers and grandmothers and when they discover that no one is really too old for dolls, they merely pin on a new label and call themselves doll collectors.

But it is a mistake to think of a doll collector only as "she," because men share the hobby of doll collecting. They may do so in the name of research in connection with history, costume design, stage production, war games (for toy soldiers are of course dolls), art, ethnology, archeology, anthropology, geography, or for other serious reasons, but they are nonetheless doll collectors. One of the most distinguished doll collectors in the world is Samuel F. Pryor, vice president and assistant to the president of Pan American Airways, whose collection numbers more than 2500 dolls. So we must not assume that dolls are exclusively for small girls, or even that the hobby of collecting them is an exclusively feminine one.

Although dolls have been made and enjoyed since ancient times, doll collecting as a popular hobby is rather new, for it was not until the 1930's that adult doll collectors began to be numerous.

Now, doll collecting is high on the list of popular hobbies, along with the collecting of stamps, coins, and glassware. The result is that the prices asked and paid for old dolls are fantastically higher than they were 25 years ago. Although scarcity and quality have something to do with price, demand is of course the deciding factor. For example, a Shirley Temple doll which sold originally for four or five dollars in the '30's is now priced at several times that amount. And some of the Parians, which originally sold for a few cents, now command prices in three figures. The true doll collector remembers, however, that the mere monetary value of a doll is not the sole reason for owning it.

It has been said that a doll which is worthy of collecting must tell a story, and that every doll in a collection should have a definite reason for being there. A collection is not the same thing as an accumulation, and therefore should never be judged by size alone. I once saw a large collection of life-size bisque dolls, all about the same age, dressed in almost identical clothes. Propped against the wall, sitting on the floor, in chairs or on tables, they filled a room. It was a dreary sight. The boring story the collection told was simply that this collector owned a great many bisque dolls, and that she had entirely missed the point of doll collecting. If the dolls had varied in size, in material, in dress, or in age, they could have been called a collection. As it was, they were just an accumulation.

Dolls are made in many sizes, but most collectors choose those measuring from six to ten inches in height because they fit nicely on display shelves. Extremely large dolls are awkward to store, so if there is a choice, select the smaller rather than the larger ones.

There are many collections consisting entirely of foreign dolls—favorite homecoming gifts of travelers—and these popular dolls will increase in interest as time goes on and the world's people dress more and more alike. Other collections can be based on costumes of specific times or cultures. Good examples of these are the extremely popular categories of English queens, and wives of the Presidents from Martha Washington to the incumbent, dressed in replicas of their inauguration gowns. These have been repeated in various materials, sizes, and qualities by dozens of manufacturers and doll artists; and they have been used for the dressing of dolls by hundreds of collectors because of the appeal of their historical interest and often colorful costumes. Groups of dolls dressed in authentic period costumes, from the style of ancient Egypt through medieval times to the Victorian era and dolls dressed to represent famous characters of history or fiction, also make worthwhile collection.

Some of the most educational doll collections consist entirely of dolls made of various materials—one each, perhaps—of wood, wax, paper, china, cloth, papier-mâché, metal, plaster, celluloid, composition or rubber.

The best sources for finding dolls are other collectors, friends, relatives, antique dealers, doll hospitals—which not only repair dolls but also sell them—and, if you are very lucky, thrift and salvage shops.

These shops, however, are no longer the rich sources of rare dolls they were in the days before doll collecting became such a popular hobby. Now, in large cities, trained experts sort the treasures from the trash whenever donations come in, and you can seldom find anything but fourth-rate plastic dolls to choose from. Even so, it always pays to look, for someone may have failed to realize that a wigless doll in a dirty dress is a genuine Schoenhut wooden in original clothes, and that the price tag of fifty cents should be astronomically higher. A gentle bath for the doll, a rinse for its clothes, a new wig, and perhaps a few minor repairs will give you a doll worthy of any collection.

When you happen to be in a salvage shop, watch for old materials—fine silks in tiny patterns, old calico, seed pearls, buttons, jet trimming, lace, soutache braid in loops and swirls, brocades, satins, taffetas, batistes, velvets—anything that can be used to dress dolls in authentic garb. It seems a sacrilege to dress a lovely old doll in orlon or drip-dry gingham. She should not only wear the fashions of her time, but the fabrics as well.

Although some people feel that their collections should include only rare antique dolls, beautiful dolls are being made today that not only rank with the best dolls of the past, but often surpass them. The National Institute of American Doll Artists, whose members are skilled craftsmen and portrait painters, make exquisite dolls which are available to doll collectors. The dolls produced by these artists are described in detail in Chapter 16.

Charming commercial dolls are also being made today, and certainly the best of them merit a place in modern collections. These plastic and composition dolls will become the treasures of the future, not only because of their historic interest, but also for their beauty. It is wise for collectors to look over the new dolls manufactured each year, and to add some of the best to their own collections.

Potential doll collectors often ask how they may identify dolls they own. My suggestion is to visit a local library and talk to the librarian. Libraries not only have books about dolls, but many of them own collections of rare dolls presented to them by patrons, frequently thoroughly classified as to age, origin, etc. Librarians will also often pass along the names of other doll collectors in the community when they know you are interested.

Other good sources of information are doll hospitals. They are clearing houses for all kinds of doll information. You can often learn from them the name of the nearest doll club, and waste no time in getting in touch with its president. It may astonish you to discover what a vast number of doll clubs there are, for they are modest about publicizing themselves, but once you are identified as a serious collector, you will find that club members are friendly people who enjoy sharing their enthusiasms with you.

In addition to the dozens of independent doll clubs throughout the country there are a great many others which belong to the United Federation of Doll Clubs, Inc. This organization of more than 100 individual clubs consists of fifteen regional divisions, each of which has its own director. The federation also lists many regional and international members-at-large. It is impossible to give here the names and addresses of member clubs, but any doll hospital or established collector should be able to help you locate the one nearest you.

It has long been the goal of the United Federation of Doll Clubs to encourage the establishment of children's museums in every key city in the United States. Several federal and many civic organizations support this movement, and the United Nations has set up a Children's Museum Committee with representatives from several other countries, as a part of the International Council of Museums under UNESCO.

One of the best known of these children's museums is in Brooklyn, New York—the Brooklyn Children's Museum, the oldest of its kind in the United States. It was established near the beginning of this century and continues to expand and to cooperate with school systems through its exhibits and classes. Some of the finest dolls in the world are on display there.

In addition to the many children's museums, of course, are the municipal and privately endowed institutions, large and small, in both the United States and Europe, which recognize the social and educational significance of dolls. Here again, it is impossible to list the names of all museums exhibiting dolls, for there are too many. In fact, it might be easier to name those which do *not*, for there are certainly very few. Many museums also have color slide collections to be used in conjunction with their exhibits, some of which may be loaned to schools and clubs.

Historical societies scattered throughout the country often have splendid doll collections. There are perhaps more of them in New England, the Atlantic States, and the Middle West, but the Far West and South are also becoming increasingly aware of the importance of historical dolls.

But as all collectors discover, no single person can tell all there is to know about dolls. The best any one of us can do is to light candles in a few dark corners. Perhaps that is one of the delights of being a collector, for discoveries never end, and mysteries solved are followed by new mysteries. No doll collector is ever bored, once she—or he—has started a collection and become aware of the endless possibilities of adding to it.

2

ANCESTORS OF TODAY'S DOLLS

As the popularity of doll collecting increases and the availability of older dolls correspondingly diminishes, some collectors and dealers have begun to call all pre-World War I dolls *antique,* and to price them accordingly. More sensibly, it has been suggested that such dolls as the ancient Etruscan, Roman or Egyptian specimens be referred to as belonging to *antiquity*; that dolls of the seventeenth, eighteenth, and the early part of the nineteenth centuries be called *antique*; and that those made between the years 1810 and 1880 should simply be called *old.* After 1880, the actual date of the doll's manufacture should be used to indicate its age.

It would be unlikely for the average doll collector to have the chance to add any true antiquities to his own collection, but the worldwide story of ancient dolls can be traced quite easily through museum specimens. The ancestors of today's dolls, figurines made of clay, wood, and other materials, are uncovered wherever archeologists explore ancient sites. It is sometimes hard to decide, however, whether these are really dolls (in the sense of playthings) or images of magic and religious significance. Egyptian tomb figures, for example, were not playthings but small effigies of agricultural workers, boatmen, servants, or soldiers. They were buried with the dead and designed to provide for them and protect them in the afterworld. Many miniature soldiers have been found in the burial mounds and tombs of Egypt, and it has even been suggested that the first "doll" in the world may have been a soldier.

Small bronze Phoenician figures wearing helmets and carrying shields and swords have been unearthed in Sardinia and Italy. Whatever their purpose may have been—talisman or not—these ancient figures prove that the art of metal casting was well advanced some time before the Christian era. (Later castings of Roman legionnaires, cavalrymen, and footmen were also found in Sardinia and Italy and other parts of Europe.)

One of the oldest surviving dolls in western Europe is a jointed 10-inch clay doll from ancient Etruria, a power older than Rome, in central Italy. This Etruscan doll, now in the Newark Museum (Newark, New Jersey), dates from 700–600 B.C. It is crudely modeled, but has the charm of honest workmanship. The parts of the body are fastened together with metal pins, a method similar to the one used much later in assembling wooden dolls. The eyes and mouth are faintly marked, but the nose is sharp and prominent. Terra-cotta dolls, similar to this one, and apparently made about the same time, have been found in Greece. Their original purpose is not known.

In any event, we know that the making of talisman or "magic" dolls did not cease in ancient times. Voodoo dolls, spite dolls, or whatever they may be called, appear in the folk-

One of the Egyptian *ushabti,* made of coarse gray pottery and still retaining remnants of its brilliant blue faience glaze, was probably made between 3000 and 2500 B.C. These tomb figures were not toys, but represented servants who were to help their masters after death.

Left: An Etruscan jointed doll of terra-cotta (700–600 B.C.). *Right:* A terra-cotta Astarte of Babylonia (about 2000 B.C.).

Courtesy of Newark Museum.

lore of many countries. They are the evil talismans of some dark age when the effigy of an enemy was fashioned of rags or wax and stuck with pins, (the Pueblo Indians of the Southwest used—and still use—cactus spines) or cursed with wizard jargon. Almost everyone has heard about them, but no one is willing to admit that he owns one. Spite dolls have had a fairly recent modern revival in the commercial "spoof" voodoo sets sold in the '50's in New York City and elsewhere. They were accompanied by amusing "props" and instructions.

Other talisman dolls have had more pleasant uses. In Japan, clay dolls three to six inches tall were used not only as ornaments, but also as charms against sickness or misfortune. Children who played with these lucky dolls were supposed to grow up to be healthy and wealthy.

From South Africa come pairs of fertility dolls, male and female, called "Ndebele" by tribes in Transvaal. These symbolic figures have significance as fetishes for insuring fertility and the production of crops. Many of these dolls, from three to four inches high, were carved of wood, while later ones were made of wire and beadwork. Different tribes, of course, have figures of different sizes and materials.

Native hand-carved wooden dolls coming from Rhodesia also reflect primitive beliefs. Those made with movable arms attached with crude iron nails suggest a heritage from an age-old past, because they have arms and legs, but no hands or feet. A tribal taboo forbids the indication of either, so the limbs end abruptly, and the man holding a spear does so by means of a slit cut near the end of the arm.

American Indians have long used dolls as talismans. One practice of the Ojibwa Indians of Lake Superior recalls the ancient Egyptian belief that a dead child is too young to look after itself in the next world. They, therefore, made a doll of feathers to be buried with the child as a companion. In British Columbia one tribe of Indians also used dolls in funeral ceremonies. When burial was near water, a spirit canoe carrying a doll figure of the dead man was set afloat to carry his spirit. But although other American Indians made dolls for their children, for beauty and ingenuity there is nothing to compare with the kachinas of the Pueblo Indians.

Kachinas are not toys as non-Indians think of them, but likenesses of a whole assemblage of supernatural beings who intercede between man and his gods.

The Pueblo Indians of North America live in villages in northern Arizona and New Mexico. They are descendants of the prehistoric tribes that settled in the region 1500 years ago and whose original homeland is unknown. They are peaceful, conservative, creative people who have preserved their ancient ways in spite of the white man's efforts to impose his own. The most famous of the kachina ceremonies are performed by the Pueblo tribes known as the Hopis and the Zunis.

The Hopis live on three mesas in northern Arizona, overlooking the Painted Desert. On the horizon are the San Francisco Peaks where the kachinas are believed to live. Every year they come down to the villages to dance, sing, bring gifts to the children, and most important of all, to bring rain. According to tribal legends, when the ancestors of the Pueblos emerged from the underworld ages ago, kachinas helped them to learn that all life is good, and that every man is entitled to believe what is best for him, and to act as he chooses provided he lives in peace with his neighbors. The kachinas are never worshiped, but the Hopis look on them as friends with human qualities. Most of them are benevolent, but a few are feared. These are the ogres and whippers who punish offenders of ceremonial or social laws.

The Hopi calendar is divided at mid-July into two parts. Five major kachina ceremonies are held during the first period, but none are celebrated in the second. Each ceremony lasts for nine days. Most of them are held in secret, often in the kivas or underground ceremonial rooms of the village. When the weather grows warmer, the dances may be held outdoors in the plazas. Dancers dress as kachinas, and to the Hopis they actually become the kachinas, losing their own identity until they remove the masks, costumes, and body paint applied in traditional designs. These beautiful masked dances, based on ancient legends, are said to be the finest in the western hemisphere. Only men may participate. If the kachina is supposed to be a woman, she is always interpreted by a man.

A tribal priest of the village relays the prayers of the people

Brilliantly colored kachina dolls are still made by the Hopi Indians in the same tradition as this ancient kachina made by their ancestors.

This English lead soldier, the conventional 2⅛-inch height, is dressed in horizon blue trousers, black cap and tunic, and carries a sword. Only the right arm is jointed.

to the kachinas in the mountains by way of the kachina dancers —a role similar to the intercession of saints in the Christian religion.

Hopi children are not supposed to recognize their fathers and grandfathers in the dances, any more than our children are supposed to recognize the wearer of a Santa Claus costume. During the ceremony the kachinas give each child kachina dolls, miniature bows and arrows, candy, and fruit. The dolls, made by the men, are small replicas of the kachina dancers, given to the child as a part of the child's religious training so that he may learn to identify the more than 200 different kachinas. The dolls are taken home and hung on the walls or from the rafters.

The dolls are hand carved from single pieces of cottonwood root; the ears, nose, horns, and other features are then attached. After being given an undercoat of white paint, they are decorated with the same colors as those used in the body paint of the real dancers—blue, red, green, yellow, black, and brown. After the paint dries, the doll maker adds realistic touches of shells, beads, feathers, fur, or leather.

The kachinas are of special interest to us because they are native to the New World. The cultural ancestors of most American dolls, however, are those of western Europe, beginning with the toy soldier.

Although no toy soldiers are known to have survived from the Middle Ages, old wood cuts show young people playing with them and museums have records verifying their existence.

It was during the reign of Frederick the Great of Germany that a tinfounder in Nuremburg became the first person to mass produce tin soldiers. His models were engraved on both sides and stood on flat bases, like the so-called "flats" of today. Some were painted and others left unpainted. They varied in height from 2 to 4 inches. He later produced rounded figures by casting metal in forms cut in slate.

Soon, all the countries of Europe demanded toy soldiers dressed in the uniforms of their armies. As the furor for them grew, many other manufacturers began competing for business. There was such confusion over the lack of a standard size that at last all firms agreed to a uniform scale that is still maintained—30 to 32 millimeters. One reason there are still so many antique tin soldiers available is that so many thousands of them were cast. They were used, just as they are today, in military games and in actual training service, where hundreds were needed in a single operation. "Flats" are the most popular for this purpose as they can be stored compactly.

Although wooden soldiers were made in Thuringia, higher production costs made them more expensive and they never became as popular as the metal models.

Perhaps the best known literary reference to toy soldiers is in the poet Eugene Field's "Little Boy Blue," which speaks of the "little toy soldier, red with rust" whose "musket moulds in his hands," left by Field's little son when "he kissed them and put them there," long years before. Field's *Poems Of Childhood* are full of references to dolls and toys, for he was an ardent doll collector as well as a poet.

In his informative account, *Making and Collecting Military Miniatures,* Bob Bard says:

> "Ladies of the court, the fair sex, enjoy a definite place in military miniature collections—princesses, queens, and mistresses."

He reminds us that

> "there have been many dioramas made of victory marches, slave markets and battles in which women shared the scene."

We can turn the tables and say that ladies have always been bewitched by handsome uniforms. Indeed, every man is handsome when he wears one, so a man in uniform surely belongs in every doll collection.

During the Middle Ages sculpture was used to adorn the cathedrals and also to help teach Bible stories to worshipers who could not read or write. Doll-like figures were carved in the form of saints and cherubs to be used as religious symbols, rather than as toys. Figures of the Christ Child were especially beloved. One legend exemplifying this comes from Rome, to which city a Franciscan monk sent a Bambino he had carved from an olive tree grown in the Garden of Gethsemane. On the voyage a storm came up and the carving was thought to be lost, but it was in a chest which floated and was saved. It reached Rome in time for the Christmas season, where the miracle of recovery qualified the carving for a position of central importance in the nativity scene assembled there each year. To this day, special services are held on the afternoon of Christmas day to honor the Bambino, and throngs of children not only participate, but send gifts and messages from around the world.

Nativity scenes were made during the seventeenth and eighteenth centuries in all Catholic countries, particularly Italy, Germany, and France, and set up year after year in churches and homes. Many of these early nativity figures are still in use, new ones are being made, and the custom of displaying them has grown until now many non-Catholics also display nativity scenes.

People speaking different languages all use their own dis-

Crèches like this have been made in France for hundreds of years.

Courtesy, Santons de Provence.

Santon figures like these peasant dolls are still being made in France, as they have for centuries, to place in a crèche.

Courtesy, Santons de Province.

tinctive names for these groups of figures. In Italy they are called *presepio,* in Germany the name *krippen* is given to the nativity scene, while of course the French name of *crèche* is used in that country. Spain's title is *nacimiento.* The Pennsylvania Germans, who came to the United States from central Europe, have given still another name to their nativity groups and call the scene a *putz.* English-speaking people tend to accept the French *crèche* as the name they prefer, although our simple translation of *nativity scene* is becoming more and more widespread.

Presepio making in Italy reached its peak in the eighteenth century, with figures made of both wood and terra-cotta. Needlewomen in Germany and Switzerland, at home and in convents, designed exquisite costumes of fine and costly fabrics. Some of the figures had heads made of poured wax with inset glass eyes; and bodies made of wire and stuffed cloth. Hands were often of carved wood, and a common feature of *crèche* figures is their expressive hands.

Santons, or "little saints," are much-loved nativity figures first created several hundred years ago in Provence, in the south of France. There, in the city of Marseilles, a *santon* fair has been held every December since 1804, and people come from far away to buy new figures for their *crèches.* The families of the province make the same figures today that their ancestors did, of the same terra-cotta, modeled in a primitive, vigorous style and painted in rich colors. Not only are the members of the Holy Family, the shepherds, the wise men and the animals of the stable used in the crèche, but villagers, craftsmen and members of noble families are all represented by *santons.* The figures are almost always small (although some are made in an 8-inch size), and are dressed in real antique fabrics. The "flea" sizes, as they are called in Provence, are 7/8 of an inch high, 1 3/4 inches, 2 1/2 inches, and 3 1/2 inches.

In Mexico, the nativity figures are placed on a small table, with the Infant, the holy pilgrims and the Magi in a setting more reminiscent of a Mexican village than of the Holy Land. The characters are often dressed in serapes and sombreros instead of the more traditional garb of European countries. Many of them are made of painted unglazed clay.

The nativity scene in Mexico is generally a part of the annual "Las Posadas," a dramatization of the search of Mary and Joseph for lodging. The posadas begin on the evening of December 16 and end on Christmas Eve. They are never one-family observances, but include all families in the village. As soon as it is dark a procession starts, with each person carrying a lighted candle. They knock at the door of a house and ask for lodging. The man of the house refuses them. This is repeated along the way until someone finally is convinced of their importance and allows them to enter the house, where they kneel before the manger scene to pray and sing. Refreshments are served and there is dancing. Then comes the breaking of a *piñata* or clay pot gaily decorated with colored paper and hung by a rope just over the heads of the guests. Each person is blindfolded and takes turns trying to hit the *piñata* with a stick. Someone is finally permitted to break the clay jar, and a shower of candies and small gifts scatters over the floor. Everyone scrambles for a share, laughing and shouting with excitement.

Puppets also belong to the doll family. Like other members of that family, they have been found in many parts of the world. Puppets were known in ancient Egypt. They sometimes replaced human beings on the stage of Athens. They are said to have been popular in China before 1000 B.C. and have long been known in Japan, India, Java, and Bali, being used as actors in plays as well as religious ceremonies.

The tradition of the Wajang Goleks, or shadow puppets of Java, goes back 900 years. Javanese shadow plays have a ritual aspect, and spectators who watch them are reliving stories of the Hindu race, the earliest of which are derived from the Sanskrit *Ramayana* and *Mahabharata*. The puppets, which are carried on a stationary central stick or pole, are manipulated by two movable poles, one attached to each of the fantastically long jointed arms. Kimport Dolls' catalogs list three-dimensional nine-inch Javanese shadow puppets with masklike wooden heads. (Also available in America are antique flat shadow puppets made, usually, of buffalo hide, elaborately carved and decorated, and held and manipulated by the same arrangement of three light wooden poles.)

The ancestors of our present-day American puppets are of course those of western Europe, puppets designed to appear in plays of domestic comedy, sharp comment on current affairs, or even political satire. In France puppets became the mouthpieces of malcontents and political satirists. During the French Revolution puppet acts quite often showed victims being beheaded—an entertainment purveyed almost in the shadow of the guillotine. In Germany puppets created so much political unrest that on several occasions performances were banned. England's Punch and Judy shows are traditional favorites, and poets from Chaucer to Byron have written about puppets.

The story of puppets and marionettes began in the childhood of mankind. But though puppets may be considered ancestors of some of today's dolls, the world of puppetry itself has survived the centuries, and its unique appeal shows no signs of diminishing.

3

PAPER DOLLS

About 1634, Netherlanders went slightly mad over tulips, and about a hundred years later, Frenchmen went equally wild over paper dolls. Pantins, they called them, for the name of the suburb of Paris where they originated. These jointed, often life-size figures were sometimes made of wood; but more often they were paper or cardboard and were always made by hand. Ordinarily, the head and torso of the figure were in one piece; arms were in one or two pieces, with a joint at the elbow; legs were made in two sections, jointed at the knee. The different body parts were fastened together with a kind of metal staple so that they were movable. In order to make the figure easy to manipulate, small holes were pierced in the tops of the upper arm sections and a length of string was run through the holes and across the body; another pair of holes, made in the tops of the upper leg sections, accommodated another length of string; then a string was tied to the middle of the one that ran from one arm to the other, and was brought down and tied to the center of the string that connected the legs. It was left to hang a few inches below the feet. By pulling this hanging string, the pantin could be made to perform all kinds of antics.

Artists created pantins to represent shepherds, shepherdesses, harlequins, ballerinas, Scaramouch, and a galaxy of fanciful characters. It was the fashion for members of the French court to carry their pantins to balls and parties, on the street, and wherever they went. The common people did the same. The craze lasted from about 1745 to 1756, and ended with an edict

Modern paper pantins or Jumping Jacks are printed in England. The cut-out pieces are pierced with a needle through the dots shown, and strung together as pictured in the diagram.

A pair of 11-inch Dennison paper dolls of the 1890's. The heads were embossed colored pictures and the dresses were made of crepe paper.

Photo by Korday Studio.

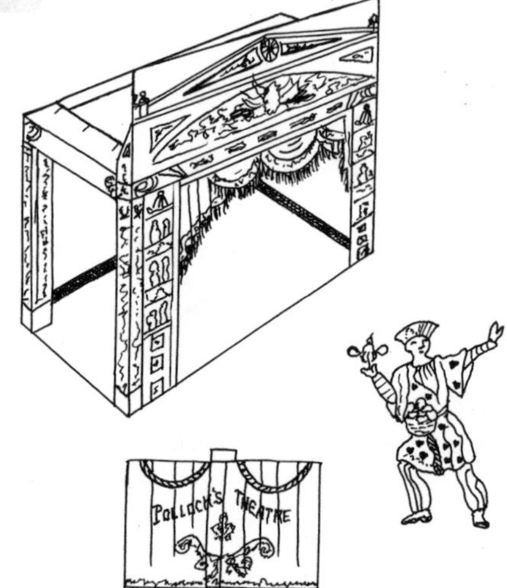

A paper doll theater, as printed in London and designed by P. Adams Turner from original engravings by J. K. Greene. It measures about 11 by 8 by 11 inches. Slots in the extensions at the top hold the curtain and scenery in place. Paper strips are attached to the feet of the actors so they can be manipulated from the side of the stage.
The character shown is Aladdin, one of the fourteen actors in the cast of the play "Aladdin," or *The Wonderful Lamp*, as performed at the Theatre Royal, Covent Garden, in 1826.

from the Paris police prohibiting the display of pantins on the grounds that it was dangerous for prospective mothers to see the twisted limbs of the pantins, for fear of their children being disfigured.

In Germany this same kind of figure was called a Hampelmann; and in Thuringia, world center of toymaking, it was a Zappelmann. In England and America the name was Jumping Jack, and still is; even today people like them because they are action toys. Their primary importance is that they gave a boost to the popularity of paper dolls.

Paper soldiers were another important kind of paper doll. The province of Alsace first manufactured printed paper soldiers, and they became so popular that for years all cardboard toy soldiers have been called "Alsatian soldiers." The typical Alsatian soldier is about 5-inches tall, and is made to be slipped into a wooden base to hold it upright. Some of the older ones were printed in black and white, while others were hand-colored. Paper soldiers in a variety of sizes were printed in America, and were often used as premium inserts in packages of candy or cigarettes. A collection of paper dolls should certainly include a few men in uniform—from this country or another.

It was in 1790 that paper dolls as we know them were first sold in Germany, France, and England. One of the earliest sets of that period included an 8-inch boy and girl on the same sheet of paper with several changes of costume, including hats for each one. Another set featured separate wigs to cut out and slip over the dolls' heads.

Early in the history of paper dolls, sheets of them were bound together in sets, resembling our paper doll books. Because they had to be tinted by hand, the price was high, and it was not until about 1880 than an economical process for printing in color was introduced. In speaking of early paper dolls, therefore, hand coloring must be taken for granted.

About 1806 both French and English story books for children were made with separate pockets to hold paper dolls illustrating the story. Many of them were made in the form of headless, dressed figures. The doll heads were printed with a pointed tab that fitted into the back of each outfit.

Paper dolls soon appeared in fashion magazines, and in 1859, *Godey's Ladies Book* printed a series of six boys and six girls with complete costumes and changes. Other magazines had beautiful fashion plates, and while they were not always intended to be dolls, they could certainly have been used that way, and undoubtedly were.

Among dozens of paper dolls printed commercially after 1860, those created by Rafael Tuck and Company, Ltd., London, New York, and Paris were particularly beautiful. They were in full color, and one series is called, "Six Famous Queens and Martha Washington." "Merry Marion" which could possibly be one of a Robin Hood series was patented in 1894. This later Tuck doll was quite different from the earlier specimens, for the head was made separately, then fastened on the neck, so the costume might be slipped under the doll's chin. This was an effective way to supplement the shoulder tabs which were made to hold the costume in place on the dolls. It is reported that all plates for the Tuck dolls were destroyed by the German blitz, and are therefore no longer available for reprint. A collector who numbers Rafael Tuck dolls among her treasures should appreciate them doubly, for they were among the finest paper dolls ever made.

Far too many advertising dolls were made, year after year, to attempt to list them all. Fortunately, most of them are plainly marked with the name of the company that offered them, and many also show the date. Another boon to doll collectors is the fact that because so many premium dolls were printed, there are likely to be more survivors than of any other kind. Some of the advertising dolls were those made for the Duplex Corset Company, Woolson Spice Company, McLaughlin's Coffee, Pope Mfg. Company (makers of Columbia Bicycles), Barbour's Irish Flax Thread, Diamond Dyes, Clark's O.N.T. Spool Cotton, Worth of Paris, Bull Durham, Cordova Coffee, Enameline Stove Polish (dolls representing flowers—water lily, sweet peas, poppies), Lion Brand Coffee, Singer Sewing Machine Company (men and women of many nations using Singer Sewing machines), Wheeler and Wilson Sewing Machine Company, Spalding Sporting Goods, Worcester Salt, Arbuckle's Coffee, William A. Rogers, Ltd. (silversmiths), and a great many others. Since paper dolls were given away to attract buyers of highly competitive merchandise, it is easy to form a picture from them of various facets of American life during the latter part of the Victorian era. The fact that these dolls were giveaways does not mean that they now have no value. In fact, the present value of many old advertising dolls now exceeds the original price of the products they were made to advertise.

Another type of paper doll made during the same period was printed in Germany about 1880. These brilliantly colored, lithographed and embossed paper dolls, which were sometimes 14-inches tall, had movable arms and legs, attached to the bodies with tiny metal fasteners. The dolls were modestly clad in bloomers, corset, and slippers, and with the exception of a wisp of feathers or bits of lace or satin, were not sold with complete costumes. They were printed on high-gloss cardboard in half a dozen styles. Photographic likenesses of actresses such as Nellie Melba, Emma Eames, and Lily Langtry, were used as heads although their names were not printed on the dolls.

About 1889 the Dennison Paper Company introduced sets of American-made paper dolls of men, women, and children. Enough Dennison crepe paper was included in each set to dress the doll. Unfortunately, copies of Dennison's 19th-century catalogs are no longer to be found outside museums and rare collections, but we have been given permission by the company to quote from their 1892 and 1894 issues.

> No. 9 Size 11 inches Price $1.25
>
> A doll 11-inches high has arms and legs cut in one with the body. The stockings are made of black tissue neatly gummed on the cardboard. The shoes are of bronze paper, with gilt lines to mark the foxing and gilt dots for buttons. An easel rest is gummed to the back of the body, near the shoulders.
>
> The head is an embossed picture; but before it is attached to the body, a fine plaiting of white tissue is gummed to the other side and finely plaited and shirred through the middle. The pink is then gummed to position, and the white placed inside of it and secured. After both are entirely dry, the ruching is carefully pulled into shape as a rose plaiting. Long loops of

pink and white paper ribbons are placed on each end of the waistline.

Suggestions on the instruction sheets that accompanied the doll were:

> . . . the dress forms (foundations) for a doll this size should be cut of stiff white paper, and be 7 inches long, 5 inches wide at the bottom, and 2¼ inches at the waistline, which is a little less than 2 inches from the top. Do not forget to leave small tabs on each form, by which to hang the dress from the doll's shoulders. Each form should be covered with plain paper of the shade of which it is intended to make the dress.
>
> A dainty house dress is of pale blue. Cut a plain piece of tissue 8 by 7½ inches, and fold and gum a narrow hem and three tiny tucks near one end. Under the hem gum a fine plaiting which has been made of paper one inch wide. Shir this dress along the top, and also along a line 2½ inches from the top, and gum these shirrings to the top edge and the waistline respectively of the dress form which has been previously prepared, forming a waist of the blouse or "Fedora" style. Before the dress is attached to the form, however, the latter should have fine plaitings of white gummed in the arm-scyes to answer for sleeves. At each side of the waist, a bunch of blue and white ribbons—strips of tissue ½-inch wide—should be placed.

The Dennison instruction manual refers to the material used to dress the dolls as "tissue paper," but the illustrations show what we now call "crepe paper." This type of paper is ideal for making paper doll dresses, for it can be ruffled by pulling between thumb and finger, and so turned into flounces and ruffles by gathering it across the grain.

Refinements in color printing in 1880 had brought about a drastic reduction in the cost of manufacturing paper dolls, and so newspapers and magazines printed more and more of them. In 1901 the *Chicago Record-Herald*, in addition to its color pages of comics of Buster Brown and his dog, Tige, the Katzenjammer Kids, and Happy Hooligan, also printed paper dolls in color. Magazines soon followed suit, and before long they were competing for reader interest. Paper dolls reached their heyday.

The first, and among the best of magazine paper dolls, were the two series drawn by Sheila Young, Lettie Lane and Betty Bonnet, which ran in the *Ladies' Home Journal* from 1908 through July 1915. "Betty Bonnet's Dearest Dolls" followed in the same magazine.

In 1909 the *Ladies' Home Journal* introduced Rose O'Neill's Kewpies, with drawing both in the form of paper dolls and also as illustrations for a full page of her rhymes. Her Kewpie-like children illustrated advertising for Jello in the same magazine.

McCall's magazine printed several series of paper dolls: Dolly Dimple, Billy Bumps, and others, designed by Grace Drayton, whose plump children also appeared in ads for Campbell's Soups. This association of paper dolls and food advertising, following as it did the profusion of paper dolls given with all kinds of household products, is a reminder that advertising itself is different from what it was fifty or sixty years ago. At that time most advertising was in women's magazines or in newspapers, so the bonuses were of a kind to appeal to women and girls. When radio and television assumed the bulk of food and household advertising, the audience changed, and advertising is now designed to appeal to children of a speed and space-conscious world, boys as well as girls. A little girl is far more likely to beg for a package of cereal offering a spaceship than a small boy is to be won over by a doll premium.

It is sometimes possible to find a copy of one of these old magazines still intact, but the paper doll pages almost always have been removed. Never fail to check old magazines, however, and if you do find one that is complete, do not remove the pages; place the entire magazine in your doll collection. You can almost put your own price on it.

Collectors who remember the early 1900's may recall the many small tailor shops in towns and cities, and the big fashion sheets which hung in their windows. There might be a dapper gentleman with a waxed mustache, dressed in a Prince Albert coat, striped trousers, and a silk hat, staring at pompadoured ladies with 40-20-20 measurements who wore tailored suits, "waists" with frothy lace and ruching, and ostrich-plumed hats. A girl lucky enough to salvage one of these fashion sheets had a status symbol on a par with the Paris label in her mother's hat.

Another outgrowth of paper dolls was the paper theater—more appealing to boys than to girls. The earliest paper theaters were probably made in England, but with the invention of lithography Germany took over their manufacture, and "kindertheater" sheets of the old fairy tales were printed: Sleeping Beauty, Hansel and Gretel, Cinderella, and Kasperle (the German counterpart of Punch). Toy theaters were also made in Denmark, Spain, and France and imported to England.

The first flurry of popularity was succeeded by a gradual deterioration in quality, until finally it was almost impossible to find a toy theater. Then Benjamin Pollock came along. Pollock, born in the East End of London in 1856, had been apprenticed to the fur trade. He abandoned that business after he married a Miss Reddington, whose father kept a toy shop in Hoxton Street, London. In 1876, a year or so after the death of his father-in-law, Pollock began a career as toy maker and publisher, devoting the rest of his life to the revival of the toy theater trade for the toy shops of England. Even in 1876 few of these shops were left. The theater shops specializing in toy theaters had been popular more than sixty years earlier, in the days of the Regency, to supply a demand for so-called "juvenile dramas." Not many new plays had been written for them since the middle of the 19th century, and, by the time Pollock took over, paper theaters were considered old fashioned and a bit stuffy. But Pollock was enchanted with their possibilities, and went about reprinting such romantic dramas as *The Miller and His Men,* musical extravaganzas like *The Flying Dutchman,* and oriental plays like *Aladdin* and *Bluebeard.* He colored the plates by hand, assisted by his daughter, and sold them for "a penny plain and twopence colored."

Each toy theater consisted of a compact folding theater, ready to be cut out and fitted together by means of an ingenious arrangement of slots and tabs. The entire thing could be folded into a thin 8 x 11-inch box that would fit on any bookshelf. The play sheets were complete including both actors and scenery.

In addition to Pollock's new versions of the plays mentioned above, he published twenty-three old stage favorites, and owned the plates of another thirty-three, including *Wreck Ashore,* and *Sixteen String Jack.*

Robert Louis Stevenson had owned a paper theater when he was a child, and when he came to London as a man he discovered the Pollock shop and renewed his hobby by buying toy theater sheets, particularly those concerned with pirates and highwaymen. His essay, *A Penny Plain and Twopence Colored,* first published in 1884, is devoted to Benjamin Pollock and the "dim shop, low in the roof and smelling strong of glue and the footlights," where he "wandered in a ghostly street with a dream that is not all a dream."

G. K. Chesterton was another great man who played with toy theaters both as a child and as a man, and who often wrote about them. Indeed, Chesterton is said to have felt that the toy theater was the real theater, where he could best see life in bright colors and exaggerated forms, and where all philosophy was sharply divided between the good and the bad. Winston Churchill, still another devotee, had a model stage and produced many plays for several years when he was in his early teens.

After World War I Benjamin Pollock was discovered by writers, actors, and artists. Among the plays written for his revived paper theater series was J. B. Priestley's *The High Toby,* with characters and scenery drawn by Doris Zinkeisson, and an adaptation of Shakespeare's *Hamlet.* Color photographs of Sir Laurence Olivier as he appeared when he played Hamlet were used for the paper actor.

After his death in 1937 the Pollock theater business was taken over by Allen Keen, a dealer in books and rare manuscripts, who was associated with Sir Ralph Richardson and George Speaight. Once again it is possible to obtain modern reprints of both Pollock's plays and his toy theaters. These are being sold in many book and toy shops in America, as well as in the Pollock's Toy Theatres and Toy Museum at 44 Monmouth Street, London, W.C. 2. Admission to the museum is free; here you may see not only the original sheets, both lithographed and hand painted, of the old plays described by Robert Louis Stevenson, but also the new stages and plays now being published.

This avenue of doll collecting might appeal to collectors who want their dolls to *do* something, instead of adorning cabinet shelves. A toy theater project would be a good one for a class, club, or even neighborhood entertainments. Little theater plays could also be tried out on a toy stage before actual production. It is intriguing to think of all the modern techniques that might be applied to paper theater plays to make them even more creative and exciting than anything Pollock dreamed of.

Furniture for paper theaters can be made of paper, or can be regular doll house furniture, if it is the correct size. The entire illusion of reality depends on furniture, scenery, and actors being on the same scale as the theater itself. The Pollock play sheets include actors—also made of paper—but small bisque, china, or wooden dolls may be used instead, provided their legs are stiff enough to hold them upright.

Thoroughly modern examples of this combination of paper theaters and "in-the-round" dolls is found in the Barbie doll theatre shown here, with Barbie and Ken dressed in medieval costumes as the actors. These twentieth century fashion dolls will be discussed in Chapter 21, but as dolls, not actors.

The Japanese have, for a long time, made tiny theaters and houses of paper which are worthy of a place in any doll collection. The people of that small country are expert at using materials the western world often overlooks; they waste nothing. As an example, an eggshell, a few scraps of paper (printed and plain) and a bit of cotton cloth are converted into a doll. Another Japanese doll is made of carefully folded paper fastened to a stick. Both types, as well as many others, are used as actors on the Japanese paper theater stages.

Collectors should be alert to the present possibilities of acquiring paper dolls at most reasonable prices. Every dime store is now selling "coloring books" which will some day be prized by collectors. The name is not entirely descriptive, for they are also "paper doll" books. One reason they become valuable is that they are printed in small editions which never are republished. Since the characters selected for the books are

Courtesy, Mattel, Inc.

Modern Barbie and Ken dolls in their own paper theater.

Japanese paper dolls have a cloth head, stuffed and fastened to a wooden stick. Kimono and *obi* are made of colored paper, printed with small designs, cut, folded, then pasted together. *Bottom right:* Two Japanese eggshell dolls, made of eggshells, paper, and cloth. White shells are used for making the girl dolls; brown ones for the boys.

celebrities of the moment, they often change when circumstances take them out of the limelight. This makes a pictorial record of the times of the books, which are also frequently a great help to anyone who wishes to dress a doll in an authentic costume.

The very fact that paper doll books are inexpensive is almost a guarantee of their value to collectors with an eye on the future, since it is often the commonplace things which are originally the least appreciated.

For instance, the paper doll book, "Victory Dolls," which Kimport printed in 1948, was offered only a few years later for $2 a copy—many times the original price. These books are documentary treasures. They contain three women and three men, each about 9-inches high, and thirty-four full uniforms including those of the WAC, Navy Admiral, Fire Watcher, American Red Cross, Decontamination Squad, Bomber Pilot, Outdoor Worker, Ambulance Driver, Military School Cadet, Armored Tank Division, Air Raid Warden, Sea Scout, Sailor, First Aid Warden, WAAC winter uniform, Messenger, Nurses' Aid, as well as evening dresses for the women. All the dolls and their uniforms are in full color. The books, which cost less than fifty cents in 1948, are impossible to buy today. Think of the valuable information in a book like this, unobtainable from black and white photographs. Many of the dolls show the back as well as the front of a figure, which in costuming is almost as helpful as being able to see the costume itself.

Other paper doll books on sale during the past thirty-five years show motion picture actors or other celebrities: Shirley Temple, Sonja Henie, Jane Withers, Blondie, Dagwood, Baby Dumpling, Judy Garland, and the Royal princesses. One of the most notable of these books was published by the Saalfield Publishing Company at the time of the coronation of Elizabeth II. The figures of the Queen, Prince Philip, Prince Charles, and baby Princess Anne are printed in full color on the back cover, scored so they may be removed without cutting. The grown-ups are about 10-inches high; the children are three- to four-inches. The book contains four full pages of costumes for the family including several for each of the children, as well as the coronation gown for Elizabeth and dress uniform and regalia for Philip. The inside pages, which are supposed to be colored with crayons or watercolors, show the Queen and her consort in various costumes, the trumpeter of the Horse Guards, the coronation chair, the ampulla and spoon used in the coronation ceremony, the scepter, the Archbishop of Canterbury with the royal crown, St. Edward's crown, the orb, a building decorated for the coronation, military representatives of foreign countries who took part in the procession, a Royal Navy ship, a Scottish piper, street decorations, periscopes for viewing the coronation, a trooper of the Grey Regiment, the Tower of London, the State coach, coronation souvenirs (a Beefeater doll and wooden soldier among them), Glamis Castle, an old inn, Westminster Abbey, and other famous landmarks of London. This pictorial gem cost twenty-five cents.

Paper dolls are always favorites for making at home. This one is dressed in white tissue paper and lace-paper doily sections and a veil made of cellophane.

Quite apart from the commercial paper dolls are the home-made cut-outs that adults and children can make and dress for themselves. They can be made out of smooth, thin card-board using watercolors, crayons, or pastels for coloring the body, and colored paper, fabric or lace for the clothing. One of my own fondest memories is of a paper doll someone made for me when I was only four. She had a dozen dresses, all made with little tabs to hook onto her shoulders; one of them was white, trimmed with a lace insertion run through with black ribbon. Every doll of my childhood had at least one dress de-signed the same way.

There are also the strings of paper dolls holding hands that anyone can make by accordion-pleating a strip of paper and cutting out one half of a doll through the entire thicknesses,

A string of paper dolls holding hands is cut from an accordion-folded strip of paper.

allowing the hands to come on a fold, so that when opened up, the dolls are fastened together.

In my previous book, *Here Is Your Hobby, Doll Collecting*, there are many other suggestions for making paper dolls, as well as patterns for copying.

Dolls made of paper often have a special attraction for collectors because they can be stored in a minimum amount of space. For example, one drawer in a chest or cabinet will hold hundreds of them; placed in scrapbooks or folders, they may be kept on a book shelf; while choice individual paper dolls, or groups of them, may be framed and hung on the wall.

Certainly no other dolls are as well suited to our modern trend toward compressed living as are those made of paper, whether they be antique or modern, French pantins or portraits of today's motion picture and television personalities.

4

FABRIC DOLLS

DOLLS WITH cloth heads run the gamut from the simplest homemade rag dolls to those of finely modeled felt and stockinet, but all can be grouped under the general term, fabric dolls.

Tillie, pictured here, is one of the first commercial dolls made of rubberized cloth, and although she is not marked, her owner, the late Alice Kent Trimpey, believed the doll was made about 1831. The doll is now included in the Trimpey collection owned by the State Historical Society of Wisconsin.

Other early commercial cloth dolls made in America were those of Miss Izannah Walker, who was born in 1817 in Central Falls, Rhode Island. Miss Walker, a typical Yankee tinkerer, was skillful at many crafts. Her interests included raising canaries, dabbling in real estate, and perfecting a parlor stove that rivalled Franklin's. Having mastered these more simple money-making projects, she was ready for her true career, and turned her attention to inventing a cloth doll, which she patented in 1873. The patent papers describe the doll as follows:

> This invention has relation to the manufacture of dolls; and consists mainly, in the secondary or double stuffing next to the external or painted layer, whereby, with a sufficient soft surface, the tendency of the paint to crack or scale off is obviated.
>
> My doll is inexpensive, easily kept clean, and not apt to injure a young child which may fall on it. It will preserve its appearance for a long time, as the soft, secondary stuffing under the stockinet or external webbing enables it to give under pressure, so that the oil paint will not scale off.

Courtesy,
State Historical Society of Wisconsin.

Tillie, illustrated in Alice Trimpey's *The Story of My Dolls,* was made of rubberized cloth in about 1831.

Photo by Pinto Photo Service.

Three 18-inch Izannah Walker dolls from Mrs. Hugh Dyer's collection. The seated doll has been restored, but the others are in original condition.

The drawings accompanying the patent papers show a two-piece die, probably made of iron, for a doll's head and torso. The internal layer of cloth was placed over the mold, a layer of stuffing covered it, then the final, or external stockinet webbing was laid on top. A hand press with exactly the same shapes as the mold, but in reverse, clamped the layers together and shaped the doll. The inner cavity of the body was next packed tightly with stuffing. The process was so successful that even today Walker dolls are remarkably free of cracks and peeling.

The earliest Walker dolls were of almost life-size children, but later ones were made in greater quantity in smaller sizes. The dolls were both boys and girls, and all of them, as a rule, had painted hair, except for the few Negro dolls Miss Walker made with wool hair. Bodies are almost always made of sateen, except for those recovered with some other material at a later date when the original body became worn.

The story of Izannah Walker's dolls is important in itself, but also because of the part they played in the creation of the far better-known Chase dolls. Miss Walker's home town of Central Falls, Rhode Island, was only a few miles from the home of Martha Chase's family in Pawtucket.

Martha Chase was born in 1851, the daughter of a physician —Dr. James Wheaton. As a child she owned, and played with, a Walker doll. When she married, it was to another physician, Dr. Julian A. Chase. The eventual use she made of this double association with the medical profession is important.

When her own little daughters were at the doll age, Mrs. Chase made dolls for them suggested by her own Walker doll, but her dolls were more natural looking and easier for a child to carry about. The dolls were correctly jointed at hips, elbows, knees, and shoulders; the feet were shaped with a flat sole and natural looking toes; the hands were cupped with separated fingers. After much experimenting, Mrs. Chase perfected a head which satisfied her, with a pretty, lifelike face covered with the same kind of spring-knit cloth that was stretched over the underbody. The doll was painted with oil colors so it could be cleaned.

About 1891, after the buyer of a Boston store saw some of the dolls and sent in an order, the Chase family set up a factory. In a business that prospered for almost twenty years, the Chase dolls were made in sizes from ten inches to life size. When she designed half a dozen Alice in Wonderland figures for the store, Mrs. Chase became, as far as we know, the first dollmaker to create dolls which portrayed characters in books. In addition to Alice herself, she reproduced Tweedledum, Tweedledee, the Mad Hatter, the Queen, and the Frog. A popular colored Mammy doll and pickaninnies in two sizes were also advertised. But Mrs. Chase's best sellers were babies and children.

Chase dolls were already famous when their designer, then almost sixty, began to make life size demonstration dolls for hospital and clinic training, filling a need she recognized through her lifelong knowledge of hospitals and the care of the sick. She created baby dolls of four sizes, from newborn to one year; a child of about four years; and a five-foot, four-inch woman. Some of these dolls were made with waterproof inner compartments so that various treatments could be demonstrated. They were also used in training nurses to put on bandages, splints, and slings. The Chase family continued to make these hospital demonstration dolls for years after Martha Chase died in 1925. The Chase toy dolls, however, have not been made since the early part of this century.

Apparently a patent to cover the making of these dolls was never applied for, but they are marked with a trademark in the form of a circle with the name "Chase" inside it, a head under it, and swirling over all, a banner strip like a cap-brim, printed with the words "Stocking Doll." This label was printed on the left side of the doll's body or on the left leg. An additional sewed-on label reads:

> "The Chase Stockinet Doll. Made of stockinet and cloth. Stuffed with cotton. Made by hand. Painted by hand. Made especially by trained workers."

While Chase toy dolls are not particularly pretty, they are sturdy and well made and any collector who has one should be grateful.

Among other fabric dolls made during this period, less famous than those of Martha Chase, were the Columbian dolls, made by Miss Emma Adams in New York in 1892. They were shown at the World's Columbian Exposition in Chicago in 1893 where they received an award and acquired the name Columbian. Made until about 1908, they resemble the Chase dolls so closely that, except for the kind of cloth used, it is hard to tell them apart. Chase dolls were always made entirely of stockinet, while Columbian dolls had heads of stockinet and bodies of woven cloth.

Other fabric dolls, too rare to be owned by most collectors, are the Sheppard doll of about 1898, the Hawkins doll head, and the controversial Philadelphia Baby—controversial because no one knows whether it was made by Sheppard or some other manufacturer. None of these dolls are as attractive as more modern dolls, and their main appeal is due to their rarity.

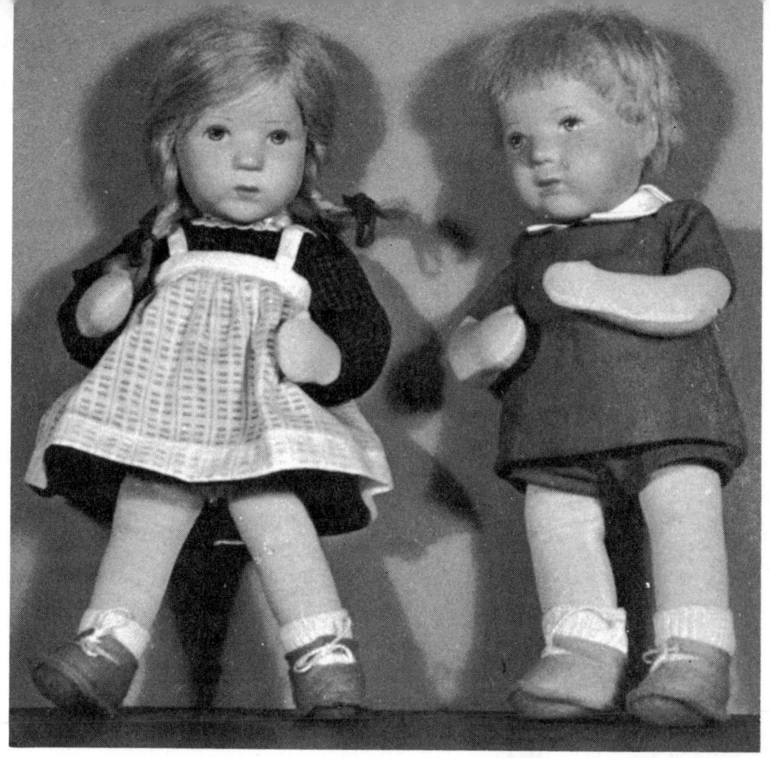

These Kathe Kruse children in Miriam Denton's collection are of modeled and stuffed cloth and are jointed. They are dressed in their original clothes.

The "play doll" is essentially the play "child" of its little girl owner, who is playing house or playing at being a mother. The dolls made by Kathe Kruse exemplify this idea; in fact, it must have been her main consideration in making them, for on the original box in which a Kathe Kruse doll was packed, the label reads: "All my dolls are 43 cm—17-inches high. They are made entirely out of waterproof material and can be washed with soap and water. They are made under my constant personal supervision, in my own workshop and every doll has my name and current number on the sole of the left foot. They are soft, warm and my aim in making them is education toward motherliness." There was no date, but it was signed in script, "Kathe Kruse."

The story of Kathe Kruse and her dolls spans the years 1910 through two world wars to the postwar world. She was born in Switzerland, and at seventeen married Max Kruse, thirty years her senior. Just as many other doll makers have done, Kathe Kruse made her first doll because she was not able to find one in the stores which she thought would please her small daughters. This was in Berlin, in 1905. The first doll was crude, but Kathe Kruse worked hard to improve her technique until she was eventually able to sell her dolls. She turned her apartment into a workshop, refusing to create her dolls in a factory atmosphere for fear they might lose the personal touch she wanted to give them.

In 1910, she asked permission to show some of her dolls in the windows of a large department store in Berlin. Overnight she became famous. The next year she sent a shipment of Kathe Kruse dolls to the United States; they were so popular that she had to enlarge her workshop. She moved to an East German city, Koesen, but continued to make her dolls at home, with her entire family helping.

Frau Kruse had thirteen children, and she made only thirteen types of dolls. Her own favorite and best-known doll is called "The Dreamer." Her dearly loved son Peter was the model for it, and the doll looks so alive that, if put among real children of the same size, he would be indistinguishable from the others. During World War II, Kathe Kruse lost her husband and two of her sons—one, the beloved Peter. Heartbroken, she moved to Donauwörth in western Germany, now making only a limited number of dolls. Although she had lost her zest for dollmaking, and materials were scarce and of poor quality, her dolls still retained their appealing qualities and expressions. Their shaped cloth faces were painted with oil colors just as they had always been painted; they still had soft, childlike bodies. Even a cynic once came to believe that a person who disliked children would nevertheless be forced to love them after holding a Kathe Kruse doll. We can re-read the legend on her box tops and reflect that Kathe Kruse fulfilled her ambition of "education toward motherliness," not only in her work, but in herself.

Here, in discussing fabric dolls, and later, those of other materials, we find dolls with story books written especially around them. So the relationship between dolls and books must be divided into two parts: dolls made to represent characters found in works of fiction, like the Alice in Wonderland dolls mentioned earlier in this chapter, and dolls which became the subject of books, like the golliwog.

Every beginning piano student who has drummed out the *Golliwog Cake Walk* has probably wondered where its composer, Claude Debussy, got the name, and what a golliwog is. England was the probable birthplace of golliwog dolls, although the name itself seems to have been the invention of Bertha and Florence Upton, authors of the children's best seller, *The Adventures of Two Dutch Dolls and a Golliwog*. The golliwog story was so popular that a series of others followed.

This 12-inch golliwog was made of felt in London between 1955 and 1960. His felt clothes are the typical black tailcoat, red shirt, green trousers, and purple spats.

Elio, a felt Lenci doll, was made in about 1929 in Italy.

Courtesy, Newark Museum.

Whether the stories or the doll came first is debatable, but the two appeared almost simultaneously about 1910. The dolls were made in both England and Germany, and before long, almost every English child owned one. They were never as popular in the United States as they were abroad.

Golliwogs, which resemble the members of minstrel shows, were made in a variety of sizes and color combinations—the most common of which were red, yellow, and purple—and often wore black tailcoats; some little black figures wore striped trousers, and others were in gay costumes of brighter hues.

Golliwogs are still being made in England by Deans Rag Book Co. of London, and the one pictured here is a splendid example. It is about 12 inches high, with both body and clothes made of felt, and it is firmly stuffed and extremely well made. It was purchased new in London between the years 1955 and 1960, and sent by relatives to a little girl in America. It happens to be the doll which started Lori Silverwood's collection—a collection that has since been added to by her world-traveling aunts and uncles with dolls from Africa to Hawaii.

The use of felt as a dollmaking material has by no means been confined to golliwogs. Signora Elena di Scaveni of Turin, Italy, began to make child dolls of felt before World War I. At first this was a hobby, but during the war she turned dollmaking into a business. Her intention in doing this was not only to keep herself busy, but also to increase her income while her husband served in the Italian army.

She took out her first patent in September, 1921. For her trade name she chose Lenci, the pet name given her as a child, and continued to make dolls until the mid-30's. Lenci dolls were made entirely of felt—both bodies and clothes. Typical of Lenci's doll children, with their wistful, appealing little faces and their beautifully made clothes, is Elio, purchased at Liberty's in London in 1920. He is 18-inches tall and wears a sleeper; his name is embroidered on one of the pockets, and he carries a toy monkey in the other pocket.

Former employees of Signora di Scaveni, including one who labeled her dolls "Margurin," later went into business for themselves in Turin and began making felt dolls representing the people of Italy and Sicily. Many souvenir dolls now sold in Italy are the productions of these artists who learned so much from "Lenci."

Bernard Ravca was a French dollmaker who specialized in making character and peasant dolls of silk stocking material, sometimes on a base of bread dough or crumbs. During World War II his studios in Paris were looted, and he emigrated to the United States, where he eventually became a naturalized citizen. He traveled throughout the country lecturing and displaying his dolls, contributing the proceeds of his exhibits to French charities and French War Relief.

Many of Ravca's dolls were miniatures of foreign dignitaries —British, French, and American. Because he delighted in expressing human character, his whimsical dolls have all the individuality of real people and reflect his own humor, pathos, and gentle satire. Ravca never duplicated his dolls, but he made hundreds of different figures of American life. These included representations of American Indian tribes, cowboys, hillbillies, and other regional characters. He made world leaders (Churchill, Roosevelt, Stalin, Chiang Kai-shek), artists, musicians, writers, and dancers familiar to everyone, so that in the fullest sense of the word, his dolls were "characters." Nevertheless, M. Ravca considered his most popular dolls to be the peddler women and organ-grinders of French provincial life, and certainly he is best remembered for peasant dolls. These may have also been his own favorites, for he had a tender feeling for old people with gnarled hands and seamed faces, and made a great many of them, often grouping two or more together as friends or cronies.

The humblest type of fabric doll—sometimes set apart from those commonly called fabric—is the rag doll. As traditional bedtime favorites and childhood playmates, rag dolls bring fond memories to almost everybody.

Raggedy Ann and Raggedy Andy, sometimes called "The Indomitable Rag Dolls who thought lovely, kind, beautiful thoughts," are now close to their fiftieth anniversary. A collector who compares the originals with the latest toy department specimens will find them practically identical. The new Raggedys have the same shoe-button eyes, wide smiles, ragged red yarn hair, and red and white striped socks as the first ones did. Ann wears a blue and white print dress just like her ancestor's, and Andy's checked shirt and blue cotton trousers are in the familiar style of the original Andy. They each wear a little red heart with "I Love You" printed on it.

Johnny Gruelle, their creator, was a political cartoonist whose career began in 1889. Years later he found an old rag doll, badly worn and its face obliterated, in the attic. He sketched on a new face and gave the doll to his small daughter calling it Raggedy Ann—a name that came to his mind when he remembered the poem his old friend, James Whitcomb Riley, wrote about Little Orphant Annie, who's

Come to our house to stay,
An' wash the cups and saucers up, an' brush the crumbs away,
An' shoo the chickens off the porch, an' dust the hearth, an' sweep,
An' make the fire, an' bake the bread, an' earn her bread an' keep.

After a short time Gruelle had to make a companion for Ann, and what name could be more suitable than Raggedy Andy, suggested by Riley's "Raggedy Man," which told about the tramp he found asleep in the barn, and chased through the back lot, shouting at him,

You're a *purty* man, *you* air!
With a pair of eyes like two fried eggs,
An' a nose like a Bartlutt pear!

Gruelle used the name and character of Raggedy Ann in a cartoon he drew for the New York World, and about the same time wrote his first book, *Raggedy Ann Stories,* published in 1918. This was followed in 1920 by *Raggedy Andy Stories.* Before his death in 1938, Johnny Gruelle had written more than twenty Raggedy Ann and Raggedy Andy books, which altogether sold more than ten million copies.

The Knickerbocker Toy Company now holds the contract for making the dolls, just as they have been made for two generations. It is a pleasure to walk into a modern toy department and see two old familiar figures smiling over the heads of plastic and synthetic dolls.

While the design and sale of the dolls is the exclusive right of the publishers of the books, it is safe to estimate that many hundreds of Raggedy Anns and Andys have been made at home by mothers and grandmothers, and will long continue to be. No Parian aristocrat priced at hundreds of dollars can wear with honesty the heart tag, "I Love You."

These famous rag dolls are far from being the only fabric dolls made at home. It is hard to catalog homemade dolls, for most of them are not even marked with the name of the person who made them. It is best, therefore, to guess at the age and birthplace of the doll in question from the kind of materials used in making and dressing it. The fact that a doll is made by hand is not conclusive evidence in establishing its age, because it is easier to sew dolls that way than on the sewing machine. Since sewing machines were not in common use until the middle of the nineteenth century, a machine-stitched doll probably is not older than that, but a hand-stitched doll can be of any age.

Almost every little girl who was born after the middle of the eighteenth century, and before World War I, played with one of the printed rag dolls offered by various food and clothing manufacturers. These dolls have never been taken seriously by doll collectors, and at best have been called "secondary" dolls; but if they have personal associations, or are in good condition, they should not be ignored, for they too, are a part of the American scene. Although no well-loved doll made of cloth can be crisp and bright after seventy or eighty years of active existence, it does have one of the requirements of a collector's doll—it means something. Their very reputation at present as lesser dolls, insures that someday their importance will rise by reason of their eventual scarcity.

These rag dolls sent out by manufacturers were printed on cloth, ready to be cut out, sewed, and stuffed at home. A few of the best known were Rastus, made by Cream of Wheat; Aunt Jemima, by Aunt Jemima Pancake Flour Company; Sunny Jim, by the makers of the cereal, Force; Puffy, by the Quaker Oats Company; and the Palmer Cox Brownies. Cox also designed a series of dolls of different nationalities: German, Scottish, Canadian, John Bull, and an American sailor.

Soon after 1900, Buster Brown and his dog Tige came out of the funny papers to become rag dolls, and so did Foxy Grandpa and Boys, as well as the many rag doll patterns made by the Adams Print Works of North Adams, Massachusetts.

In *Woman's Home Companion* for December, 1907, there are two full picture pages of patterns for making cloth dolls and their wardrobes, a cloth Teddy Bear, and a cloth Buster Brown's Tige. The following excerpt from the magazine describes the patterns:

> Christmas marks the changes of Fashion in Doll Land just as distinctly as Easter does for grown folks. Little mothers watch anxiously for magazines that will illustrate dolls and their latest outfits. Every new detail is noted carefully, for last season's dolls must be thoroughly up-to-date in order to associate with the dolls of 1908.
>
> Here we have the pattern of a rag doll, which may be cut out and stuffed and will stand the hardest sort of wear without showing any signs of injury. Included in the pattern is a pretty little party dress made to fit the rag doll.
>
> Every well-ordered doll's wardrobe should include a short reefer for pleasant days, and an automobile coat, too.
>
> To wear in her own doll's house there should be kimonos, long and short, and dressing sacques, that any little girl may make with tiny pieces left from her own frocks.

All of these patterns were made for 22-inch dolls, and cost ten cents each. No wonder so many girls learned to sew by making doll clothes! And that is, no doubt, what both the magazine and the little girls' mothers had in mind.

Homemade rag dolls are still being made, with and without patterns, in spite of all the mechanical toys and miracle synthetics. Therefore, modern dollmakers should take care when they sew together the pieces of a rag doll, for it may some day find its way into a museum. It is important to label every doll with the name of the dollmaker and the date, so that no future collector will puzzle over the doll's origin.

Many cloth dolls are being made in Europe, Mexico, and South America. In fact, the greater part of all collectors' dolls

Patterns for 22-inch rag dolls as shown in *Woman's Home Companion,* December, 1907. The price of each pattern, including complete instructions for choosing material, cutting and sewing the doll and her garments, was ten cents.

This pair of homemade rag dolls follows a long tradition of toy-making.

Peasant dolls like these, with stuffed cloth bodies and faces covered with stockinet material, are still made in France.

made for the tourist trade are of cloth. In a later chapter we shall say more about them under the heading of foreign dolls.

In addition to the particular fabric dolls discussed here, there are of course thousands of unidentified ones, both homemade and commercial. Such dolls can be accepted or rejected according to preference. Sometimes, indeed, a nameless orphan may come to hold a place of special affection in a collection. And because fabric dolls are so easily made by the amateur, orphans naturally abound.

5
WOODEN DOLLS

PEOPLE ON ALL continents have been making wooden dolls for hundreds of years, and are continuing to make them, particularly in the Orient. Some are all wood; others have wooden heads, and bodies of some other material. Especially when the figure is an extremely old one, it is sometimes difficult to be certain whether we are looking at a doll, a figurine, or an idol. Several years ago, for instance, one of the large doll import companies advertised a shipment of Chinese household figures as dolls; they were so old that the cedar of which they were made had become as lightweight as balsa wood. Who can say whether they were originally dolls or idols? But perhaps one answer is to say that the proper designation depends upon what we would like the figure to be. If a figurine is called a doll, and is treated like a doll, it thereby becomes a doll. When children pull off hollyhock blossoms and call them dolls, that's what they become. And surely, in the end, it is preferable to be an admired doll than an unworshipped idol.

African dolls made of native wood may once have been idols, but they fit into a doll collection very nicely. The wire-wrapped collars, shields, spears, and fantastic headdresses may be even more interesting than the figures themselves. Dolls from the islands of the Pacific, from Mexico, South America, and Alaska, and those of the American Indians, are often made of wood, but so many of them are one-of-a-kinds that it is impossible to classify them.

The making of true wooden dolls has a long history in Europe. So many of the families living in the forests of Germany during the fifteenth century were carving wooden dolls, that dollmaking had already become a recognized craft. By the middle of the eighteenth century the fine quality of German dolls was recognized by a doll-conscious world, and in order to keep up with the demand for them, German dollmakers were turning the craft into a village or cottage industry. The forests of Germany supplied the material for thousands of dolls shipped to other European countries; and before long *all* wooden dolls were being called *Deutsch* dolls, which was soon corrupted into *Dutch* dolls. Wooden dolls have borne more names than any other kind of doll. At various times they were known as Flanders Babies, peggitys, Penny Woodens, Penny Gretchens, Wooden Bettys, woodentops, and Timbertoes.

It is amazing that, in their long history, so few changes have been made in the construction of wooden dolls. The method of attaching arms and legs to the body of early wooden dolls by means of pins or pegs inserted through the body at the shoulders and into the top of the legs, is quite similar to that used in making the Etruscan doll described in Chapter 2. The more elaborate ball and socket joints came later.

Antonio Filarete, who designed the big bronze doors of St. Peter's in Rome, wrote a book about architecture in which he mentioned lay figures or manikins—those faceless, unpainted, jointed wooden representations of the human body, made to be set in any position a person can take. Filarete's mention of lay figures is the first account of them on record. He did not invent them, but he did use them, just as artists use them today when they work without a model and want to experiment with different poses and effects. Lay figures are not dolls, and were never intended to be. Yet, the figures have been very useful to makers of dolls, for the unknown genius who invented them devised ways of articulating joints so they could be turned freely, yet remain where they were set. Almost all wooden-bodied dolls have been made with some variation of the lay-figure joint principle.

Doll collectors interested in trying their hand at dollmaking will find wooden ones good to begin with, since they require few tools and only small pieces of wood. A doll from 14- to 20-inches high is both easier to make and to dress than a small

A crude and unusual jointed wooden doll whose age and origin are unknown.

Courtesy, Franks Doll Museum.

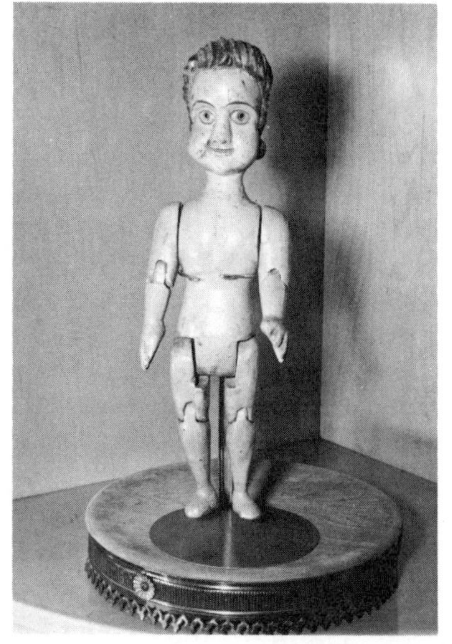

This type of peg doll can be made by home craftsmen using only a piece of soft pine or balsa wood, a sharp knife, and a few small nails.

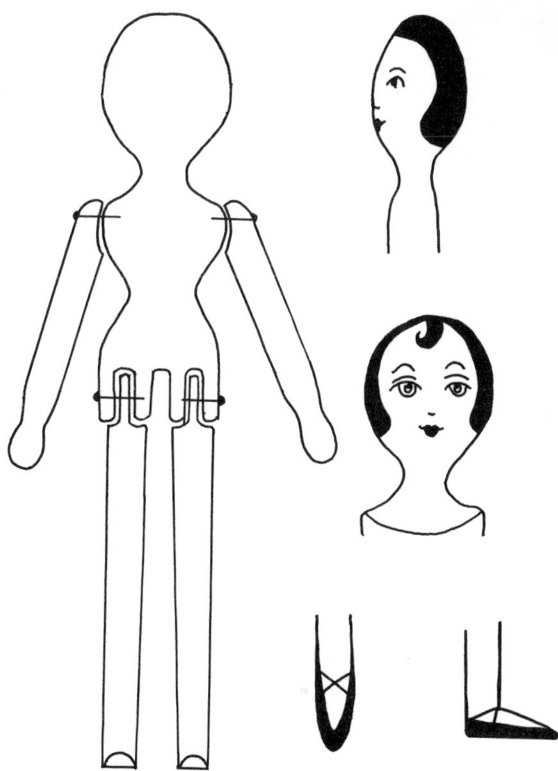

one. Soft pine or even balsa wood is easy to handle. The balsa is easier to carve, but the pine will not splinter so easily and will hold the pins or nails for the joints more firmly. Carve the head and torso in one piece, and the arms and legs separately. Sand the pieces thoroughly before painting them, and then assemble the doll. Insert small wire brads through the tops of the arms and shoulders into the body; drive other wire brads or nails through the tops of the legs and into the lower part of the torso, as in the illustration.

One of the finest qualities of wooden dolls is their durability, for even if the paint flakes off, the wood remains. If that were not true, there would be far fewer wooden dolls remaining from earlier centuries.

The oldest dressed wooden doll in the great collection of the Victoria and Albert Museum in London dates from 1690–1700. The family of the "Old Pretender," James Stuart, is supposed to have given the doll to a loyalist supporter. It is dressed in a pink satin dress, and wears a fashionable towering headdress of silk and lace. The doll's expression is quite unpleasant, and several large beauty patches on her face add to her sinister appearance. She is the extremely common type of wooden doll which has come to be known as a Queen Anne, and her greatest value is in her personal history connecting her with James Stuart. The doll's head is over-sized, out of scale with her body, as was characteristic of dolls of the period, and her hands are formed in the scoop shape so often found on early wooden dolls. The so-called Georgian doll shown in our illustration and called Lady Candour, is similar to the Victoria and Albert Museum Queen Anne in both appearance and construction, although a much finer doll and in better condition. This conflict of names is confusing—what is a Queen Anne doll, and what is Georgian?

Queen Anne of England was born in 1665 and died in 1714. Her reign was followed by that of George I, from 1714 to 1727; and his by that of George II, from 1727 to 1760. George III was king from 1760 to 1820.

The division of 18th century wooden dolls which are identical into two groups—Queen Anne and Georgian—is both misleading and inaccurate because wooden dolls similar to

This Queen Anne doll of the Georgian period is 23 inches tall and is made entirely of wood except for inset glass eyes. As with many eighteenth-century dolls, she has a separate wig of real hair and an elaborate, fanciful headdress. She is costumed to represent Lady Candour of Sheridan's *School for Scandal.*

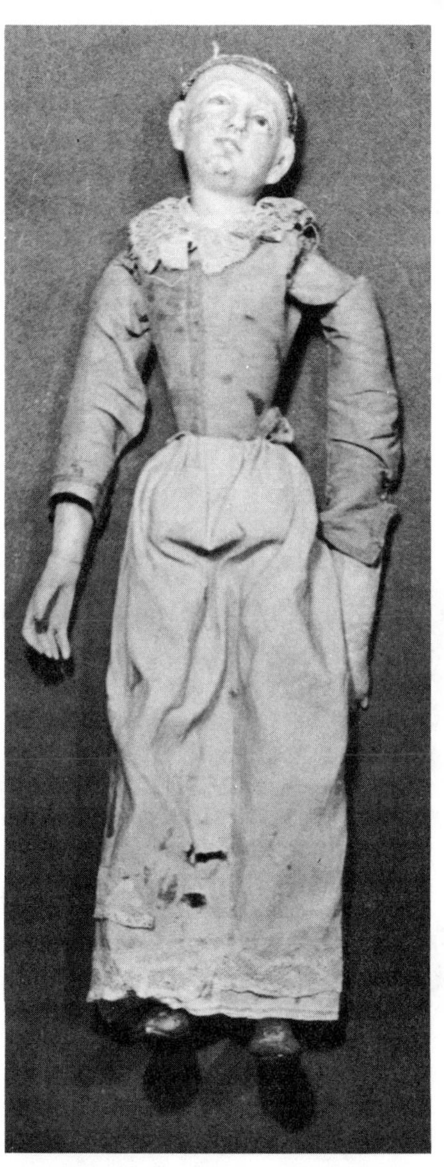

This old wooden doll (1780–1790) is from the province of Liguria or Piedmont, Italy. The doll is jointed and has set-in glass eyes.

A group of wooden dolls from Mrs. Walter Wagner's collection. *Upper left and top center:* Queen Anne dolls with real hair. Others are English peg dolls dated about 1800.

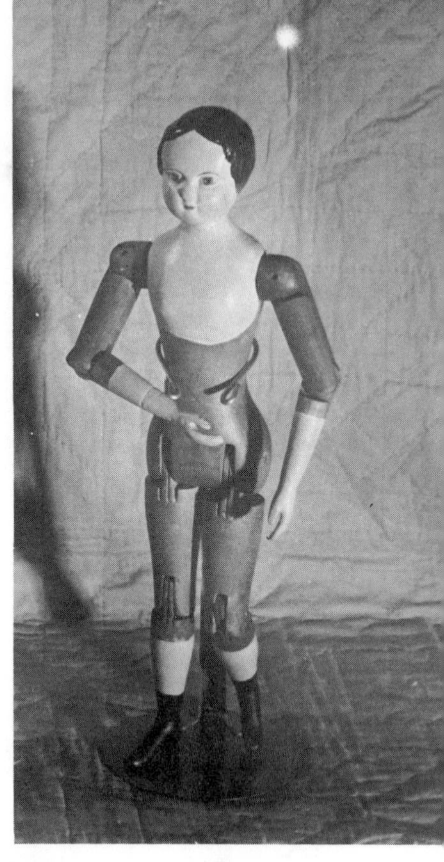

A Springfield wooden by Joel Ellis.

This Schoenhut girl doll with wig and well-shaped feet is made of painted wood.

Courtesy, Franks Doll Museum.

the known Queen Anne doll in the Victoria and Albert Museum continued to be made after the death of Queen Anne and all during the reigns of the Georges, with few changes.

It therefore seems preferable to designate as the Queen Anne type *all* wooden dolls similar to Lady Candour, even though they may have been made in Georgian times, rather than to insist on a strictly chronological placement.

Queen Anne type dolls were usually made with lathe-turned bodies and peg-jointed limbs. The paint on the heads extended down over the shoulders, and the lower arms and hands were painted, as well as the lower legs and feet. Eyes were generally made of glass and inserted in the heads in such a way as to give the dolls an earnest, unblinking expression. Most of the early dolls had wigs of real hair, but the later ones were painted with bangs, curls, and swirls. The thumbs on the dolls' scoop hands were slightly separated from the fingers. These dolls all wear prim, stoical expressions because of their staring eyes and tight little mouths.

It is sometimes said that museums contain the failures of the doll world: dolls which their original owners thought were too finely made or too well dressed to be loved. Such dolls were spared the rugged existence of more lovable dolls, and have therefore survived far longer. This theory could easily apply to the Queen Anne type, although what these dolls lack in emotional appeal, they now more than compensate for in historical value. From them we discover just how an eighteenth century corset was laced, what objects people carried in their pockets, and how a baby's diaper was fastened. These old dolls have the same rigid charm found in the "primitive" paintings of early America.

One of the famous doll collections of the world is that with which the little Princess Victoria played not many years before she became Queen of England in 1837. In childhood she and her governess, Baroness Lehzen, dressed the 132 dolls which make up the collection. Most of these dolls are wooden, of the type just described—Dutch dolls—peggity dolls; we can only wonder why the princess chose crude woodens instead of the fine waxes and papier-mâchés that were so popular in England at the time. Victoria's dolls, now in Kensington Palace, are from 3- to 9-inches tall, have small sharp noses, bright red cheeks made by dabbing on circles of paint, tiny full-lipped mouths, and broad brows framed by elaborate painted curls. The dolls are dressed in elegant replicas of dresses worn by ladies of the court and by theatrical personages of the day.

Even in the days of the Pilgrims, children had wooden dolls, for early settlements were built in the midst of the raw materials needed for making them. Most of these dolls were made at home, carved of wood from the forest or woodpile.

A great number of Scottish, Irish, and English immigrants settled in the Appalachian Mountain area of the United States. They naturally brought with them the dolls, legends, and songs of their native lands, and many of them have not been forgotten by their descendants. Because of their similar appearance, it is just as easy to trace the colloquially named "wooden poppets" of the Appalachians back to English wooden dolls of the eighteenth century, as it is to identify the American ballads of Barbara Allen and Lord Randall with their origin in the British Isles.

In the nineteenth century Americans worked out improved methods for the commercial manufacture of wooden dolls, and so created the curious story of the Springfield wooden dolls. It began with a man named Joel Ellis.

Born in 1830 in Barnard, Vermont, he was an ingenious inventor but a man with little business ability. Having moved to Springfield, Vermont, he and two partners, Britain and Eaton, organized the Vermont Novelty Works there in 1859.

It was in their factory that many of the early Ellis inventions were manufactured. His numerous patents included those for a toy cart, a baby carriage, the first American-made violin and guitar cases, a steam shovel, and a wide variety of wooden toys, many of which were designed to make use of scraps of waste wood.

In 1869, a flood carried away the entire plant, all stock, and tools. Ellis reorganized the company and rebuilt the factory. In 1878, the factory was destroyed by fire, and was again rebuilt. Meanwhile, on May 20, 1873, Ellis was granted a patent for a double mortise-and-tenon joint to be used in wooden doll-bodies.

While the patent was pending, Ellis organized another company, called the Cooperative Manufacturing Co., for the manufacture of dolls. He apparently planned from the start to keep the doll manufacturing business entirely separate from his other factory, for he built a two-story factory building and bought a saw and planing mill for it.

As soon as the doll patent was granted, Ellis turned it over to the new company in exchange for capital stock. The dies used in making the dolls were so costly, and the royalty paid to their owner so high, that after only one year the factory closed, and Ellis left Springfield.

It is not clear who took over the operation of the doll factory for the next nine years, but it was probably Mason and Taylor. Mason had been an early partner of Joel Ellis.

Then followed a most confusing situation. It seemed that every toymaker in Springfield, Vermont decided to make wooden dolls. They sometimes patented improvements, but just as often neglected to do so, as if determined to donate inventions and lose their identity in the common cause of doll-making. That is why the name Springfield dolls includes the work of Henry H. Mason, Luke Taylor (probably one-time partners of Joel Ellis), F. D. Martin, George W. Sanders, and C. C. Johnson.

In 1879 Martin patented a doll with hemisphere joints which fastened at the shoulders with elastic or string run through the body. His doll has a papier-mâché head and was prettier than the all-wood Ellis dolls had been. During the following year, Sanders improved the Martin doll by using the ball-socket mortised joint used in all subsequent Springfield dolls. Three years later, in 1882, C. C. Johnson produced a doll that had all the previous improvements, plus a Mason and Taylor invention of a neck that could be turned. He used a wooden foundation for the head and covered it with a mixture of composition and glue that could be molded into shape.

The Joel Ellis wooden dolls were made in only three sizes: 12 inches, 15 inches, and 18 inches. He used only one style of head, but it could be painted for use as either a boy or girl blond or brunet as the market demanded. Black-haired dolls were made for special orders.

Springfield dolls made after Ellis stopped production were in a variety of sizes and styles. Some were of rock maple; others were made of poplar or beech wood. At first all hands were made of wood, but later either iron or pewter took its place. While the feet of all the Ellis and some of the Martin dolls were painted black, all the others were painted blue.

A great number of dolls made by the various inventors and manufacturers of this one small town has survived, in spite of a few weaknesses in their construction. Especially weak were the mortise-and-tenon joint used in the Ellis dolls; the way the feet were attached to the legs in other dolls, and the quality of the paint used which resulted in leprous complexions for many surviving specimens.

In 1872, just before the Springfield era, one Albert Schoenhut left his native Germany and settled in Philadelphia. His family had been toy makers for generations, and he immediately went into the toy business in his adopted country, specializing in the making of toy pianos. He was a good businessman, and soon other members of his family had to join him in order to fill the demand for Schoenhut toys.

The Schoenhut Humpty Dumpty Circus was put on the market in 1903, and was even marketed in Europe with astonishing success. A Schoenhut advertisement of 1907, which framed a picture of the circus' animal acts, performers in action, and animals, reads:

TOYS THAT GLADDEN THE HEARTS OF OUR DEAR LITTLE ONES—THE TOY WONDER

"100,000 clever tricks, circus performers, acrobats Max and Moritz, the greatest show on earth. Menagerie, hippodrome, tight rope performers. You can start a circus with a few pieces, then keep adding to them until your Greatest Show on Earth is complete. THE NEWEST AND BEST UNBREAKABLE TOY. . . . The figures are made of solid wood, jointed like French dolls, painted in oil colors; the clowns and others are dressed in fancy costumes. Will stand the roughest kind of treatment. . . . Sold in sets, 50¢ to $25 and over, according to the number of figures in a set. If your dealer cannot supply you, send us his name and we will mail you literature with

Courtesy, State Historical Society of Wisconsin.

This typical "Dutch" or wooden peg doll is in its original condition, but has new clothes.

Courtesy, Franks Doll Museum.

A wooden clown and his horse, made as part of the famous Schoenhut circus, are jointed to be set in many positions.

latest illustrations, free. Do not send money. WRITE FIRST! The A. Schoenhut Co., Manufs. and Patentees. Manufacturers of the world renowned SCHOENHUT Toy Pianos. Established in 1872. 2225 Adams St. Philadelphia, Pennsylvania.

The basic patent for Schoenhut's next venture—what he hoped would be a virtually indestructible doll—was issued in 1911. According to the catalog the doll was made of hardwood, and all parts were held together with "patent steel spring hinges, made with double spring tensions and swivel connections." The doll's head and body was made of solid wood; the feet had two holes in the soles to receive "the post of our unique metal stand that goes with every doll. The shoes and stockings have two holes to correspond with those in the feet. The one hole is straight, to hold the foot resting flat, and the other hole is oblique to hold the foot in a tiptoe position . . . only one stand is necessary to support the doll on one foot or the other." The dolls were all made with wrist and ankle joints, and as no rubber was used in their construction, they never needed re-stringing. Furthermore, since they were painted with enamel colors, they needed nothing more than a little soap and water to make them look like new.

The first Schoenhut dolls were 16-inches tall, but eventually other sizes were made, some as large as 22 inches. An Italian sculptor modeled the faces of the first dolls, but when people complained that he made the supposed children's faces look too mature, Henry Schoenhut, son of the company's founder, took extensive art training and after 1916 did all the modeling himself. The dolls were delightfully lifelike, and now had really childlike faces. Some were made with mohair wigs; others had carved wooden hair. The eyes of some were carved in the wood so delicately that they looked like glass; others were made with sleeping eyes.

Albert Schoenhut died in 1912, and in 1914 came the war with Germany. The Schoenhut factory survived both tragedies, as well as the influx of cheap toys that flooded the market after the war. In 1924, to reduce the cost of manufacture, elastic cord was substituted for the sturdy metal springs. Soon after, the metal stands were eliminated. Stuffed dolls with "Mama" voices, hollow wooden heads, and mohair wigs were the final efforts of the company to cheapen manufacturing costs. The Schoenhut story finally ended in June, 1928, with the introduction of a push-toy.

There are modern examples of wooden dolls, and while they do not bear any resemblance to those of the Springfield toymakers, or to those of Schoenhut, they are all related. There seems to be an essential quality of honesty about wooden dolls. They have always had a special appeal for collectors and writers as well as for children. For in addition to the two Dutch dolls who share the title and exploits of Florence and Bertha Upton's *Adventure of Two Dutch Dolls and a Golliwog,* wooden dolls are immortalized in Frances Hodgson Burnett's beloved story of *Racketty Packetty House* which has charmed several generations and is still on the library shelves despite a trend toward more factual prose. There seems to be little danger that dear old Peter Piper, Ridiklis, Meg and Peg and Kilmanskeg will be forgotten. What a relief when they were all saved from destruction, and their "nice, queer faces, and their funny clothes" were restored to beauty again, and they went to live with "the little girl princess in her splendid palace."

It is more tempting to cuddle a rag doll, perhaps, but a wooden doll is a trustworthy friend, capable of enduring from generation to generation.

6

PAPIER-MÂCHÉ AND COMPOSITION DOLLS

ONE OF THE BEST materials ever used for doll-heads and bodies is papier-mâché, a substance not only important in itself, but as a forerunner of modern composition.

Papier-mâché (the French words mean "chewed paper") is a material familiar to many because it is so commonly used by children in various school crafts. Because it is light in weight, easily shaped, and is inexpensive to prepare from materials available everywhere, puppet and marionette heads are often made of papier-mâché. There are few adults interested in crafts who have not had some experience in making papier-mâché by tearing newspaper into bits, soaking it in water, and mixing it with paste to form a dough. When dried it is tough and hard, and may be painted with either oil or tempera colors. Sometimes it is then covered with clear varnish or lacquer to protect the paint and give it additional gloss. Commercially, other materials are also added to the dough, such as glue or sizing.

Papier-mâché may have come first from Sindh and other parts of India (where it was used in making boxes, trays, and other small objects), or from China and Japan. It was probably first used in Europe in 1740 by a German named Martin in the manufacture of snuffboxes.

All Europe promptly approved the material, and soon it was being used for larger projects than those attempted by Martin. The ceilings and interior cornices of houses and public buildings, for example, were often made of papier-mâché. As dif-

Irene is a 36-inch doll, probably German, with a papier-mâché head, stuffed cloth body, and wooden arms and legs. Her molded hair, painted black, is in a popular 1830's style.

Courtesy, The Newark Museum.

This doll from the 1830–1840 period has a papier-mâché head and the typical molded hairstyle with side curls and a high comb at the back. The body is kid, and the arms and legs are wooden.

Courtesy, State Historical Society of Wisconsin.

ferent uses were explored, improvements were made in the composition and preparation of the material, until eventually three distinct forms developed. The first, and true papier-mâché, was made solely of paper pulp. The second involved the pasting together of sheets of paper, and then subjecting them to pressure. In the third method, sheets of thick millboard cast from paper pulp were put into a heavy press to be shaped.

Dollmakers quickly saw the possibilities of the material,

and developed their own methods of manufacture—sometimes secret ones. Wastepaper was often shredded and boiled until soft, and the excess water squeezed out, leaving a kind of dough. Clay and glue were added to make the mixture, stiff and sticky. It was spread in thin layers in two-piece metal molds, pressed firmly, and then allowed to dry. The two sections were then put together, sealed, and the seam covered with strips of cloth or paper. Complexion, features, and hair were painted on next, and the doll-head was ready to be attached to a cloth or kid body. It is important to know that many early papier-mâché and composition doll-heads were sold separately, to be attached to homemade bodies. Therefore, many dolls made from these heads are truly one-of-a-kind.

Since most dolls were not marked in any way until 1891 (when a U. S. law required that all imports be marked with the country of their origin), it is only guesswork to give Germany credit for making the first papier-mâché doll-head. But what was more logical than for Germany, a country already busy making dolls, to welcome this new material?

The doll collection of the Newark Museum, Newark, New Jersey, includes a beautiful 36-inch papier-mâché named Irene. The span of time between the late 1820's and the 1840's is as close as the museum will come to setting her age. Like almost all papier-mâché dolls, she is not marked with the manufacturer's name, and the name Irene was probably given to her by a former owner. The personalizing of dolls by giving them names when they were shipped from the factory did not begin for a number of years, and then only when the doll was made to represent a famous person, such as Jenny Lind or a queen or an empress. Irene's papier-mâché head is attached to a stuffed cloth body. Her arms and legs are made of wood and her feet are carved separately, then attached to the legs at the ankles. Her painted eyes are turquoise blue, and her dark hair is also painted, as are her blue slippers. She wears a full-skirted dress of sprigged muslin, with pantalets to match. And she carries her own 5-inch peg doll.

Another papier-mâché in the Newark Museum's collection has a slim-waisted kid body with long spindly arms and legs of carved wood. Her hairstyle roughly dates her, for it is the one known as the "Apollo knot" or "plaited arcade" which was the vogue in Paris for several years from about 1826.

Many of these European papier-mâché dolls were entirely factory-made, and their kid or cloth bodies were often stuffed with hair. Some of them had leather arms, sewed-on leather shoes, and made use of endless combinations of materials. Few papier-mâché dolls, however, had both heads and bodies made of that material. Homemade bodies were of cloth, leather, or whatever other material was available. Probably far more doll-heads were purchased to be attached to dolls whose bodies were made at home, than were ever put on factory-made bodies. While the same thing is true of other dolls, both European and American prior to World War I, the greater individual care in making and varying papier-mâché heads seems to have added a special charm to them, especially those coupled with non-commercial bodies.

The difficulty of identifying early papier-mâchés is a challenge to doll collectors. The dolls marked with a "Superior" label are good examples, for nobody can decide whether the dolls were made in Germany or America. Judging by their hairstyles, they were German; yet the labels (with a gold background and black letters) were printed in English. Often, in addition to the "M & S Superior" label, numbers such as 2015, 2020, 1020, 4515, and 201 are included. These may have been the numbers of styles or manufacturing lots, which apparently did not follow any consistent sequence of size. "M & S" dolls were made in 20, 25, and 32-inch sizes, in addition to the most popular 11-inch size; and one example of 42 inches has been reported. In some instances, the letters used with "Superior" were not M & S, but A.F.N. & Co., A.F. & Co., or G.L. A "Superior" doll, owned by one collector, has the letters DD stamped inside the head. These initials, which are impossible to identify, may indicate that these dolls were produced by several different dollmakers to be sold under the "Superior" label.

"M & S Superior" dolls had a fine high luster; they were either blonds or brunets, and the eyes were always of a painted blue or brown, never of glass. All "Superior" bodies appear to have been factory-made, stuffed with hair waste, fashioned with leather arms and with leather shoes that were sewed on as an integral part of the feet. Most of them have white stockings striped with red, and red shoes.

It seems quite unlikely that actual manufacturers' data will ever appear to solve the mystery of "Superior" papier-mâchés. Only by piecing together authentic bits of individual information about them can collectors, dolls' clubs, and museums hope to establish any kind of accurate history of these very satis-

Courtesy, Franks Doll Museum.

Left to right: A pre-Greiner with black eyes; French papier-mâché with black pupil-less eyes and stiff pink kid body; Greiner with painted eyes and wooden legs and arms.

factory dolls. Not even the exact dates of their manufacture are known, although the hairstyles indicate that they were made during the period of about 1850 to 1870.

Coinciding with the making of "Superior" dolls, if these dates are accurate, are the papier-mâchés made by Ludwig Greiner. Greiner dolls, however, are easy to identify because they were carefully labeled and, although they followed the European tradition in styling, had the distinction of being the very first dolls of any kind to be patented in America (No. 19770 in the U. S. Patent Office).

Ludwig Greiner was a German immigrant who had undoubtedly learned his trade in his native land. His patent, dated March 30, 1858, covered some of the styles and methods of German papier-mâchés, but added improvements of his own. Other manufacturers learned a great deal from his excellent work, and so can we, for the details of his dollmaking methods are clearly explained in the patent papers, for all to read.

Greiner's ambition was to make a naturalistic doll-head, so sturdy that it would be practically indestructible. Except for scuffed paint and a nose that almost always has a badly worn cloth-filled tip, he was successful. There are a great many Greiners still in existence.

The patent application explained his method of molding the head in two parts and of reinforcing the inside of the joining by pasting strips of linen or muslin over the seam. The papier-mâché he used was made of white paper, cooked to a pulp and beaten, then mixed with glue, whiting, and rye flour. The nose was strengthened by filling with linen or muslin, saturated with paste. The heads were allowed to become about half dry, and were then replaced in the molds, saturated with more paste, and again reinforced with cloth at the seam. They were next put in a press, to force the features into a clear-cut reproduction of the mold. After drying, another layer of papier-mâché was pasted on the outside of the seam, and the head was dried once more. The finish consisted of oil paint. On some Greiner dolls a small label pasted on the back under the last coat of finish reads: "Greiner Patent Doll Heads. Pat. Mar. 30, '58." The size number was printed directly under the name. Other labels have the additional words: "Ext. '72," which of course means that the original patent was extended in 1872.

Ludwig Greiner has been cherished by collectors, not only for his good workmanship, but also for his thoughtfulness in applying his labels so securely. Even if the label is missing, it is often possible to see the place where it was once fastened between the shoulders.

Greiner made and marketed his doll-heads for at least twenty years, with several factories operating at the same time. As he made only heads, the very ease of making them encouraged him to produce a large variety of styles and sizes. Sizes varied from a small head to one for a 36-inch doll. There were both boys and girls, blonds and brunets, and at least eight different hairstyles. The eyes were almost always painted on the face, although a few had inset glass eyes.

The inner reinforcing of the heads cannot alone be depended on to identify Greiner dolls, for other manufacturers often copied it, but once you have examined a genuine Greiner, it is not hard to recognize others. There is a certain strong family resemblance as well as an intangible "something" about the dolls, even though the bodies were made of whatever material happened to be on hand, or appealed to the home dollmaker. Proportions of the bodies are likely to be quaint, with heads often too small for the rest of the body, or arms and legs, hands and feet out of scale. Material of all kinds was used for the bodies, including cotton, linen, wool, or leather; and they were stuffed with either cotton, wool, hair, or scraps of cloth. These variations actually add to the charm of old homemade dolls and tend to personalize them in a way impossible for factory-made dolls.

It is easy to understand why so many Greiners have survived, for he must have made a vast number. There are probably many, many others, still packed in old trunks in family attics and forgotten. If you happen to find an old papier-mâché, even if its paint is worn and its seams are ripped, think seriously before attempting to restore or repair it. In gathering illustrations for this book we reluctantly had to reject several dolls from a most worthwhile collection because they had been so energetically restored by their owner that all personality had been covered with fresh paint. There are experts in various parts of the country who do masterly restoration jobs and who know when to stop.

Other manufacturers followed Greiner's lead in making papier-mâché dolls, sometimes changing his methods a little, but seldom making drastic improvements in them. Unfortunately, many were poorly marked, or not marked at all, so that collectors often disagree about a doll's origin. Among the less important papier-mâchés of the nineteenth century are those credited to G. H. Hawkins, made about 1868, on a buckram base; the dolls marked "W A H NONPAREIL," of about 1870; those of Lerch and Klagg, also of about 1870; Philip (or Phillipp) Goldsmith, of 1875; Joseph Schön, 1887; Solomon Hoffmann, 1892; and George Doebrich, 1895. And there are many others, still.

A man named Lazarus Reichmann of New York City put an end to the large-scale use of papier-mâché for dolls, and took a giant step forward in dollmaking. In 1877 he invented the first composition material: a mixture of glue, sawdust, and dough that seldom contained either paper or paper pulp.

Occasionally, only the heads of dolls were made of composition, and the bodies were made of cloth or leather, but most often the entire doll would be made of composition. This was because the material itself was easily adapted to factory methods, and doll-bodies could be made of it at a cost lower than was possible with cloth or leather stuffed bodies. Before long almost all doll-bodies, for use with all kinds of heads, were made of composition, enameled in flesh-color. This continued to be the case from the late 1800's until World War I. Sometimes the hands were made of wood; the center section of ball-joints was almost always machine-turned wood.

Composition still remains the best of time-tested materials used for making dolls; it is unbreakable, can be repainted and repaired, is not affected by extremes of temperature, and only its surface finish ever cracks or splits. Perhaps modern-day plastics will prove to be as enduring—we shall be able to say in thirty or forty years.

It is easy enough to tell the difference between china and celluloid, or wax and wood, but it is not always so easy to say whether a doll is made of papier-mâché or composition. Composition, however, is heavier, and the surface is generally smoother because the composition substance is of finer grain than papier-mâché. A simple way to become familiar with this difference is to examine the unpainted inside parts of a doll-body, where it is not hard to see the difference between macerated paper and dough-like composition.

Composition head, arms, and legs were used with a cloth body for this doll of the late 1800's. She has a mohair wig and sleeping eyes.

A Shirley Temple doll in her original clothes. When new, the doll's hair was in ringlets. She has sleeping eyes made of plastic and a beautifully modeled body.

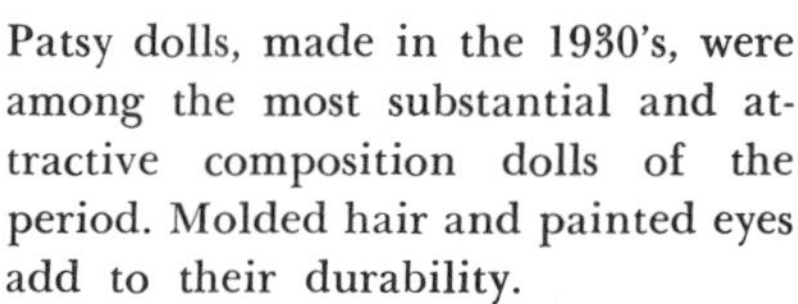

Patsy dolls, made in the 1930's, were among the most substantial and attractive composition dolls of the period. Molded hair and painted eyes add to their durability.

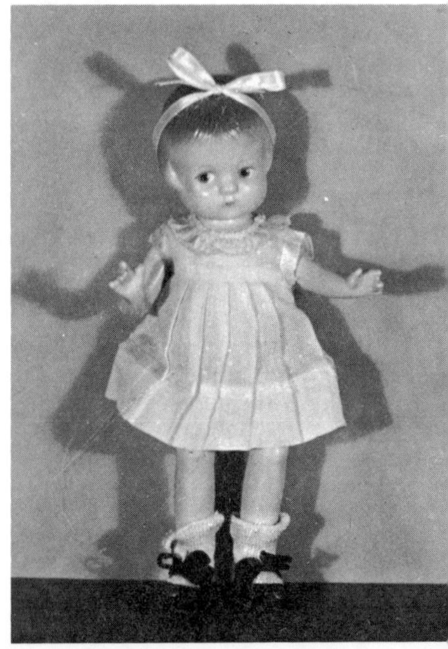

Most of the dolls between the two world wars were made of composition, for plastics were still only a matter of experiment. Some of the most popular were the small, inexpensive ones, often unmarked, whose clothes were more important than their bodies, thereby encouraging the sale of "sets" of dolls. Other excellent ones were the many kinds of German character dolls, and the English Pomona doll-heads used on cloth bodies.

Perhaps the most famous of all composition dolls was the Shirley Temple doll introduced by the Ideal Novelty and Toy Company of New York in 1933. Based upon the dimpled, curly-haired child star of motion pictures, the doll designed by Herr Bernard Lipfert was made in composition in sizes ranging from 11 inches to 27 inches, and became a tremendous seller.

A 16-inch Shirley in the author's collection has greenish hazel sleeping eyes, an open mouth showing five tiny white teeth, and a curly wig of silky blond mohair, from which the original curl has vanished. The neck is modeled in one with the shoulders, and the head swivels on it by means of a concealed wire loop through which elastic is run. The same piece of elastic is strung through the arms, just as was done with the bodies used on German bisques. This device of joining the head to the neck at a point directly under the chin and ears, eliminates the unsightly join at the base of the throat which was customary in earlier dolls. The entire body and head of the doll are composition, well shaped and smoothly finished. She even has tiny dimples at the back of each knee. There can be no mistake about who she is, or who made her, for in raised letters on the back of the head just under the wig the trademark reads: "Cop Ideal Nat Co." On the body itself, under the number 16 (the size), and again in raised letters: "Shirley Temple." This doll suffers from two major faults of many composition dolls of the 1930's—her body color has faded a little, and there are several fine-line cracks in the material of the face.

Some of the 18-inch and larger Shirley Temples are said to have had "flirting" eyes, and one collector claims to have seen specimens without *any* identifying marks. However, it would be strange if such a popular doll had not been copied by unauthorized manufacturers.

For a long time Shirley Temple dolls were not considered important enough to merit serious attention by collectors, probably because so many of them were made. But collectors are now quietly gathering them in, and it is no longer easy to find one in a thrift shop bin and take it home for a dollar. The Deanna Durban and Judy Garland dolls were contemporaries, but never as popular as Shirley Temples—a tip for collectors looking for rarities. There were many other composition dolls inspired by celebrities, fortunately well marked and easy to identify.

It was also during the 1930's that the durable and popular Patsy dolls appeared. It has been claimed that they were the first dolls with a wardrobe to be marketed, a statement hard to prove. At any rate, these sturdy little girls with molded-on hair and lifelike proportions were, like the Shirley Temples, made of composition. There was also Patsy's twin brother Skippy as well as Patsy-Joan, Patsy-Ann, Wee Patsy, Pasty-Lou, and Patsy-ette. These are all harder to find than Patsy.

The 1930's were the days of composition dolls; many were produced right up to World War II, when dollmaking virtually stopped. Some of the favorites were the Walt Disney characters of Snow White and the Seven Dwarfs, Prince Charming, the Blue Fairy, and Pinocchio. Of course these characters have inspired doll artists through the years, and have been made in all media, but the ones mentioned here were all of composition.

Other outstanding composition dolls of the period were those created by the Madame Alexander Doll Company of New York, which concentrated on dolls inspired by characters from books and motion pictures. The Madame Alexander Dionne quintuplet babies were among the best of those produced to fill the market demand developed by admirers of the famous children. Like some of the Shirley Temples and other composition dolls made during the 1930's, they have a tendency to develop hairline cracks in the finish, but this was a fault of the material rather than the manufacturer. They are dolls well worth collecting.

The many composition dolls made prior to World War II

are too numerous to list in detail, but they are clearly marked with the name of the manufacturer as well as the date of their patents. Collectors would be wise to add a few of the best to their collections before it is too late, always remembering that quality rather than quantity is the criterion for choosing dolls.

7

WAX DOLLS

Wax, like wood, was used in the making of images and figurines of religious significance for centuries before it was applied to the manufacture of figures that we know for certain were intended as dolls. The world's museums contain wax burial figures, statuettes, and effigies from ancient Egypt, Greece, and Rome, and from medieval Europe. During the Middle Ages, the Roman Catholic Church in Italy made use of wax in several ways. For example, at one time the walls of the Church of the Annunciation, one of the incomparable churches in Florence, were said to have been completely covered with wax votive figures. Wax dolls, or more accurately wax religious figures, were sold outside this church for centuries.

Beeswax was probably the first kind of wax used by man, although there are a great many other kinds. Indeed, the story of wax is as fascinating as the story of spices, and is worthy of serious study. Wax is found everywhere; it is easy to manipulate, has a lovely texture, and is easy to color. If given reasonably good care it is permanent. Pure beeswax has the unfortunate tendency of turning dark with age, so that many of the oldest wax dolls are almost black. That is why, as far back as the Middle Ages, various additions have been made to wax to improve it. One Italian formula, thought to have been used by Cellini, calls for 3 or 4 ounces of Venice Turpentine, 2 ounces of flake white, and dry vermilion for color. These materials were ground together and added to one pound of fine white wax "of the kind used for candles," and melted. Animal fat was sometimes added to beeswax to give it a softer consistency, and other colors could be used instead of the vermilion.

The making of wax religious figures was only a short step away from wax dollmaking, and we know that by the sixteenth century wax dolls were being made in Europe. Most of these early wax dolls were of solid wax and were thick and blunt-featured, looking more like masks than dolls. While England led in the making of wax dolls, no one knows where or when the first one originated. Although Germany, France, and Austria all contributed to the techniques used, it is impossible to be definite about the first European wax dolls, as few old wax dolls are marked in any way.

The Victoria and Albert Museum has many specimens of wax dolls, as might be expected in the country where wax was so popular, and where so many wax dolls were made. The museum's earliest exhibits of these are in a collection formed by the Powell family, begun in 1754 by Letitia Powell when she dressed a wax doll with a legless wooden body in an ivory brocade gown. A contemporary label fastened to the doll's petticoat reads: "fashionable full dress for spring 1754." The doll's eyes are similar to the eyes found in wooden dolls of the same period—the "Queen Anne type." Letitia dressed another wax doll seven years later, marking it as a replica of her own "wedding suite 1761." Letitia's thoughtful custom of marking and dating her dolls was continued by her descendants, and is one reason the museum's collection is so valuable for doll collectors. It covers the years from 1754 to 1912.

Much credit for stimulating the English and French in the use of wax as a material for dollmaking must go to Madame Marie (Grosholtz) Tussaud's famous waxworks exhibit on Marylebone Road in London—even though her wax figures are perhaps more accurately cataloged as portraits than as dolls.

This artist, born in Bern in 1760, learned the art of wax-working in Paris. She shared her knowledge with Madame Elizabeth, sister of King Louis XVI, and their association may have been the reason Mme. Tussaud was imprisoned for three months during the French Revolution. After her release, she managed to leave France with her collection of life size wax

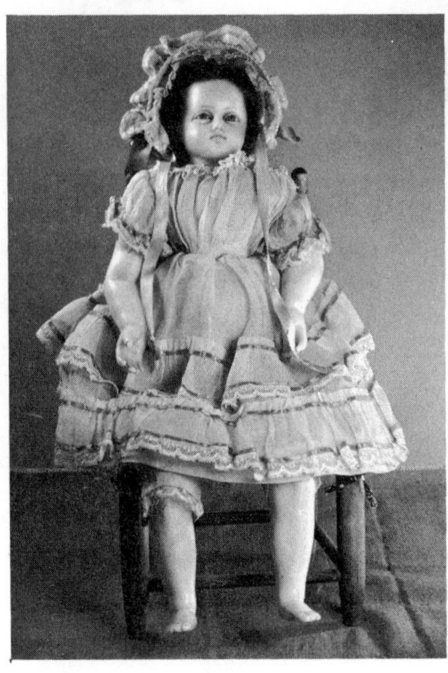

This blue-eyed 23-inch doll in Mrs. Hugh Dyer's collection has hair set strand by strand and lashes and brows set in individually. The doll is unmarked but has all the Montanari characteristics—a short fat neck, three eyelets in the arms, two creases in each elbow and wrist, and dark-rimmed eyes.

Photo by Pinto Photo Service.

figures and went to London where she set up her gallery, eventually adding to it until she had about three hundred exhibits. There were gory, morbid replicas of victims of the guillotine, and notorious criminals, with the relics and implements of torture connected with each one, that filled what she called her "Chamber of Horrors." This display was enormously popular, and at the time of its founder's death in 1850, the impetus was already strong in the manufacture of wax dolls. Increasing numbers of artists and sculptors experimented with this age-old material. However, with few exceptions, their names are unknown.

One family, the Montanaris, dominated the rest, and set a standard of excellence with dolls of the finest workmanship and beauty. Biographical records are sketchy, but it is generally agreed that the family consisted of Madame Augusta Montanari, her husband M. Napoleon Montanari, and their son Richard. Napoleon was a wax modeler of medals and figures, probably one of the craftsmen who followed the lead of Madame Tussaud, for he was her contemporary and also lived in London. Mme. Montanari and Richard are thought to have been the dollmakers. Practically all that we know about the family comes from the reports of the Crystal Palace Exposition of the World's Industry held in London in 1851, (where Montanari dolls won an award), and from the Paris World Exposition in 1852.

Montanari dolls were made in a variety of sizes, according to these exhibition reports, representing ages from infancy to adulthood, and were of great beauty, with fine modeling, beautiful glass eyes, and the inset natural hair that has always been used to identify them. This distinctive method of setting individual hairs in the wax scalp of a doll, however, was not the invention of the Montanari family, for there are ancient Egyptian images and effigies with inset hair. It is also certain that there were some English and European dollmakers previous to this and others who were contemporaries of this clever family, who used the same method. Therefore it is only fair to be a little cautious in claiming that a doll is a Montanari. In many such dolls, a hot needle was used to insert each tiny strand of hair in the wax, the doll's head being fastened to a block so that it could be worked on from all sides. Sometimes a very small slit was cut in the wax and a few hairs inserted in it; they were then fixed in place by pressing with a miniature metal roller. Or, on occasion, wisps of hair prepared as for wigmaking might be inserted into grooves cut in the doll's scalp. Not all hair was set in concentric circles toward the crown; a center or side part was sometimes used instead.

The Victoria and Albert Museum in London has a rare 14¾-inch doll dated about 1853, with a wax head, bust, arms, and legs, and a stuffed cloth body with an inked mark, "Montanari Soho Bazaar." It is thought to be a model of Princess Louise, later Duchess of Argyll, and is not as good an example of Montanari dolls as are some of the unmarked specimens. It is possible that this doll may have been re-waxed sometime during its history, and in the process something of its personality, as well as its modeling, may have been lost. This is one reason many collectors refuse to touch the marks of age and wear, and will not restore a doll. As far as we can learn, this is the only wax doll ever found with a Montanari mark, and it has, therefore, become customary to call dolls which approach the quality of the known Montanaris, "Montanari type."

Beside the inset hair, eyebrows, and eyelashes, Montanari dolls may be identified by the solid poured wax of the head and shoulders, delicately colored and exquisitely modeled; by the fine quality of the inset glass eyes; and by the impression each doll gives of being an individual character study with a personality all its own. For thirty-seven years after the first Montanari doll was produced, the family made this limited, but famous line of dolls, and there are a surprisingly large number of known Montanaris still in existence.

Some of the Montanari competitors also used *poured* wax for the heads, while others made what are in reality "waxed" heads. Papier-mâché was used for the base of the latter type, which was dipped in wax after shaping. The advantage of this method was that it was much less expensive than the use of solid wax, and permitted finer detail in modeling. Charles Marsh, a London contemporary of the Montanari family, was one of the manufacturers who adopted this combination of papier-mâché and wax. His dolls are so different from the Montanari all-waxes that there is no chance of mistaking one for the other.

All Marsh dolls appear to have been labeled, and one in the London Museum has a stamp on its chest in an oval shape which reads, "From E. Moody, Soho Bazaar. Chas. Marsh. Sole Manufacturers London. Dolls cleaned and repaired." Below it, in another oval are the words, "Warranted to stand any climate."

All Marsh wax dolls had long blond hair, set into the heads in thicker clumps than the Montanaris, and in a way to suggest a part. The inset glass eyes, with natural hair lashes and brows, are a bright blue. The mouths are painted pink, and there are two red dots in the nostrils. The hollow heads and shoulders are one piece, and are sewed at each side to the white linen bodies through two holes in the back and front.

The story of another well-known wax dollmaker, Pierotti, begins when Domenico Pierotti came from Italy to England in 1780, bringing with him the knowledge of wax dollmaking; it continues through three generations of the family, ending in

1935 when Domenico's two grandsons suddenly stopped making dolls for Liberty's and for Hamley's Toy Store in London and disappeared.

It was apparently about 1793 that Domenico Pierotti began to make wax dolls at an address on Oxford Street. By the year 1853, his son, H. Pierotti, was listed in both the Watkins Commercial and General Directories as a wax dollmaker at 33 Great Ormond Street, Queens Square, London. In 1862 the Pierotti Royal Model Wax Dolls were awarded a medal of honor at the International Exhibition. From 1871 to 1935 the two sons of H. Pierotti continued to make dolls in the family tradition. Although there were probably a great many Pierotti wax dolls made during this long period of manufacture, they are rare finds today. It is possible, however, to see a few authentic Pierottis in museums. There is a beautiful example in the Toy Museum at Rottingdean, England. It has natural blond hair and dimpled wax hands, and is dressed as an infant, although the face is not that of a baby. The feet of Pierotti dolls were almost always made of wax, and the bodies were of white calico. Their complexions were lovely, the wax colored by a secret process; the cheeks, lips, and corner of the eyes were tinted pink. An outstanding detail of modeling was the realistic little roll of flesh at the back of the neck of baby dolls, as well as the baby-creases at wrists and ankles. The hair was inserted in tiny slits cut in the wax to hold clusters or small strands, thus circling the head up to the crown.

While there was no authenticated label for Pierotti wax dolls, the characteristics already described would help determine a doll's identity. There are certainly enough differences between Montanari, Marsh, and Pierotti dolls to set them apart.

The jury of the 1862 International Exhibition commented that although it appreciated the lifelike and delicate finish of the dolls of Montanari, they felt that it diminished the "necessity of any effort of imagination." This same criticism can apply to the wax dolls of Marsh and Pierotti, and may account for the fact that there are so many surviving wax dolls; they were too beautiful to be played with, and had to be kept safe from children's hands. Or perhaps these delicate and perfect wax dolls were not made to be played with by children, but for adult appreciation.

The method of making doll-heads of poured wax, as the Montanaris and some others were made, began with the modeling of the head in clay. From this, casts or molds were made. The liquid wax was poured into the molds and allowed to harden. Holes for inserting the glass eyes were cut in the wax and the eyes were held in place with a little melted wax. When the wax for these poured heads was already tinted pink or flesh-color, little additional color had to be used except for lips and nostrils, and sometimes the inner ears and corners of the eyes.

Dipped wax heads were made quite differently. They were often based on molded papier-mâché, which was sometimes painted before being dipped in wax. Sometimes, however, the features were painted *after* being waxed. This latter method was not as enduring, for the paint often rubbed or wore off the surface.

An early example of this "waxed" technique is an unmarked doll, whose date is given as 1851, in Mrs. Hugh Dyer's collection. Only the head is waxed. This method is used by many present-day wax dollmakers; good examples are those of Gladys MacDowell.

It seems proper to explain at this point something about the eyes, wigs, and bodies used in making wax dolls. Much of the same information also applies to dolls made of materials other than wax.

The glass eyes used for many years in European dolls, and up to World War I in dolls made in other countries, were beautiful. The best ones had "threaded" irises, and were made and colored to look exactly like the artificial eyes made for human beings. They were probably manufactured in the same factories. Most of them came from Germany, which may explain why blue was for a long time the most common color for doll-eyes, except when the dolls were to be marketed in one of the German or French colonies where brown eyes predominated, as in Africa and the West Indies. Apparently Anglo-Saxon markets preferred delicate shades of blue and violet. Glass

Photo by Pinto Photo Service.

This beautiful 22½-inch wax over papier-mâché doll in Mrs. Hugh Dyer's collection is dated about 1851. It is in mint condition. The stuffed body has wooden arms and legs swiveled at the wrist and ankles.

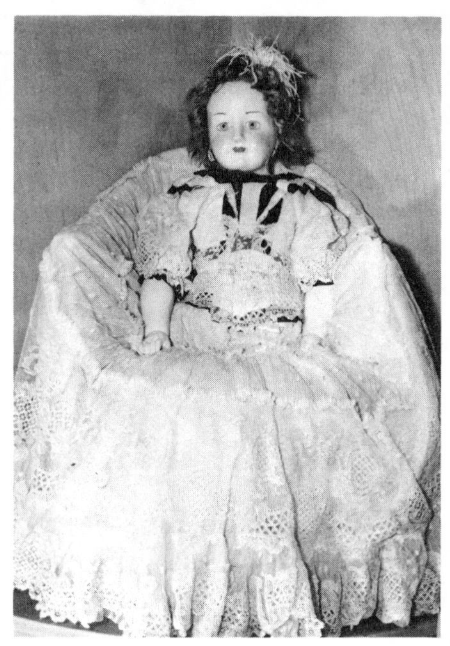

Courtesy, Franks Doll Museum.

An excellent, very large wax doll with pierced ears whose maker is unknown.

Two charming modern wax dolls made by Gladys MacDowell.

eyes were not only lovely to look at, but were also permanent, for there was no paint to peel off, as was sometimes the case when a doll's eyes as well as its mouth and hair were painted on.

Between the years of 1850 and 1875 the first attempts were made to animate dolls by having the eyes open and shut, or even turn from side to side. With wax dolls, this was done by means of a wire fastened to the small blocks of wood on which the eyes were mounted. The opposite end of the wire ran through the body and emerged at the upper part of the hip. When the wire was pulled the eyes moved, or opened and closed. The popularity of these "wire-eyed" dolls lasted for a number of years, until the sleeping-eyed dolls, whose date of origin is unknown, came to be used almost exclusively. It is a mistake to think that these eyes which moved by means of a counterbalance weight inside the head originated as late as the 1890's, as has sometimes been claimed, for dolls with sleeping eyes are known to have been made early in the 1800's.

There is a technical reason why dolls made with glass eyes, either fixed, wired, or sleeping, must also have wigs. Without a head opening at either the top or the base, it would be impossible to insert and fasten separately made eyes. Fixed eyes were held firmly in place with dabs of plaster of Paris. Wire eyes and sleeping eyes were also fastened to the heads with plaster, but there also had to be enough space inside the heads to insert and adjust the lead weights used in their opening and closing mechanism. The doll's wig, then, was made to cover the open top of the head which was sometimes first fitted with a cork or cardboard disc.

For many generations doll wigs were made of various kinds of fur, from sheepskin to monkey-fur, and from different kinds of fibers such as hemp and jute, as well as from human hair. During the sixteenth and seventeenth centuries all fashionable Europeans wore wigs, and it was inevitable that the same methods were used when doll wigs were made. Tiny strands of hair were tied to a net cap with a special tight, imperceptible knot, covering the mesh completely. Hair set in this way could be brushed and combed. Modifications of this method have been in use for generations. Natural human hair was used for black wigs, and after the earlier years, mohair for the Saxon blonds of England and Germany was the most popular.

Bodies for wax dolls varied greatly. Either pink or white kid was the most common for really expensive dolls, and for the rest, the bodies might be of linen or cotton cloth. All were stuffed with hair, cotton, or sawdust. A rather late example of a doll with a wax head and limbs and a stuffed cloth body is "Princess Daisy," a 17½-inch English baby doll in an elaborate Dutch dress accompanied by clothing, toys, utensils, and dressing table essentials. It is dated about 1890, and is now in the Victoria and Albert Museum collection of wax dolls.

There was a lull in the production of wax dolls when bisque, glazed china and Parians replaced them, but as may be seen in the discussion of the work of modern doll artists in Chapter 16, the art is not dead.

As elusive as any kind of dolls we have ever tried to trace are the large waxen old people to be found in Mexico. They may be related to the Vargas dolls of New Orleans, or perhaps were made by another branch of the Vargas family. The Mexican figures are usually at least 20-inches high, and are often sold in pairs. An elderly man and woman with overly pink complexions and harsh expressions, somehow lacking the mellow charm of earlier Mexican dolls, were recently noticed in a shop in a border town. They were priced at $20 each, so could probably have been bought for $12 or $15 if the buyer had persisted.

An alert traveler could probably find worthier dolls than these in the interior of the country, at a much lower price. One should also watch for the smaller and even more charming solid wax dolls of Mexico, which are dressed in cloth, then waxed again.

As it was, even in medieval times, the making of wax dolls or figures overlaps the making of candles, and doll collectors will find there are many small seasonal wax candle-dolls offered each Christmas, Easter, Hallowe'en and Thanksgiving which are suitable for their collections. These bright little figures are made to withstand extremes of temperature and if given reasonable care, should survive for several generations, just as their ancestors have done.

Photo by Peter Klein.

A dentist's office scene from *The Awful Truth*, one of the life-size exhibits at the Movieland Wax Museum. Notice the board with names of actors, director, producer, and scene number.

If any doll collectors are inclined to try their own skill at making wax dolls, there is a modern synthetic modeling wax called "Microcrystalline," much used by artists and sculptors. Although it looks like beeswax, it is considerably cheaper; made in several degrees of hardness, it can be purchased in many art supply shops.

It is possible that the making of wax dolls may become common again. Some impetus in this direction was given by the creation of the Movieland Wax Museum, in Buena Park, California, near Disneyland. While the museum was being planned, experts studied everything known about wax figures, tested materials and methods, and often improved them. The words used by Mary Pickford on May 4, 1962, when she dedicated the museum were:

"Dedicated to the artists of the entertainment industry who, through their talents and efforts, have contributed so much to the enjoyment and understanding of the people of the world."

This would also be an apt dedication to all the dollmakers whose skill through the centuries has contributed to the same ends.

This stars' hall of fame culminated years of planning by Allen Parkinson, whose original inspiration came when he visited Madame Tussaud's Waxworks in London. His idea was to let the public see likenesses of great motion picture stars in scenes from their most famous pictures, incorporating the actual costumes and props used in the filming, or making exact duplicates of them. Sophia Loren gave the torn dress she wore in *Two Women* for her wax replica; Gloria Swanson's $10,000 Russian chinchilla wrap and Buster Keaton's porkpie hat were their own. Liberace's tuxedo and the candelabra used in his first television appearances are a part of his scene. When a garment had deteriorated, as occurred with the robes Charles Laughton wore as Henry VIII, an exact duplicate was made. To give a visitor the further illusion of being in a motion picture studio during the making of a picture, the real equipment used in filming the production was positioned just as it had been during the filming of the scenes. Therefore, in addition to the stars and other actors, wax figures of the cameramen, technicians, and their lights and sound equipment were also made a part of the set.

There are about one hundred wax figures of Hollywood personalities in this museum, and more will continue to be added as results come in from surveys of fan mail, theater owners, exhibitors, and visitors to the museum, indicating that certain performers or pictures should be included.

The museum is of great interest to doll collectors, and will perhaps lead to a revival of wax dollmaking, since those who planned the exhibits decided that the age-old medium of wax was still the most effective material to use. Madame Tussaud's wax figures inspired dollmakers in France, Germany, and England more than two hundred years ago. Who knows what will result from this twentieth century exhibit?

FASHION DOLLS AND FRENCH BISQUES

IT HAS BECOME the habit of some dealers and collectors to invent names for particular kinds of dolls, and too often these names persist. A good example is the designation "fashion doll," used in conjunction with French bisques as if this were a specific kind of doll like a rag doll or a baby doll. In fact, fashion dolls are not necessarily limited to the French bisques with kid bodies and wasp waists, dressed in elaborate costumes. Instead, any kind of doll, which is used for the purpose of selling or displaying fashions or styles is a fashion doll. In a sense, modern American "Barbie" dolls are fashion dolls. Store window mannequins are fashion dolls. Instead of saying, for instance, "a Spanish fashion doll," one might better state, "This unmarked wax doll was bought in Spain and is dressed in a costume popular in Paris in the eighteenth century." It is possible, for instance, such a doll might have been sent from Paris to Spain in the eighteenth century to display the fashions of the moment to a Spanish queen who wished to order a costume, see the latest mode in hairstyles, and find out what accessories should be worn at a court ball. On the other hand, it might have been a French doll brought home to Spain for the daughter of a wealthy Spaniard.

Fashion dolls have been made of wood, wax, bisque, glazed china, paper, and porcelain. Nothing about the doll or the way it is made, or the material used makes it a fashion doll: only the use to which it was put.

France has been the source of world fashion for so long that hundreds of years ago a queen of England sent to France for

An exceptionally fine French fashion doll in Mrs. Hugh Dyer's collection. It is not marked but is said to be a Huret, dated about 1850.

Photo by Pinto Photo Service.

a sample of Parisian styles. Since there were neither fashion magazines nor photographs, the easiest way to pass along this information might have been to send living models, wearing actual clothes, but instead, there is a fourteenth century

Group of fine French bisque and fashion dolls in Mrs. Walter Wagner's collection. *Top, left to right:* French fashion doll with body of kid over wood; an F.G. doll; a Belton. *Center, left to right:* French fashion with kid body; Jumeau marked on head, body, and shoes; a Steiner; a Société Française de Fabrication des Bébés et Jouets. *Bottom, left to right:* Bru, circa 1879; Jumeau, unmarked; French walking doll.

record of a tailor to the court of the king of France, sending a doll and her wardrobe to the queen of England. A hundred years later, Queen Anne of Brittany ordered a doll to be dressed and sent to Queen Isabella of Spain, to show Paris fashions. There are other records of similar dolls, and it is curious to discover that many of these early fashion dolls were much larger than those used later—some of them even life size. Every detail of dress was duplicated, hats, jewelry, coiffure, shoes, dresses, gloves, and laces. Nothing could surpass this way of showing and recording the details of dress, for there can be no argument when the evidence is tangible. It was good for its time, and a valuable record foı present-day research.

England was not the only country dependent on French fashions; for centuries, all European elite turned to France for leadership. Not even the French Revolution put an end to the exchange. Fashion dolls were not always feminine; replicas of elegant gentlemen are also mentioned. These are much rarer, however, and many collectors have never seen one.

As we study the dolls of the eighteenth and nineteenth centuries, it becomes increasingly difficult to draw the line between play dolls and fashion dolls. For this reason, some doll experts are inclined to hedge and call them "lady types," or "style dolls," instead of fashion dolls.

During the height of the French enthusiasm for fashion dolls, there were shops on many Parisian streets devoted entirely to dressing and selling these dolls, the materials for their elaborate wardrobes, and their costly accessories. One street was actually named "La Rue de la Poupée," and here every shop offered something exclusively for dolls. There were doll dressmakers, wig makers, milliners, flower makers, fan makers, lacemakers, jewelers who made doll jewelry of gold and precious stones, weavers who specialized in fabrics for doll clothes and doll shawls.

At this time, French bisques were the kind of doll most commonly used for the display of fashions. Perhaps the reason that even now they are sometimes erroneously classified as the *only* kind of fashion doll has to do with the mystery and confusion surrounding their manufacture.

Bisque, a contraction of the word biscuit, is the name potters use to describe unglazed pottery and porcelain. When applied to dolls, it refers to the flesh-colored ceramic dolls made in quantity in Europe during the Golden Age of Dolls, 1860–1890. Few bisque dolls have been made anywhere since World War I, except for a small number in Japan and a few made by American doll artists, described more fully in a later chapter. Since World War II, unglazed china, or bisque, has been replaced by composition or plastic. But good pink bisque, smooth and satiny, with a warm lifelike color, is far more natural looking than any other material used for dolls. It is strong, and although not unbreakable, will survive quite rough treatment. In addition, the pigments used for painting features on bisque dolls are fired on in high-temperature kilns, and are practically permanent.

Many French bisque dolls of the 1860–1890 period have blown glass eyes, and wigs of real hair. While sizes varied, they averaged about 10 to 32 inches in height, the favorite sizes being 12 to 16 inches. Bodies were most often made of pink or white kid, either rigid or with gusset-type joints. Less often, bodies were made of cloth. Early French bisques had heads and shoulders modeled in one piece; but after Emile Jumeau invented swivel-heads in the early 1860's, most bisque dolls were made with heads that turned, and were fitted into the deep shoulders and busts.

Trying to establish a logical time sequence for the making of early French bisques is as frustrating as trying to identify the makers, because most of the dolls are not marked. We therefore have a great many lovely dolls to be matched up with a few manufacturers' names. Among these names are Belton, Gauthier, Greffier, Broiliet, Mauger, Huret, Jumeau, Voit de Hildburghausen, and Steiner.

Dolls marked with the initials F.G. may have been made by Francois (or Francis) Gauthier, or by F. Greffier, one of the first makers of French bisques; there is disagreement among experts as to the meaning of the mark. It is possible that Gauthier merged his business with that of Jumeau, or perhaps he was the maker of some of the bisque heads which Jumeau

This 17-inch doll and costumes are probably Jumeau about 1867. Expressive face with full cheeks and double chin, construction of body, shaped and curved fingers are all typical of him, and his early dolls are rarely signed.
Courtesy, Newark Museum.

Group of Bru bisques. *Left:* A kissing Bru (by pulling a string at her side, she will raise her hand and throw a kiss); second doll from left has stiff kid body, with bisque hands and arms.
Courtesy, Franks Doll Museum.

This "Whistling" Bru in Mrs. William Foster's collection spent World War II in a French convent. She wears her original coat and bonnet.

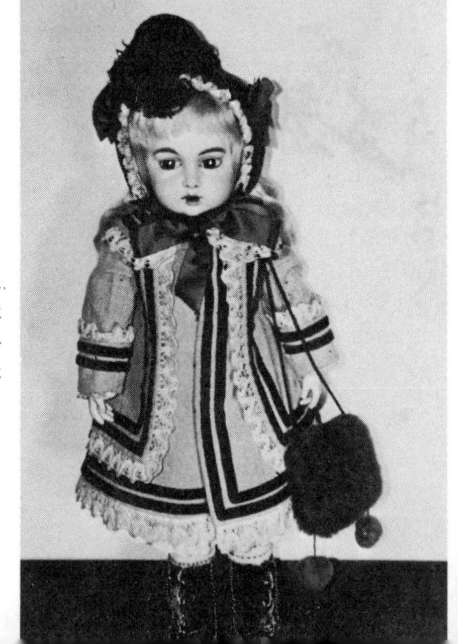

put on his own kid bodies. Kimport once mentioned having seen a doll with Jumeau's stamp on the body and F.G. on the shoulder. If there really was a merger, Gauthier may have made bisque heads after it, as well as before and marked them with his initials. Perhaps some day a clue will appear to help unravel this mysterious business. At any rate, F.G. dolls are always spoken of with respect by collectors, for they are of the finest quality.

The first firm ground we reach when studying French bisques was the year 1844, when Monsieur Emile Jumeau won a prize at the Paris Industrial Exposition for his dolls of flesh-tinted bisque. Then in 1851 he was awarded a prize for doll costumes at the London Crystal Palace Exposition. Jumeau dolls received many awards from 1844 through 1886.

Perhaps the most complete and authoritative history of the Jumeau firm is to be found in the 1957 translation by Nina S. Davies of a French booklet written by J. Cusset and printed in Paris in 1885. Published under the title, *The Jumeau Doll Story*, the book contains photographs of the Montreuil factory, Emile Jumeau, Jr., and descriptions of the methods he used in manufacturing his two lines of dolls, Poupées Parisiennes, and Bébés.

The Jumeau business was founded in 1843 by M. Emile Jumeau, Sr., and the only dolls made for a number of years were those with kid bodies, called the Poupée Parisienne. It was not until 1878, when the founder's son, Emile, Jr. headed the firm, that the unbreakable Bébés appeared.

The Jumeau factory in Montreuil employed about 350 workmen, and Jumeau operated a shop in Paris on Rue Pastourelle where he had at least fifty workers; in addition there were many dressmakers, milliners, etc., who worked for him in their homes. Employees in the Jumeau factory served a five-year apprenticeship without pay before they were fully qualified. Even the women who lived at home and brought their work to the shop or the factory were required to receive training in the factory. There were twenty young women who made the glass eyes used in the dolls, and it therefore seems unlikely that eyes were imported from Germany, as has been claimed in the past. Some of the dolls were blonds with blue eyes, and others were brown-eyed brunets. He often used a simple spring device for the dolls' eyes to turn them into sleeping-eyed Bébés.

The process for making bisque doll-heads was approximately the same in all factories, including Jumeau's. Heads were first modeled in clay; from this, two-piece plaster molds were made. Kaolin, an extremely pure form of white clay was steeped in water for a long time; the longer the steeping, the finer the porcelain that resulted. When the clay paste was finally taken from the water, it was kneaded like dough, and rolled out into thin sheets, the thickness of the doll's head. It was next pressed firmly into the plaster molds to assume the exact modeling of the original head. After the molds had been used 50 times they were replaced, so the modeling was always clear-cut. As soon as the clay had hardened slightly, the two parts—front and back of the head—were removed from the molds and joined to make a head which was hollow inside. The larger sizes had ears applied at this time, while smaller dolls had ears molded together with the rest of the head. Holes for inserting the glass eyes were carefully made while the clay was still moist, and the area surrounding each eye was shaved as thin as possible so that later, when the eyes were set, they would show off to the best advantage. The heads were fired at an extremely high temperature, then coated with two applications of pale pink mineral paint, and given pink cheeks, lips, and nostrils and the heavy eyebrows and lashes characteristic of Jumeau dolls. The last firing was followed by the fixing in place of the blown glass eyes, and finally, the addition of a wig.

The method Jumeau used for making his later papier-mâché doll bodies is also like that employed by other doll-makers of the period. Thick gray paper was soaked in paste and placed in layers in cast iron molds. The back and chest required more layers of paper for strength than did the legs, while the hands and feet were almost solid. The torso was molded in two parts (like the head), front and back, which were then glued together. After the paper was dry, the "cups" were placed. These were the small rings of metal, wood, or cardboard inserted in the torso, arms, and legs, to which elastic would be fastened when the doll was eventually assembled. The papier-mâché body was then coated with thick white paint, dried, sandpapered, and given five successive coats of flesh-pink paint. Varnish was applied, and the parts were dried. Finally, the doll was assembled by running elastic through the various sections.

There are some variations in the makeup of Jumeau dolls. Early ones often had leather hands and feet, as well as leather bodies. Some of the rarest Jumeau's were made of jointed wood, covered with kid; others were entirely of wood, and a few had cloth bodies.

In the late 1870's, Jumeau shifted from his wasp waisted ladies with adult faces to the childlike bodies and faces that made him immortal. It was after this change that he took the lead among dollmakers, and his production jumped so much that he had to increase the size of his factory.

In spite of the insistence of the author of *The Jumeau Doll Story* that all Jumeau dolls are marked, there are opposing claims made by authorities who maintain that there were *unmarked* Jumeaus. It is very possible that there were imitators of Jumeau who did not identify themselves with a trademark, for, of course, anyone as successful as Jumeau was certain to have been copied. It is safer, therefore, to claim authenticity only when a doll is marked with Jumeau's name. A common mark on French bisque dolls was "Tête Jumeau's," meaning Jumeau head and indicating that the head by Jumeau was made to be used on the doll body of another manufacturer.

Jumeau's most important rival was perhaps Anton Bru. He made exquisite bisque heads that were quite different from Jumeau's. Bru dolls were usually marked with the BRU incised vertically in the left shoulder, at the back. Bru dolls were probably first made with wooden bodies; later he began to cover them with kid, and finally produced bodies of kid ingeniously cut in one piece and shaped by means of darts at waistline and joints. Feet and hands were most often of wood or bisque.

The relationship of Jumeau and Bru has been explained by M. J. S. Moynot, president of the Société Française de Fabrication des Bébés et Jouets (French Society for the Manufacture of Dolls and Toys), in discussing the toymaking situation of

France. According to M. Moynot, the houses of Bru and Jumeau merged, to form La Société Française de Fabrication des Bébés et Jouets. The two daughters of M. Jumeau and the son-in-law of M. Bru were among those named as directors of the new corporation. In 1938 the manufacture of Bru dolls ceased, but as late as 1951 the Jumeau doll was still being made. It was different from the earlier Jumeaus, having been improved and changed through the years. While it was still a beautiful doll, it bore little resemblance to the older ones.

The dolls of Jules-Nicholas Steiner present a peculiar problem. His trademark, registered in the French government office in 1889, shows a picture of a doll with bangs and long curls holding a banner printed with the words, "Le Petit Parisien, Bébé Steiner." Yet not all Steiner dolls are marked, and even when they are, the markings vary. Some consist of the same words stamped in ink together with the additional phrase "Medaille d'or Paris, 1889." Moreover, in spite of the labels, many experts doubt that the Steiner dolls were French, believing instead that they were originally made in Germany and assembled in France. Still other authorities contend that Steiner had factories in both countries. But whatever the geographical truth, Steiner's work was of outstanding quality. A characteristic of many of his dolls is an open mouth revealing two rows of tiny teeth, instead of the usual single row.

Early French dolls were made with holes drilled all the way through the ear lobes to permit the insertion of earrings. German dolls of this period also had pierced ears, for it was fashionable for little girls as well as grown women to wear earrings.

Except for Jumeaus, the eyes of most French dolls were imported from Germany and were made of blown glass—or as it is sometimes called spun glass or paperweight glass—colored gray, light or dark blue, violet, and brown. A few French dolls had eyes made of enamels.

Wigs might be made of human hair, mohair, silk, or from Angora goatskin with its long wavy hair attached. Hair was almost always blond and very thick, so that it might be dressed in fashionable and elaborate fringes, curls, and puffs. Most of these wigs were made by highly skilled wigmakers in a day when wigmaking was a recognized trade requiring a long apprenticeship.

The United States first saw some of these exquisite French bisques at the 1876 Centennial Exposition in Philadelphia. This event, like the 1893 World's Columbian Exposition in Chicago, gave many Americans their first glimpse of European artistry, in a way hard for today's more sophisticated fair-goers to appreciate.

The name "Centennial doll" probably came from the French bisques which parents brought home from the Exposition to their children, who were often not allowed to play with it—only look. French dolls everywhere served quite a different purpose from the comforting rag-babies, or the durable woodens and papier-mâchés.

Luella Hart is an expert researcher, writer and doll authority, who has gathered doll trademarks and patent records for more than a quarter-of-a-century through her studies of dolls in Europe and America. She has contributed to many magazines, including *Spinning Wheel, Toy Trader, Hobbies,* and *Doll Talk,* and wrote the chapter on modern dolls in the 1956 revised edition of Max von Boehn's *Dolls and Puppets,* from the point where von Boehn left off, 1930 to 1955. A complete list of her books is listed in the bibliography, but because Mrs. Hart publishes them herself, they must be obtained from her directly, or from Kimport Dolls, Paul Ruddel, or the Mark Farmer Co. Collectors will appreciate that she is qualified to answer all their questions about the marks and makers of French dolls, as well as the dolls of British and German manufacturers.

Any collector who can contribute authentic, indisputable information about unmarked European dolls will be doing other collectors a favor by passing it along. Old letters, old advertisements, old bills of lading, etc., might furnish just the bit of information needed to confirm or clarify some disputed point.

An Adams, Massachusetts collector, Mrs. William Foster, has done just this. In order to encourage other collectors to share information about their dolls, and also to record an intriguing story, I quote from a letter Mrs. Foster wrote to me recently about her whistling Bru doll:

> This doll and her nine Bru sisters were in a collection before World War II, and belonged to a girl who became a member of the French Underground. When the Germans took over Paris, she took all her dolls to a convent for safekeeping and told the nuns that if anything happened to her, she wanted them to sell the dolls when the war was over, and use the money for the convent.
>
> She was later captured and shot as a spy. When the war was over, an American collector went to Paris and while on tour, her guide took her to the convent where the dolls were, and she bought the ten Brus. She later on sold eight of them, and just now has released the one I have. The last one she is keeping for herself, and says she will keep her as long as she lives.
>
> While the American collector was at the convent, she also bought the embroidered lace which was handmade by the French nuns. She took it home with her and used it to trim the doll's lovely dress, which she made 20 years ago when she bought the doll.

This 18-inch doll is of very pale bisque for a Bru and has a swivel head on separate bisque shoulders, both head and shoulders incised "BRU JNE 6T." Her expressive brown glass stationary eyes are of blown glass, and her original pale blond mohair wig is cut in bangs in the front, and reaches almost to her waist in back. The slightly open mouth, modeled in a whistling position, has a small metal disc inside, with a pinhole opening in it. A key at the back of her neck at one time activated the bellows inside her head. This forced the air to make a whistling sound as it came out.

The doll wears her original bronze tab earrings in her pierced ears; the fine white body is made of kid; arms and hands are of bisque; the legs and feet are of wood. Around the chest, which is molded with little bosoms, a part of the original paper label still remains. She's dressed in a coat of light taupe wool with brown velvet and ecru lace trim, she wears a matching bonnet of brown velvet, rust-colored ribbons, and brown ostrich-tips. The rest of her outfit includes high-button brown leather boots, handworked stockings, and a little brown fur muff with pompoms. Her dress is a copy of the original—very detailed, with a square neck, rows of tucking on bodice and sleeves, insertion lace, and two tiers of gathered flounces on the skirt. These flounces are made of the wide, handmade lace obtained from the convent, as Mrs. Foster mentioned in her letter.

All collectors will understand what was meant by the doll's owner who sold her to Mrs. Foster when she said, "You have a real treasure. I hope you will love her as much as her original owner, who thought enough of her to protect her from the enemy."

9

GERMAN AND AMERICAN BISQUE DOLLS

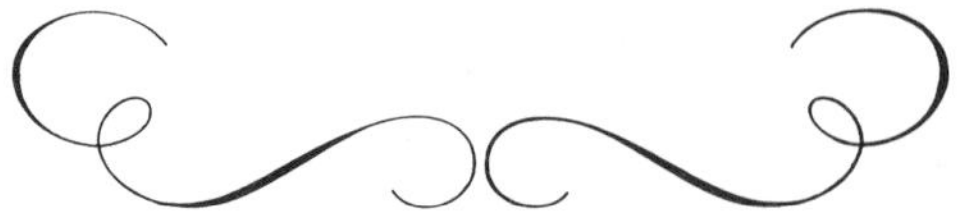

FOR HUNDREDS OF YEARS until World War I, most of the dolls of the world came from the forests of central Europe, with Graefenhain, Thuringia, and the town of Sonneberg recognized as the primary centers of dollmaking. So it is not particularly surprising that some of the most famous dolls created by American designers at the beginning of the twentieth century should have been commercially produced in conjunction with German manufacturers.

Germany's domination of the doll and toy market was the result of its cheap peasant labor and the skill of its generations of trained craftsmen. It has been said that the output of German village toymakers was limited only by the smoke nuisance created by the firing operations of making bisque and china doll heads.

It must be remembered that nineteenth century German toy manufacturing was not the construction-line operation we have come to associate with a large volume of production, but was rather a network of cottage industries in the small villages located in the heavily forested areas of Saxony and Thuringia. The bulk of the work was done at home by families. The father, perhaps, molded the different parts of the dolls; the mother took over the painting and wigmaking; the children assembled the dolls. After completion, the dolls were taken to a central collection point, and from there sent to city buyers who shipped them to markets all over the world.

So long as Germany could cut costs and increase volume far beyond French capability, and still maintain quality, there could be little serious competition. At the time modern interest in doll collecting began, thirty or forty years ago, twentieth century German-made bisque dolls were snubbed—there were so many of them. But that has changed, and now German dolls have come to be appreciated.

Fortunately for collectors, it is generally easier to identify the German bisques than the early bisques of France. The U. S. law of 1891 requiring that all imports be marked with the country of origin, helps doll collectors a great deal. Even though the name of the manufacturer was not also required, it is an advantage to know at least where the doll was made. Many dollmakers, however, did begin to add their names and sometimes initials and numbers as well. This occasionally causes arguments among collectors, but more often helps to identify the dolls more exactly. However, when a German-made head was put on a French-made body in a French factory, just exactly which country *should* be given credit for it?

German bisques were the "play dolls" just as the daintier waxes were the "show-off" dolls, of Europe and America. Because so many thousands of them were made, there is still a good chance to buy Simon and Halbigs and Armand Marseilles at moderate prices. Some day they will all have gone into collections, and it will be too late.

When identifying and fixing the dates of specific German dolls, it is helpful to consult Luella Hart's *Directory of German Dolls*, listed in the bibliography, which covers the years 1875 to 1960.

One of the most prolific German doll manufacturers was the firm of Simon and Halbig, identified by the initials "S & H." On some dolls the initials were combined with "K & R" and a six-pointed star (Kämmer and Reinhardt); with "H H" (Heinrich Handwerck); or the mark of C. M. Bergmann, among many others. Two names on a head probably meant that the firm made the heads for some other manufacturer who supplied the bodies. One German authority claims that Simon and Halbig made no complete dolls. In addition to initials, most of the heads were also marked with numbers—probably sizes or styles.

The Simon and Halbig Company was making doll-heads in

Courtesy, Franks Doll Museum.

Boy dolls made in Germany. *Bottom rear:* A pre-Greiner with black pupil-less eyes. *Left to right:* Blond china; glass-eyed Parian; luster china; painted hair china; Heubach; and Heubach character doll.

Right: Author's childhood bisque Simon and Halbig doll in original dress sits beside her contemporary Armand Marseille cousin. Both dolls have sleeping glass eyes, natural hair, and jointed papier-mâché and composition bodies.

The author's "laughing doll" is a Gebruder Heubach made about 1910. It has a fine bisque head, sleeping eyes, and ball-jointed composition body.

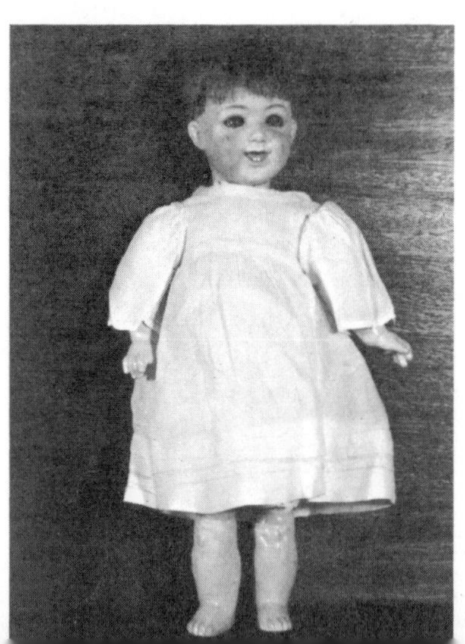

Thuringia long before 1891, and continued to operate at least into the 1930 period. Sizes varied from very small to quite large. Some were colored as Negro dolls, but most of them were the usual blond German type with blue eyes. A few had brown eyes. The satiny bisque of many Simon and Halbig dolls is as fine as that of most French dolls. Some have closed mouths, while others are open-mouthed, giving the doll a slightly expectant expression. Closed mouths are rated higher by collectors, which is odd, for a row of little white teeth showing between a doll's smiling lips often gives it a most engaging touch.

The McKims of Kimport Dolls have spent a great deal of time trying to untangle the confusion of doll marks and labels, and Ruby Short McKim once wrote an excellently documented article for *Doll Talk* about the German dolls marked "K & R" —the firm of Kämmer and Reinhardt, which operated the largest doll factory in Germany. The firm was organized in 1885 by Franz Reinhardt, a young salesman, and Ernst Kämmer, an expert modeler. One of their most famous dolls was the "Kaiser Baby," made in 1908. Many legends have been spun about it, such as that the doll was suppressed by the German royal family because it was an unflattering representation of Kaiser Wilhelm as an infant, even showing his withered arm. This was one of the earliest of the so-called character dolls, not pretty, but with much personality. Some of the firm's other character dolls according to Ruby McKim were named Marie, Gretchen, and Hans. Kämmer died in 1901, and the K & R Company bought out the rival factory of Heinrich Handwerck when its owner also died. Still later, K & R merged with the firm of Simon and Halbig.

Armand Marseille, in spite of the French name, was a German firm; a contemporary of Simon and Halbig, it also made dolls for the mass market. The quality of Armand Marseille dolls did not always equal that of Simon-Halbig's, and was definitely inferior to that of J. D. Kestner dolls (which will be discussed later in this chapter). Armand Marseille's output, on the other hand, was at one time larger that that of any other company, and included the greatest variety of bisque heads. Many of them, but not all, carry the initials "D.E.P." or

"D.R.G.M.," indicating that they were patented or registered in Germany.

The firm was in business before 1891, and there are A. M. heads dated as early as 1894. The doll called Miss Columbia, in honor of the World's Columbian Exposition in 1893, is an Armand Marseille, and so is the Floradora Girl of 1905. The same doll was patented in 1921 by the George Borgfeldt Company, which took out patents on many A. M. dolls and became their sales agent. Other Armand Marseille dolls were their Kiddie Joy, Nobby Kid, and Baby Betty. Nobby Kid, introduced in 1915, was probably the last German doll patented before World War I wiped out the foreign doll trade.

The marks on Armand Marseille dolls varied greatly. Sometimes a horseshoe was part of the trademark; sometimes only the initials of the name were used. There were different combinations of numbers under the name. Some late specimens carry the numbers 390 or 391.

My first bisque doll was a Simon and Halbig—a typical example of the German bisques made about 1908–1910. The pink bisque head has "sleeping eyes" of blue blown glass, waxed eyelids inset with real hair eyelashes, and pierced ears for earrings. The mohair wig was replaced many years ago by a wig made from my own hair, when it was cut to shorten my pigtails. Incised in the back of the head, just below the wig, are the initials, "S & H," and above them, a six-pointed star. On either side of the star are the initials "K" and "R," and on the tapered base of the head—hidden from sight when the metal hook in the head is slipped through the elastic used to string the body together—are the incised numbers "58." The head is on its original 22-inch composition, ball-jointed body. Alice has such a bright, alert expression that even after all these years I sometimes think she is about to speak.

Sitting under the Christmas tree with Alice, was my sister's German bisque doll, purchased in the same store. It is an Armand Marseille with the word GERMANY incised under the name, and the number 300 under that. The additional figures X3 are under the number. The bisque is smooth and fine, the sleeping eyes are of brown blown glass, and the features are smaller in proportion to the face than those of the other doll. The unmarked composition body is identical with that of my Simon-Halbig; indeed they may have been made in the same factory. Both dolls have been restrung only twice in the more than fifty years since they were purchased, and the only sign of age is the slightly worn paint on the fingertips and toes.

These composition doll-bodies are typical of those found on many German bisques, although bisque heads were sometimes placed on bodies of cloth, kid, and occasionally wood. On these particular bodies, only the ball sections of the arm and leg joints are made of wood. This was a practical material to use at the places receiving the most wear. All that was said in the last chapter about doll-bodies, is equally true of those used on German dolls and it is more than possible that they were all made in the same factories.

Gebruder Heubach, another contemporary, used as his trademark an incised circle with a fan-like center. He made excellent bisque heads, but probably did not manufacture entire dolls. His greatest distinction lies in the fact that he was one of the first bisque doll manufacturers to create "character faces." Up until about 1909–10, dolls were made in the conventional way, to look like dolls and not individuals. Heubach changed this, introducing a line of dolls that were sometimes not even pretty but were full of individuality. One of these, "the laughing doll" from the author's own childhood was purchased about 1911 or 1912. It is a 12-inch doll with a bisque head and papier-mâché or composition ball-jointed body. The mischievous face has a wide-open laughing mouth, showing two tiny lower teeth. The sleeping eyes are of blue glass, and the wig is light brown mohair (trimmed by my imaginative sister), which was originally shoulder-length. The body is not marked, but the Heubach circle is on the back of the head.

Some of the finest and most highly prized German bisques are those of J. D. Kestner, Jr., whose dolls were made in Walterhausen, Thuringia. We know very little about this company, but it is thought that Kestner's were made for almost a generation before the first Simon-Halbigs, or from about the year 1860, and that they continued to be made up to World War I. In any event, it is certain that J. D. Kestner, Jr., first registered his trademark in the U. S. Patent Office in 1896. The trademark is a Royal Crown with two ribbons streaming from it, the one on the left printed "J.D.K." and the one on the right "Germany." The patent was for a bisque doll head with a kid body, and was the only one ever issued to Kestner in this country.

In the 1890's, the George Borgfeldt Company took over as exclusive agent for Kestner in the United States and Canada, and the joint operations of these two firms was a great advantage to both of them during the many years they were associated. Many of the most famous and popular dolls on record were suggested by the New York house of Borgfeldt and turned over to Kestner for manufacture. Three of the most successful of these were the Gibson Girl of about 1900, copied from the drawings of Charles Dana Gibson, the Kewpie of Rose O'Neill, and the Bye-Lo Baby of Grace Story Putnam, any one of which would have made a doll manufacturer both wealthy and immortal.

The direct merging of Kestner and Borgfeldt with Rose O'Neill, designer of the famous Kewpies, continued from 1912 until World War I. Rose O'Neill was born in Wilkes-Barre, Pennsylvania, and moved with her parents in 1872 to the Ozark country, where she lived the rest of her life. She was a writer and an artist whose work was full of the light, whimsical spirit of her Irish father. She not only wrote the sentimental and delightful poems and stories about her Kewpies, but also painted their pictures, and finally sponsored their appearance in the round, as dolls, instead of drawings.

The name Kewpie is the diminutive of Cupid. The elfin look of the little figures with their fat baby stomachs and golden topknots is accented by a pair of tiny blue wings. Kewpies, possessing the very essence of infant charm, first appeared as drawings to illustrate Rose O'Neill's poems in a series appearing originally in the 1909 *Ladies' Home Journal.* After this initial series started, paper doll Kewpies followed, as we have seen; then by demand, and sponsored by George Borgfeldt of New York, arrangements were made with the J. D. Kestner Company for the manufacture of bisque Kewpies. This international venture was one of the most successful in the entire history of

Three Kewpie dolls. Left and center are celluloid; Kewpie at right is bisque. Rear view shows the famous little blue wings on the shoulders.

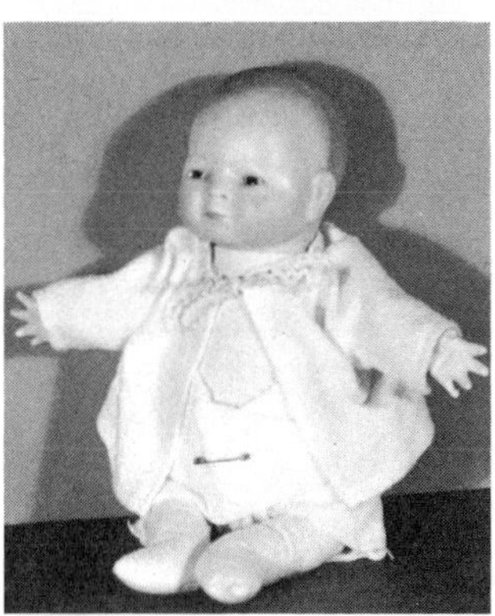

The "Million Dollar Baby," a bisque Bye-Lo is one of the greatest dolls of all times. This is in Miss Miriam Denton's collection.

dollmaking, for it is said that by 1913 some 5 million Kewpies had been sold. True to Kestner tradition, the quality of the dolls was exceptionally fine. Most of them were bisque, but a few were made of celluloid, stamped with the tortoise trademark, which identified only the best celluloid products. On the bisque Kewpies the name O'Neill was stamped on the sole of the foot, a red and gold heart-shaped paper label was glued on the chest, and on the back was a small circular label reading, "Copyright Rose O'Neill." There is little chance of finding an original bisque Kewpie with both of the paper labels intact, but the incised name on the foot serves to identify the doll forever.

During the sad days when World War I blocked all trade with Germany, American manufacturers replaced bisque Kewpies with those of celluloid, composition, cloth, rubber, and metal. In recent years a few bisque Kewpies have come on to the market from Germany, cast in in the original, copyrighted molds, and painted in equally careful detail on a bisque of perhaps a little different texture from the first ones. They are marked with the word GERMANY stamped in ink in tiny letters on the back.

Early Kewpies were as popular with adults as with children, and were often used decoratively, sometimes with a huge bow of ribbon tied around the tummy, or in conventional doll clothes. One popular custom was to dress a pair of miniature Kewpies as bride and bridegroom, and place them atop a wedding cake.

Kewpies were generally made in sizes ranging from one to 12 inches, but there were a few life size, and others as small as half-inch ivory charms. Some collectors specialize entirely in Kewpies, inspired by their great variety. Action Kewpies have been in great demand, and there are many of them, for Rose O'Neill claimed that Kewpies helped get people *out* of, instead of *into* trouble, and made them like busy little people, singing, teaching, flying, working.

Rose O'Neill died in 1944, and her three-story frame house in Taney County, Missouri, in the Ozarks, was completely destroyed by fire in January, 1947. Her brother was living in the house alone, but because of a washed-out bridge could not help to save the building. A newspaper account of January 7, 1947 relates that while Mr. O'Neill was able to rescue a dog and cat, all of his sister's antique furniture, original manuscripts and personal treasures were lost. These included original Kewpie and Scootles doll models, a carton of German-made Kewpies in their original boxes, Ho Ho statuettes, and original drawings and paintings of the dolls. Scootles and Ho Ho, designed by Rose O'Neill never achieved the popularity or wide distribution of her Kewpies, and are therefore even more valuable than original Kewpies. These kinds of dolls, which collectors have for so long called "secondary," are often more worthwhile to own than are the better-known varieties.

Another great German-American doll was the beloved Bye-Lo Baby. It was the creation of Grace Story Putnam, an American sculptor and artist who had previously made a doll named Peter Pan, and a later one called Helen Pan. She dreamed of making a really lifelike baby doll, and spent many days searching for the baby she visualized to use for a model. She visited scores of hospitals, looked at hundreds of babies, and then in a Salvation Army day nursery she found the one she was seeking—a newborn infant. Working swiftly, in the nursery she modeled the head in clay.

In her studio, Mrs. Putnam made a plaster mold from the clay model, and from it, a finished, life size wax copy. Completing the doll with a soft cloth body, Mrs. Putnam set out to find a sponsor for it. George Borgfeldt, already so successfully allied with the J. D. Kestner Company in the making and sale of Kewpies, was interested, and he and Mrs. Putnam entered into a ten-year contract. The molds went to Kestner in Germany, and in 1923 the first Bye-Los went on the market. They were all-bisque with swivel heads and glass eyes. The naturalistic bisque bodies were also designed by Mrs. Putnam. However, only a few of this type were manufactured, for it soon developed that they were too expensive for the market. Mrs. Putnam then redesigned the head with a flange at the base of the neck, so it could be sewed into a cloth body. This style was used in the future more often than any other. The alive feeling of the cloth-bodied Bye-Los is most appealing, giving one the sensation of actually holding a real baby, however small. In spite of the fact that they are not as rare as the all-bisques, they have always been the favorites of Bye-Lo collectors.

Mrs. Putnam and the manufacturers did a certain amount of experimenting with the babies and tried using other materials for the head, but bisque was always the favorite. The dolls were made in about ten sizes, from seven inches to life size. A few were made as Negro babies with dark skins. All were conscientiously marked with the incised name, "Grace S. Putnam" on the head; the same name was stamped on the soft cloth body.

Hands on these dolls are sometimes made of bisque, but are often of celluloid stamped with the tortoise mark. The usual style of hands has widely spread fingers, and the hands are inserted in the cloth arms just as the flanged heads are inserted in the cloth bodies. Bye-Lo Baby eyes were either of glass (fixed or sleeping), or were painted on, either blue or brown. Molded-on, painted hair was the most common, although a few had wigs. The painted hair is natural looking and attractive. In one series of all-bisque Bye-Los, the head and torso were modeled in one, instead of with the swivel-head. These were jointed at hips and shoulders. The all-bisques range in size from about 3 inches to 9 inches. (Oh for a 3-inch Bye-Lo Baby!)

Mrs. Bernice Large of Arcadia, California, owns one of these rare all-bisque Bye-Los. The legs are bent in a natural, baby position. Measuring the doll over-all, from the tips of the toes to the top of the head, without allowing for the bent knees, the length is about 9 inches. The bisque is beautifully finished and is a delicate flesh-color. The doll has brown glass eyes, a head open at the top covered with a wig of brown natural hair.

The original wax model of the Bye-Lo Baby, appearing to be a real baby asleep, is on permanent display in the Charles W. Bowers Memorial Museum in Santa Ana, Calif. It looks so alive that one walks up to the net-screened crib on tiptoe.

Just as it affected many other things, the great depression of the 1930's wrecked the doll import business. In 1934 the Borgfeldt Company tried to solve the cost problem of Bye-Lo production by making the dolls of composition, but not enough people were able to buy them. One collector has reported owning a Bye-Lo made of plastic, marked with the name of Borgfeldt, which had been listed in the 1950 toy catalog of the F. A. O. Schwarz Company; but nothing more appears to have been done since then to revive the doll.

Wars and depressions have affected dolls ever since the beginning of doll history, and the effect they have had on manu-

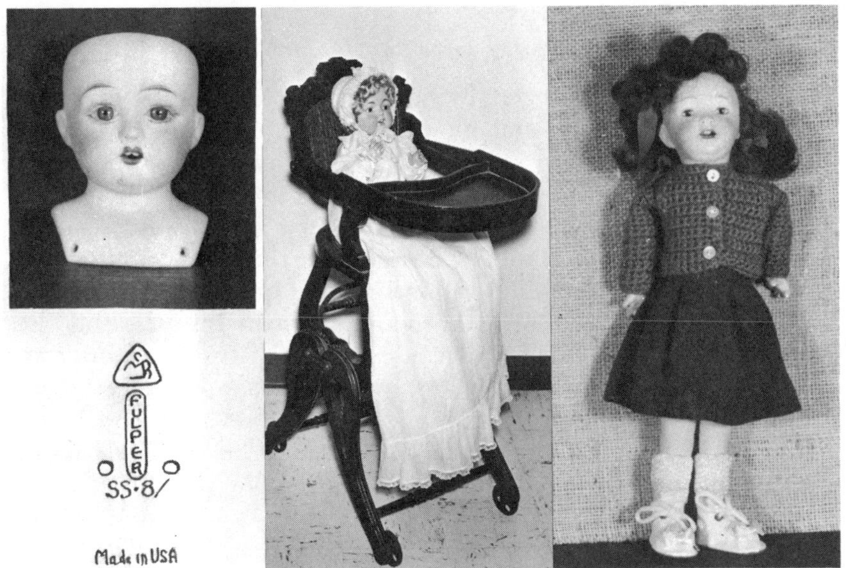

Fulper doll-head and mark impressed in the porcelain before firing.

A Fulper-head baby doll sits in chair which is combination rocker, stroller, and junior chair.

Courtesy, Franks Doll Museum.

Carol, clearly marked JAPAN on her shoulders, was probably made in the 1930's. She is good quality bisque with sleeping eyes, real-hair wig, and jointed composition body.

facturing has never been more dramatic than in the case of German dolls during World War I. After the supply of German-made dolls in the stores of America was gone, there were literally no more to sell, for German factories turned to making guns and submarines. Overnight, New York toy importers were in a slump.

With characteristic ingenuity, a few American manufacturers tried to fill the gap. Among them was the Fulper Pottery Company of Flemington, New Jersey, already making pottery and tableware in their big plant. They needed only the proper kind of fine clay, and suitable doll molds to go into the doll business. They arranged to borrow molds from the Armand Marseille Company, and by 1918 were producing the Fulper doll head. These were carefully marked by incising the name "Fulper" vertically in the back of the head, and "Made in USA" at the lower edge of the shoulders. The head was made with holes in the shoulders for sewing on to a cloth body, as many old china dolls were made. The quality of the bisque was definitely inferior to the better German bisques, and the dolls were notable only because of their historical interest. Fulper made only the eyeless, wigless heads—as many as a thousand a day. They were shipped to other manufacturers who supplied the eyes and wigs. Horsman Dolls of New York probably used more of them than any other firm, but other companies were supplied as well. Many styles were made, ranging from babies to small boys and girls, and even some young ladies. Sizes also varied, depending on the demand of manufacturers. Life size heads made by Fulper Pottery also went on to shop-window mannequins used in displaying children's clothes.

The Fulper doll-head business ended as soon as the war ended and Germany could resume its doll manufacturing, for with the cheap labor of central Europe, it cost less to make an entire doll there than to fasten a pair of eyes inside an American Fulper head. Fulper stopped offering new models after 1920, and by 1921 they discontinued making dolls altogether. Even though their one-time production of a thousand heads a day for three years seems like a fantastic number, there is presently a definite shortage of them; and collectors who value dolls with a story should be delighted to add a Fulper head to their collections.

After World War I, the German doll and toy business never regained its former dominant position, although Armand Marseille produced the Dream Baby in the 1930's, perhaps in an attempt to share the popularity of the Bye-Lo Babies. Like the Bye-Lo, it had a flanged neck designed to fit into a cloth body. But unlike the Bye-Lo, the Dream Baby never offered serious competition to other doll manufacturers. Other countries began to cut sharply into Germany's dominance—Japan in particular—making not only dolls of new design at a lower cost, but producing well-made copies of old German dolls as well. By the time World War II started, giving American manufacturers their chance, Germany had already fallen far behind.

Then, too, at the end of the war, Italy's manufacturing boom included the making of thousands of dolls for export. For the past twenty years this has continued, and Italian dolls are among the finest of all those imported today. Meanwhile, American manufacturers, with the aid of plastic, and new and more economical ways of converting it into dolls, have built up still more formidable competition for Germany. Whether or not these modern materials will be adapted by German craftsmen and used to make better dolls than they once made of bisque remains to be seen in the future.

10

THE ARISTOCRATIC PARIANS

NO ONE KNOWS how long bisque dolls have been made, but William Taylor Copeland, a potter connected with the Spode factory in England, is given credit for making the first Parian ware in the middle of the last century. His mixture of two parts of feldspar and one part of fine white china clay, ground together and fired to a high temperature, produced a ware reminiscent of the marble used by the great Praxitiles, from the Greek island of Paros; hence the name Parian. Parian was fine and silky-smooth, and could be modeled into delicate and intricate figurines. It quickly became popular with all European potteries.

The making of doll-heads seems to have been only a sideline of the big potteries in Germany and France, and there has never been any proof that china dolls were ever made by English potteries. Perhaps individual potters employed by large factories may have made a few "hobby" dolls on their own time; there is no justification for calling dolls "Dresden" or "Chelsea" because they may resemble some of the figurines made by these and other porcelain factories. As has already been said about "fashion dolls," it is unwise to attach these blanket terms to dolls, and it is better to call them "Dresden types."

For almost half a century, Parian dolls were made in limited numbers in central Europe, to be sold not as play dolls, but to be dressed and displayed by more sophisticated doll-lovers. Confectioners and jewelers sold them, and they have always been considered luxury items.

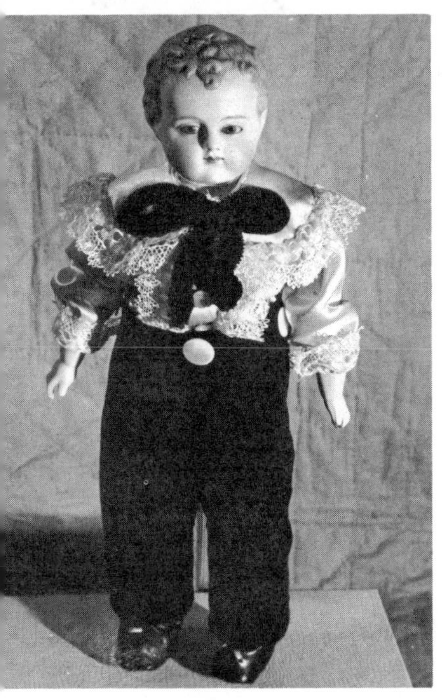

Courtesy, Franks Doll Museum.

Rare Parian boy with blond curls and ears showing. Glass eyes are of deep blue. This 11½-inch doll has an all-kid body with bisque hands.

Excess coloring on the cheeks of this Parian in Mrs. Bernice Large's collection is not unusual.

A group of fine glass-eyed Parians in Mrs. Walter Wagner's collection. *Top left:* Queen Carol of Saxony. *Top right:* "Miss Grape." All are blonds except the extremely rare black-haired lady at the left center.

Very few Parians are marked, and anyway, marks were so often faked even in nineteenth century Europe, that the quality of a doll is far more important than the person or firm who made it. For example, the famous crossed swords mark of Meissen porcelain was imitated by several other potteries, who changed the swords into similar, but different, shapes which might be mistaken for swords.

Many Parian heads were cast in the same molds used for making bisque and glazed china heads, but very few Parians were duplicated in quantity. A possible example of this may be seen by comparing the Parian boy doll owned by the Franks Doll Museum, with the Parian boy doll in Mrs. Walter Wagner's collection (see pictures page 119). If closely examined, however, it will be apparent that there are slight differences in both the modeling and the painting. This might have been the result of variations in workmanship, or it might have been accidental resemblance, or perhaps both dolls were made by the same artist.

It was difficult to cast all the fine detail of the best Parians in molds, and the combs and necklaces, ribbons, laces and flowers had to be added by hand. The fact that German labor was cheap and plentiful is one reason this particular kind of doll was made in the factories at the edge of the Thuringian forest, close to the source of fine clay and ample wood for firing the kilns.

A typical Parian doll has an elaborate hair arrangement of curls, puffs, braids, and loops. It often wears wreaths or bunches of delicate flowers, or a net snood, combs, lace frills, ribbons or beads. The popular contemporary name for them, "fancies," was certainly descriptive.

Quite often the coloring of Parian dolls is a little exaggerated, especially the tinting of the cheeks. The "clipper ship" doll owned by Mrs. Bernice Large is an example of this excess rouging, as is also the top and center doll in Mrs. Walter Wagner's group of Parians. Most Parian dolls were blond, probably because yellow pigment fired more effectively on the soft finish of the unglazed porcelain than did darker colors. For the same reason, black hair was more common on dolls made

Left and center: Rare Parian or Dresden-type dolls with glass eyes, fluted neckline ruffles, and Dresden flowers in their hair. They have stuffed bodies with Parian feet and arms. *Right:* A Parian with painted eyes, Dresden flower wreath in hair, stuffed body with kid arms and hands. Costumes by Mrs. Clara Franks.

Courtesy, Franks Doll Museum.

Group of fine Parians. *Center:* Large 27-inch Parian with painted eyes. *Top right:* 27-inch doll with glass eyes and unusual hairstyle with narrow blue Dresden ribbon across front. *Front, left to right:* two small Parians with glass eyes; Parthenia with molded earbobs, painted eyes, hair dressed with bands of ribbons; blonde with ringlet curls and blue blown glass eyes.

Courtesy, Franks Doll Museum.

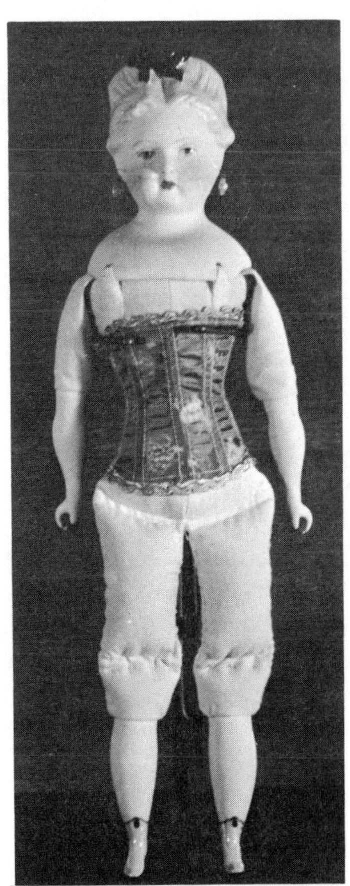

Nancy, one of Emma Clear's fine reproductions, is made of blond bisque. A black luster bow is molded on her hair.

of glazed china. Therefore, a black-haired Parian is more valuable than a blond because it is so rare.

It has been estimated that about one-fourth of all Parian dolls were made with glass eyes; all the rest had painted eyes. The glass eyes were of the most exquisite blown glass, blue being the most popular color. A superlatively fine Parian owned by one collector has violet eyes—a rare and indescribable shade. Ribbons, bows, flowers, combs and other ornaments modeled on the heads were often painted with luster, a highly iridescent form of ceramic coloring with a metallic glint. Sometimes the doll's shoes were also trimmed or painted in luster.

Some Parian heads were apparently sold separately and converted at home into dolls by attaching them to cloth bodies. Many Parians have matching arms and hands, feet and legs, indicating that they were either made or assembled in factories. Many such dolls have kid bodies, but some are of cloth. It is easy to tell whether bodies are home or factory-made.

Although Parians were probably not designed to be play dolls, one wonders why they were not, for the hard-fired porcelain of which they were made was at least as durable as pink bisque. If there was ever a time when these dolls were handled roughly it is not now, for when you own a doll valued in three figures, you treat it with care.

As already indicated, Parian ware was given the name because it resembled marble. But if a small amount of pink pigment were added, perhaps a fraction of the amount used for pink bisque, the material was called blond bisque. This is what some of the early Jumeaus were made of. If the clay used in making the doll was coarse and a trifle rough, the material is called "stone" bisque or "sugar" bisque. This is often a bluish-white color, or even has a grayish cast. Many of the inexpensive Japanese china dolls of modern times were made of this, but fine dolls—never.

Doll collectors prize the original, and reproduction dolls made by the late Mrs. Emma Clear, owner of the Humpty Dumpty Doll Hospital, once located in Redondo Beach, California. The Clear dolls were made almost exclusively of either Parian or bisque, and are comparable in quality to the best dolls ever made in Europe. No American dollmaker has approached them in variety or quantity.

Mrs. Clear first operated a doll hospital in the East. After she and her husband went to California she began not only to repair dolls but to make replacement reproductions of china and bisque arms and legs. Finally she had molds made of some of the finest antique dolls, and hired a staff of expert artists and craftsmen to create reproductions which were sometimes even more beautiful than the originals. Humpty Dumpty Doll Hospital sold these heads and parts separately, and also as finished dolls. They should never be confused with real antiques, but that is unlikely, for one of the most inflexible rules of Humpty Dumpty was that every doll made there must be clearly marked in such a way that it could never be changed. The mark on Clear dolls is in script, with the number of the year it was introduced enclosed in the flowing "C." Our Nancy, for example, has a "49" inside the "C." This insistence on marking followed an experience Mrs. Clear had with her first reproductions. In a Chicago antique show dealers demanded that she mark her work with either name or date, so it could not be artificially aged and passed off as a genuine antique, as a few unscrupulous persons might try to do.

Although she was a doll expert, Emma Clear never personally designed or made the dolls marked with her name. Sometimes, as with her George and Martha Washington, she commissioned a sculptor to design them, and had professional mold-makers work from the originals. Martha Oathout Ayres was the talented sculptor who modeled the first President and his wife, the American Madonna, Danny Boy, and other originals. The hands for Martha Washington were copied from Mrs. Clear's own delicate veined hands, and the modeling is exceptional.

Mrs. Clear's personal account of some of the techniques used in making her dolls could well apply to those of the older European Parians. As with all molded doll parts, the original models were made in clay by the sculptor, and from them plaster of Paris molds were made. Plaster is soft, and after being used forty or fifty times, the details of the modeling tend to become blurred. It was the practice of Humpty Dumpty to discard molds and discontinue making that particular doll when the mold began to deteriorate. However, with her own designs, Jenny Lind and the Washingtons, Mrs. Clear had permanent porcelain master-models made, since she intended to continue making these dolls. Then too, instead of the usual two-piece plaster molds, these three doll-heads were reproduced in eight-section molds, so that when worn pieces were replaced, it would be easier and less expensive to do so than to make entire molds. These permanent master-models are in contrast to the one-time-only clay models which were destroyed as soon as molds were made.

One characteristic of clay is that it shrinks as it dries. This shrinkage averages about 10 per cent, and is uniform in the entire piece. This gives a potter an easy and convenient way to make an entire series of sizes from one original model. Thus, a doll-head is modeled of clay, then dried; another head is cast from the first one, and dried; another is cast from *that,* and so on. This is undoubtedly what had happened to a doll-head I saw a number of years ago in a hobby shop. It was what is called *greenware,* or ready-to-fire pottery clay, a casting sold in quantity in such places, to be smoothed, glazed, fired, then painted with overglaze china colors purchased in the shop. The head was exactly like Mrs. Clear's reproduction of "Toinette"—a rare Parian, a doll which she said she obtained permission to copy from its owner, Mrs. Lawrence D. Butler of Syracuse, New York. Whether the hobby shop doll had been made from the original head, or from one of Mrs. Clear's reproductions, it was an unmarked fake. Only the ignorant or inexperienced would think that a doll bearing all the earmarks of a fine Parian in hairstyle, nosegay of flowers, and facial expression would ever be made of ordinary pottery clay, glazed, and *painted* crudely by an amateur. The details of the modeling had been blurred by many castings, and the size had shrunken with each casting, so the doll was much smaller than the original had been.

While Mrs. Clear did none of the actual painting of her dolls, she had a staff of skilled artists in her workrooms, who were adept at painting the fine details which were so important. A brush of only one or two hairs, for example, would be used for painting eyes and brows. This work was always done with overglaze (china paint) colors, instead of colored glazes as is sometimes done.

"Papa" Clear invented or adapted a special device for use in stuffing doll-bodies with sawdust to make them firm and tight. He also was in charge of the shipping department, which sent dolls all over the world. As has been said by many doll experts, there has never been anything to compare with Humpty Dumpty.

The little brocade corsets worn by Humpty Dumpty Doll Hospital dolls were most fetching, with tiny eyelets and lacings. Some collectors dress these dolls only in chemise and drawers, so the corset will not be hidden under other clothing.

Mrs. Clear kept a file card for every doll she reproduced, with the name of its present owner and as much history about it as she considered to be authentic. She gave little credence to the hearsay stories that sometimes accompany dolls, particularly when there has been a succession of owners. This is a good rule for all collectors to follow.

Mrs. Clear died in 1952, and the doll hospital was purchased by Mrs. Lillian Smith, a former employee. She continued to make dolls in the same molds used by Mrs. Clear which were marked with the name CLEAR, but she added the name SMITH as well. Therefore, any H.D.D.H. doll marked only with the name CLEAR was made prior to 1952.

In addition to Mrs. Clear's dolls, Mrs. Smith added several new models of her own design, many of them bonnet dolls. These are marked only with the name SMITH.

Mrs. Smith operated the hospital for several years, then sold it and its name to Mrs. Hazel Morgan, but retained some of the molds and replicas of doll-heads and parts. Some of these she later sold to various doll hospitals and dollmakers, but there is no list available of those who bought them or which models were involved.

Mrs. Morgan operated Humpty Dumpty Doll Hospital in Arcadia, California, where Mrs. Smith had transferred the business soon after she purchased it. Within a short time illness forced her to close the hospital and retire.

Mrs. Morgan and Mrs. Clear's husband, who had himself retained rights to some of the dolls when he sold the business to Mrs. Smith, jointly gave permission to Neva Wade Garnett, owner of Clara's Doll Hospital in Paradise, California, to use the trade name CLEAR. Today, Mrs. Garnett appears to be the only active, authorized, and available source of many of the famous line of dolls.

The dolls whose names on the following list are marked with an asterisk are those made from molds designed by Lillian Smith and marked only with her name. The others are marked either CLEAR, or CLEAR-SMITH, depending on when they were made. These lovely dolls will increasingly attract collectors, but there are few places to obtain full information about them, as may be imagined.

NAME OF DOLL	HEIGHT IN INCHES	MATERIAL USED
American Madonna	21	Parian
Alice	17	Bisque or Parian
Ann Rost	18	Parian, luster, china
Annabel Lee	15	Parian
Baby Stuart	15	Parian or bisque
*Barbara	18	Parian
Barbary Coast Gent	12, 15, 19, 23	China, Parian, bisque, and luster
*Beth Bonnet Head	13	Parian
Blue Scarf or Queen Louise	20½	Bisque
*Butterfly Bonnet Doll	13	Parian
*Christine	16	Parian
Claudia	No size given	Bisque, Parian
Coronation	18	Bisque
Curly Top	18	China, luster or Parian
Dagmar	17	Parian,bisque or china
Danny Boy	No size given	Parian or bisque
Deborah	15	Parian
Diedra	18	Parian
Dolly Madison	22	China, Parian, bisque or luster
Elizabeth	20½	Parian
Elsa	17	Bisque or Parian
Gibson Girl	18	Parian or bisque

NAME OF DOLL	HEIGHT IN INCHES	MATERIAL USED
*Gladys Bonnet Head	13	Parian
The Grape Doll	18	Parian, luster or china
*Hollyhock Bonnet Head	13	Parian
Isabel	22	Parian
*Ivy Mae Bonnet Head	13	Parian
*Jennifer	20	China
Jenny Lind	18	Parian, china, luster, bisque
Kaiserin Augusta Victoria	17	Parian
*Kathleen	18	Bisque
*Lady Carolyn	15	Parian
Linda	17	Parian or bisque
Little Girl With Curl	20	Bisque
*Louise	17	Parian or bisque
Margaret Rose	18	Parian
Mary Augusta	18	Parian or bisque
Mary, Queen of Scots	15	Parian or luster
Mary Todd types	10, 12, 16, 17, 20, 27, 32	Parian, china, luster, bisque
Mona Lisa	18	China or luster
Nancy	13	Bisque
Naomi	15	Parian
Parthenia	15	Parian, luster or china
*Sheila	18	Parian, luster or china
Sir Galahad or Dresden Gent	19	Parian or china
Spill Curls	21	Parian, luster or china
*Sue	18	Parian or bisque
Sylvia	17	Parian
Tiara	22	Parian
Toinette	18	Parian or luster
*Virginia	20	Parian
Washingtons, George & Martha	18	Parian or bisque
Young Victoria	23	Parian, china or luster

11

CHINA DOLLS

DOLL-HEADS of china were made during the same era as those of bisque. This statement is in the language of the doll collector rather than that of the ceramist, for technically they are both china. Bisque, as mentioned before, is unglazed china; "china dolls" are made of bisque which has been glazed.

China dolls, like almost all dolls of the nineteenth century, were made in central Europe, largely in the principalities which in 1871 were consolidated to form the German Empire. The rural areas near the cities of Sonneberg and Nuremberg were the chief sources of china dolls, and as explained earlier, most of the work on them was done by individual families who sent the parts to central distribution points for shipping all over the world. We take china dolls seriously, going to great pains to find marks on them to show who made them and when they were made, but to the pieceworkers in a home industry this was not important. The making of doll-heads was only a way to make a few pfennigs as easily and as fast as possible, and this probably accounts for the fact that so many of the dolls are not marked. Collectors therefore have to study those dolls which can be identified, and judge all the others by their quality and condition.

Black hair predominates among the German glazed china heads, though not among the other German dolls. Still, blue eyes are far more common than brown. There are few china dolls with brown hair, which is strange, because both brown and auburn hair were surely common, and equally easy to paint.

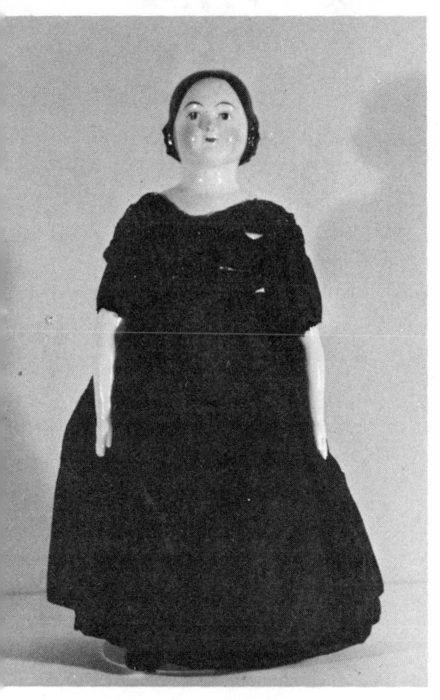

An early white glazed china doll has hairstyle found on dolls prior to 1860.

A common late type of glazed china doll with painted hair that almost covers the forehead. Glazed china arms and legs with blue garters and high-heeled boots date it after 1860.

Rare pink porcelain of 1850's–1860's in Mrs. Hugh Dyer's collection. Back and bosom are beautifully sculptured, as are hands, arms, and feet.

Photo by Pinto Photo Service.

One dependable way to determine the age of a china doll is by its hair style. Most of the really old ones have high foreheads, with hair parted in the middle and brought down smoothly to a row of curls, or looped over the ears. They have deep sloping shoulders so the dolls could be dressed in fashionably low-cut gowns. Another helpful characteristic is that practically all dolls with china legs made before 1860 wore flat-soled shoes. China dolls with elaborate hairstyles, sometimes with combs and bandeaux molded on, were made from about 1850 to 1870, the time when Parians had similar, more fanciful styles. Bushy hair, with bangs almost covering the forehead, and features a trifle too small for the size of the face are common on dolls of the 1880's and 1890's. As a rule, these same dolls have shoulders which come only to the top of the arms, and stocky necks, which give the head a more compact look than earlier dolls. In addition, the smug, stolid look of some of these later china dolls makes them far less attractive than the others.

Here again, as with "fashion dolls" and "Dresdens," we meet the name-callers. Whoever began to call certain dolls "Dolly Madison," "Mary Todd Lincoln," "Jenny Lind," "Empress Eugenie," or "Queen Victoria" started a senseless custom. What humble German workman in his tiny village in the forest had ever even heard of these ladies? The names only mean that someone in the past twenty or thirty years fancied a resemblance to some particular individual, and for convenience, tagged the doll with the name.

There is an occasional china doll which was given a little individual touch by its maker—for example, a head turned slightly to one side after it was taken from the mold and while the clay was still damp. Such a doll is another owned by Mrs. Hugh Dyer: a rare pink porcelain or china, with black hair and brown eyes, and an off-the-forehead hairstyle. The doll's head is turned almost parallel to its shoulder, and the deep shoulders are enclosed showing the top of the arms and the lovely modeling of the bust and back. The doll is 12½-inches high, and the arms and legs are also made of pink china, beautifully sculptured even to the tiny pads under the toes. One of its nicest features is the black script "G" painted under the glaze inside the shoulder, for it is seldom that we find a china doll-head marked in any way.

A china doll-head owned by Mrs. Dora Walker of Louisville, Kentucky, and mentioned by Eleanor St. George in her book *The Dolls of Yesterday*, is also marked with a "G." Mrs. Walker believes that it may have been made either by or for Philip Goldsmith of Covington, Kentucky. He took out a patent in 1885 for a cloth doll-body made with a corset, and most of the heads he used with it were made in Germany. He may have been assembling china dolls for some time before this, so the fact that the hairstyle of Mrs. Dyer's doll is most certainly older than 1885, still does not prove that the "G" is not Goldsmith's mark. It is tempting to do this kind of guessing when handling unmarked dolls, but the great danger is that someone may repeat the guess as an actual identification. That trap is as fatal for doll collectors as the "name-calling" habit.

Mother Parlington, a pink luster in the author's collection, is another example of beautiful china. She is about 9-inches high and has a pale pink glazed china head. Her brown eyes are painted, and her painted black hair is parted high over her forehead, ending in flat curls at the sides and back. The body is made of cloth, and looks as if it had been factory-made, even though all stitching is by hand. The feet are ingeniously cut and shaped as a part of the legs, though only an inch long. The white kid hands are sewn with tiny hand-stitched lines to indicate fingers, and the doll is holding a minute knitted sock, made on pins for knitting needles. A piece of wire is twisted to form spectacles which rest on her nose. There is a label fastened to her petticoat which reads, "I am Mother Parlington. I came to visit Lillie Howell in 1853 and she persisted on my staying ever since."

The pink luster we have just been speaking of is sometimes called "Chelsea," but it is neither luster nor Chelsea. Luster is the name sometimes given to pink china, which is made by adding pink oxide color to white china or porcelain, or to its glaze. The addition of this chemical tends to make clay harder. True luster is quite a different thing, and would be entirely unsuitable for coloring the surface of a doll-head. As explained in the last chapter, luster has a metallic sheen and was often

Mother Parlington is a pink luster head, cloth body, and hands of white kid.

A group of dolls in Mrs. Walter Wagner's collection. *Top:* Outstanding are the man with monocle (*center*) marked J.P. inside shoulder; to his *right*, late glazed china with glass eyes; to his *left* a Biedermeier. *Front:* Heads only; *left*, a pink luster man marked KPM; *right*, a fine head made about 1844.

used for decorating shoes, boots, ribbons, flowers and ornaments on the elaborate dolls of the Parian group.

The evenly tinted color of the best pink luster dolls was usually achieved by either mixing the oxide with the clay itself, or by coating the inside of the plaster mold with a wash of pink before filling it with white clay. Sometimes the glaze itself was tinted pink. Careful examination of the inside of the head will generally determine which method was used.

This is just as informative and not as useless as trying to decide whether a doll is made of "hard paste" or "soft paste," or wasting time calling a doll "Chelsea" or "Staffordshire." These names are particularly meaningless, since they imply that some of the great English potteries made commercial quantities of china dolls. No one has ever been able to confirm that this is true, and in the rubbish heaps of the potteries no broken dolls have been recovered, as would have been the case if dolls had been made there.

Many old china dolls were attached to cloth or leather bodies by sewing through the holes pierced in the clay at the shoulders. A large china head is heavy, and prudent dollmakers often used tape or narrow strips of cloth instead of thread or twine to fasten the heads in place.

Painting the faces of good china dolls was done with great precision, and resulted in fine and delicate work. The lines marking the eyes, eyebrows, and especially the fine red line often painted above the eyes, are unbelievably precise. This last marking is found more often on older chinas than on more recent ones. The soft tint on the cheeks is delicate and skillfully blended, and some of the best chinas have brush strokes marking the hairline, usually at the sides of the face and across the forehead.

Almost all china dolls had molded hair which was also painted with china paint or overglaze color. One of the checkpoints in buying old dolls is to notice whether this painted hair has been retouched, for it almost always wore off a trifle at the back of the head or on the tops of the curls where it received the most wear.

One of the most sought-after china dolls is what has come to be known as the ball-head, or Biedermeier, marked by a tonsure-like black spot on top of the closed head, where a wig was to be fastened. There is some difference of opinion about this doll's date, but it was probably made about 1830–40. These dolls were made in several sizes, and the older ones have cloth bodies, china arms and legs, and flat-soled shoes. This alone would indicate that they were made prior to 1860, when fashion turned to high heels.

Another popular specialty of collectors of china dolls comes under the title of "name heads." Luella Hart is quoted in *Doll Talk* as saying that only two firms, Hertwig and Company of Katskutte, and Porzellan Fabric Company of Veilsdorf, made these dolls from 1870 to 1890. Name heads are identical in style, varying only in size and name, and were always made of white glazed china. Their hairstyle was one that was common at the time, with the forehead almost covered with curly bangs and a cropped look at the back of the head. A dress or guimpe-top was molded in the china, and the edges of the Peter Pan collar were touched with gilt or gold luster. On the front of the doll, between the holes used for sewing the head to a cloth body, a girl's name was also painted in gold. Sometimes the dolls had gilded chains and lockets as well.

Name heads were sold during latter part of nineteenth century. Name and details of collar are painted in gold.

This Sandhog Baby in Mrs. Hugh Dyer's collection was found in the East River in New York. Hair was probably once painted black, but only traces of pigment remain.

Photo by Pinto Photo Service.

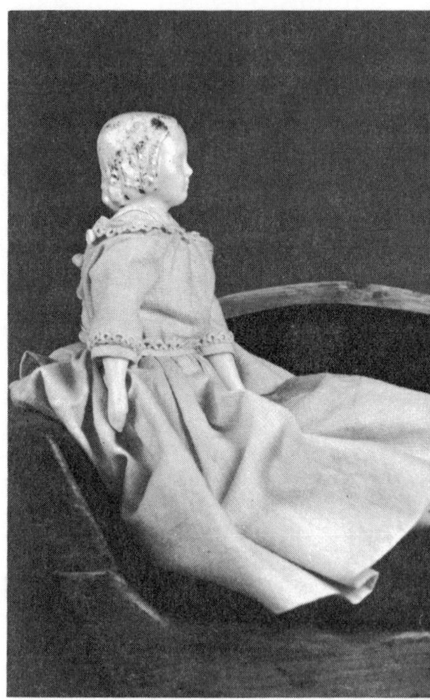

The "name heads" may have been designed to be given to children bearing those names, since only the most popular names were used. As far as can be determined, there were only twelve: Agnes, Bertha, Dorothy, Edith, Esther, Ethel, Florence, Helen, Mabel, Marian, Pauline, and Ruth. Sizes ranged from 2½ to 6½ inches. These dolls, while neither rare nor particularly valuable, are popular with collectors. A person who owns one or two can seldom resist completing an entire set, and if her own name happens to be one of the twelve, she at least must have that one.

It will be recalled that when glass eyes had to be inserted inside the doll-heads, it was more feasible to use open-top heads and cover the opening with a wig, than it was to try to insert eyes from below. Obviously, all this additional work added to the cost of a doll. When a glaze coat and firing had to be counted in as well, the added labor may be the reason so few glazed chinas with wigs have ever been discovered. Prices had to be kept as low as possible because the competition among doll manufacturers was intense.

An attempt to attract doll buyers appeared during the 1880–1890 period, when a few German dollmakers used printed cotton for doll-bodies instead of plain pink or white muslin. These "Primer Prints" were patterned with flags, numbers, flowers, and fanciful designs. While the patterned bodies of these otherwise ordinary china-head dolls are the only things which set them apart, they were very popular for a short time, and appeal to some collectors.

Hundreds of styles of china dolls were made during the last half of the nineteenth century, and it is impossible to describe or picture more than a few of them. They were made by the gross and sold for a few pennies. They were definitely intended to be used as play dolls. During recent years clumsy reproductions have been made of some of the common china heads, but they are easy to detect and can never be confused with either the old ones, or the lovely Clear reproductions. Even when modern copies are not marked as copies, the quality of the painting alone is a giveaway. We have never seen a modern copy—with the exception of those made by Humpty Dumpty Doll Hospital—which did not have heavy, coarsely painted eyebrows. No old doll was ever painted that way. Another characteristic of old dolls ignored by modern reproducers is the color of the doll's lips. The old china color is a faded orange tint rather than a true red, and the same delicate shade is used for the line above the eyes.

With china dolls as with all other kinds, a doll's value soars when there is a story connected with it. Mrs. Jean Dyer of Loudonville, New York, owns a china doll with a splendidly mysterious history. She calls it her "Sandhog Baby," for it was found in 1920 in the East River by workmen laying the foundation for one of lower Manhattan's large bank buildings. Mrs. Dyer's father was the consulting engineer for the project, and when the workmen gave the doll to him, he passed it along to his daughter.

The head, as Mrs. Dyer describes it, is only 1½-inches high, and the entire doll measures about 8½ inches. When dredged out of the sand, the head had been broken off at the base of the neck and almost all the paint had been worn away except for a few remnants of black in the hair, and the pink on one cheek. Mrs. Dyer had the doll body restored, and a muslin body with reproduction arms and legs made. A random guess would date this doll at some time between 1840 and 1860, or possibly a little later. The high forehead suggests that it was surely earlier than the '70's or '80's. Now dressed in an old-fashioned pink and white checked cotton of about its period, it is a china doll with special appeal.

12

DOLLS THAT MOVE

For hundreds of years, dolls have been made to move, performing a variety of acts, either singly or in connection with other dolls or figures. Some moving dolls are animated by means of simple manipulations of the hand, as with puppets and marionettes; some depend upon simple cranking or winding, and still others function according to elaborate variations of the clockwork principle. Dolls classified as mechanical include those that creep, walk, cry, wet, sing, speak, gesture, or are animated in any way by means of built-in mechanisms, bellows arrangements inserted in the body, or devices in the box or container supporting the doll and connected to it by rods or wires. Contrary to popular impression, performing dolls are not an invention of today's manufacturers. In fact, they have a history older than the Christian era—so remote that it is impossible to discover who did make the earliest ones, or even where and when they were made.

At any rate, mechanical dolls cannot have predated the invention of the cam. The cam is an off-center wheel, or revolving disc mounted on a shaft. It is used in all kinds of mechanisms, its shape being determined by its function. One of the most common shapes is the heart-form. A lever, pivoted at the center, with a rod at one end and a wheel at the other, moves against the edge of the cam. Teeth are cut in the edge of the cam and also in the edge of the wheel. They are arranged so the two sets of teeth mesh, and the result is what is called a "cam gear wheel": as the cam rotates, the wheel movement raises and lowers the rod by means of the lever.

The cam, enabling dolls to perform many lifelike motions, requires only some kind of force to motivate it. This force was first provided by winding, later by means of steam, water, or heat, and eventually by electric batteries or wiring.

Early clocks and music boxes, whose works activated the motions of doll-like figures, led the way toward free-standing mechanical dolls. The first Strassburg Cathedral tower clock, of 1352, provided elaborate housing for automatic figures of the Virgin and Wise Men who bow before her, as well as for a cock which moves its beak, crows, and flaps its wings. Other monumental clocks in European cities contain moving figures and devices indicating the time of day, the day of the week, the day of the month, and the phases of the moon. Few belfry clocks of this sort have been constructed anywhere since the seventeenth century, but the skills developed for their design proved vital to the making of mechanical dolls.

Pierre Jacques Droz, a Swiss mechanic who lived from 1721 to 1790, developed these techniques further, and about 1750 introduced the first music box. While they have been greatly refined since that time, the principle of their construction, involving a comb, a cylinder and a regulator, remains the same. When bells, castanets, or drums are added, and the music is coordinated with the movement of attached dolls, amazing effects are possible.

The famous Droz dolls, created by Pierre and his son Henri, survive in a museum in Neuchâtel, Switzerland. These are the same dolls shown to Louis XVI and Marie Antoinette, who marveled at the way the automatons could write, draw, and play the organ. The dolls are the work of a mechanical genius who combined past inventions with his own intricate devices, and produced dolls packed with clockwork and bellows enabling them to perform almost every lifelike motion.

For a brief time in 1961, the Droz dolls were on loan to the Smithsonian Institution in Washington, D. C.

It is dangerous to designate "firsts," but it is a fact that the first *known* talking dolls were those shown at the French Exposition of Industry in 1823. They were animated by a device patented by Johann Mälzel, born in 1772. When their right hands were touched, the dolls said "Mamma," and when their left, "Papa." Mälzel, incidentally, was also the inventor of the metronome, so familiar to all pianists. It consists of a pendulum activated by clockwork and was introduced about 1816. Thus it is possible to trace the close relationship between clocks and dolls and their inventors in still another instance.

One of the most enchanting places for doll-lovers is the doll section in the London Museum, Kensington. One of the museum's exhibits is a 12-inch Negro doll dated about 1870. One end of a wire is fastened to the doll's back and the other end to a platform on which it stands. The platform is jerked by the action of a camshaft fastened to a small wheel, which, together with the platform, is fastened to the top of a metal drum resting on three legs. When a flame is lit under the drum, a jet of steam rises from the water inside it and escapes through a narrow funnel, moving the camshaft, which in turn causes the wheel to revolve, thus jerking the wire and the platform. The doll then dances. This complicated arrangement makes use of the cam, the wheel, the shaft, and steam power in a novel way, but one suspects it was the inspiration of a mechanic rather than a doll-lover.

Some of the other exhibits in the doll section of the London Museum are more conventional. One of them is a New York-made walking doll 7-inches high, dating from about 1870. It is wound with a key and is called an "Autoperipatetikos." The china head has the conventional black painted hair of the time, and the doll's flaring skirt covers the walking apparatus so that at first glance it appears to be just an ordinary cloth-bodied doll. Indeed it is mainly because of its horrible name that the doll even merits attention—the inventor must have been a linguist as well as a mechanic. One boy doll in the museum's collection sits on a three-wheeled bicycle, animated by clockwork; another is set in motion by turning one of its wheels backward.

Antonia Fraser, in her book, *Dolls, Pleasures and Treasures,* describes many of the finest European dolls now in museums and private collections. Her account is full of illustrations and descriptions of this fascinating branch of doll collecting which flowered on the Continent. Perhaps the peak of accomplishment came with one group she mentions which was made for the Sultan of Mysore, Tippoo Sahib. It consists of a life size tiger rushing to devour a uniformed Englishman. The Sultan obviously did not care for the English.

A helpful guide for collectors of mechanical dolls is the detailed list of those patented in America, offered in Clara Hallard Fawcett's *Dolls, A Guide for Collectors.* It gives the patent, name of patent holder, and annotations by the author.

In the United States, a great many patents were issued during the period from the Civil War to 1900 for walking, creeping, crying, singing, and talking dolls. These were sometimes mounted on boxes containing the mechanism; more rarely the devices were built into the body of the doll. Because they were made to compete with products less expensive to manufacture in France, Germany, and Switzerland, it is not strange that most American-made moving dolls are less elaborate than the elegant clockwork productions of Europe. But as with other matters concerning dolls, there were many exceptions, and it is dangerous to be dogmatic.

Kimport thoroughly researches the dolls they sell, and accompanies each one with a pedigree sheet. When they first heard of a "Godwin" doll its origin was a mystery, but they finally discovered the solution in the files of the U. S. Patent Office. On August 25, 1868, W. F. Godwin of East New York, New York took out Patent No. 81491 for an improved automatic *toy*. Researchers going through patent files and looking only for dolls would probably miss this one, which Kimport believes accounts for the fact that Godwin dolls have never been numbered among other mechanical dolls. Godwin's patent covered the mechanics of making a figure walk, push or pull a cart, and perform other feats. To the inventor, the doll itself seemed to be secondary to what it could do. One described in *Doll Talk* was neither elegant nor beautiful. It was 11-inches high, with papier-mâché head and metal hands made to fit around the handle of a doll carriage that it either pulled or pushed. The feet are made of red-painted metal and swivel at the ankles.

The doll is believed to have belonged to someone in the Amana Society, a German religious group which first settled in western New York state in 1843, and then moved to form the community of Amana in Iowa in 1855–64. The first known owner of the doll was Sarah Iduma Ellis, who sold it in 1941 to Mrs. Elsie Clark Krug. She in turn sold it to Mrs. Walter White, who then sold it to Kimport. The collector who purchased it from Kimport was given a photostatic copy of the U. S. Patent Office receipt, as well as official photostats of the mechanical features of the doll and its intricate technical details. Certainly no doll could be more authentically documented than this one.

United States Patent Office records are tantalizing, since they describe so many dolls that collectors will never see. Great ingenuity went into the efforts to overcome fierce competition between dollmakers. For example, the crying doll patented in 1877 by W. A. Harwood, had a reed mouthpiece set in the doll's chest, through which one blew to make the doll cry. Another imaginative creation, the crying doll invented by J. P. King of Philadelphia, was made with two rubber bulbs inside it, one containing air and the other water. By means of an elaborate system of reeds and tubes, pressure on the bulbs made the doll wail realistically.

In addition to other methods as unusual as these, many creeping and walking dolls operated with clockwork, and were wound with a key or bar. A few simple devices could be put in motion by gently pulling or pushing the doll's hand, giving it a slight lateral nudge to help it along. A patent issued in 1902 to E. U. Steiner protected his invention of this kind. The excellent and sturdy Schoenhut doll that walked, was introduced in 1913, and in 1917, the "Dolly Walker" of Harry H. Coleman made its debut. Many others followed.

Webber singing dolls were made in the 1880's. They were operated by a bellows system—set in action by a gentle squeeze —which made the doll sing popular little tunes. A newspaper advertisement from the 1880's describing the Webber Singing Doll, which was made by the Massachusetts Organ Company, Boston, Massachusetts, claimed it was the:

> . . . finest French make, with wax head, real hair, and finest eyes, and is no different in appearance from the best of imported

> dolls; but within its body is a most ingenious machine, which, when it is lightly pressed, causes the doll to sing one of the following airs: "Home Sweet Home," "Greenville," "I Want to Be an Angel," "There Is a Happy Land," "Sweet Bye and Bye," "Bonnie Doon," "How Can I Leave Thee," "A.B.C. Song," "America," "Thou, Thou Reign'st" (German), "Frohe Botschaft" (German), "Tell Aunt Rhoda," "Buy a Broom," and "Yankee Doodle." The singing attachment is a perfect musical instrument, finely made, and will not get out of order, and the doll is sold for the same price that toy dealers ask for the same quality of a doll without the singing attachment.

The doll was made in two sizes—22 inches, which sold for $2.75, or with sleeping eyes for $3.25; and 30 inches, priced at $5.00, or $5.75 with sleeping eyes.

In addition to the bellows system there were other methods for animating dolls; among the most famous are the phonograph dolls, sometimes mistakenly called Edison dolls.

There is frequent misunderstanding over just what is meant by the term "phonograph doll," confusing it with the much older music box principle. A true phonograph doll was fitted with a built-in apparatus. Cylinder-type recordings for the *reproduction* of sounds could be placed on this apparatus, and a music box mechanism *created* sounds by striking the teeth of a metal comb against the projecting teeth of a revolving cylinder. The cylinder teeth were set in a pattern of notes for each tune, in the same way that perforated rolls of paper were later used in player or mechanical pianos. Both types of mechanism are set in motion by winding.

Thomas Edison did not patent a phonograph doll, and may never have seen one, but several other inventors made use of both Edison's name and his phonograph. One of them was William Jacques of Newton, Massachusetts, who in 1888 patented a combination doll and phonograph, assigned to the Edison Phonograph Toy Mfg. Co. Other phonograph dolls followed, and much later, in 1922, the Averill Manufacturing Corporation of New York patented the "Madame Hendron Talking Walking Doll." The standard Hendron phonograph doll was about 28-inches high, with a composition head, arms, and legs, but a simple cloth stuffed body. The body always carried the stamp "Genuine Madame Hendron Doll," and it was American-made. A sound box with a winding device was inserted in the back and separate cylinder records reciting nursery rhymes accompanied the doll.

Another phonograph doll incorporating Edison's invention is the "Mae Starr." The body, as well as the speaking apparatus, is almost identical with the Madame Hendron dolls, and little is actually known about the history of either one. Claims are made that the firm of Fleischaker and Baum had the sole manufacturing rights to the "Mae Starr," and that the phonograph parts for both dolls were made by the Universal Talking Toy Co.

An Edison doll owned by Mrs. Elizabeth Holloway of Dover, Delaware, was made about 1889 or 1890. It has a typical German-made bisque head and composition ball-jointed body, and when dressed looks just like any other bisque doll of the period. But the entire torso has been replaced with one made of metal. The mechanism is wound with a key projecting from the doll's right side, and plays nursery tunes. Although it has not been verified, Mrs. Holloway has been told that only eight of this particular model were ever made.

The cost of Edison-type dolls apparently discouraged manufacturers, and few were produced once less expensive ways to make a doll communicate were discovered. Modern talking dolls are often manufactured with some variation of the old clockwork mechanism. Although a few play records, these are made of plastic instead of metal.

Dr. Myron Merrick, a Berlin Heights, Ohio, veterinarian, has one of the largest private collections of automatons and animated toys in the United States, as well as a notable collection of Burmese glass, Staffordshire figures, lithopanes, and music boxes. Dr. Merrick was also responsible for organizing the International Musical Box Club, and was its president for two years.

When the Merrick house became too small to contain the vast collection, a room was added, almost as large as the original house. Custom-made cabinets with sliding shelves hold many of the larger boxes, and tabletops, shelves, and cabinets are covered with other pieces of the collection which Dr. Merrick

This view of Dr. and Mrs. Myron Merrick's mechanical doll collection shows the advantage of ample display space for dolls of this kind. Many of the dolls are Jumeaus of delicate French bisque.

Photo by Ewell Studio.

Group of French Jumeau mechanical dolls shows that regulation dolls were often simply mechanized. Boxes on which the dolls stand contain the complicated music box devices which animate them.

Courtesy, Franks Doll Museum.

and his wife share happily with anyone who is interested. Mrs. Merrick's pets are the mechanical Jumeau dolls. One of these lovely ladies holds an ivory-covered dance program in one hand and a lace fan in the other. After being wound, she raises the program, on which are written the names of dances and partners, turns her head from side to side as if looking for her partner, then coquettishly hides behind her fan. A standing doll playing a harp is one of the largest in the Merrick collection. Her beautifully modeled hands and fingers move across the strings of her harp, her head moves as her eyelids flutter, and her chest seems to rise and fall in a breathing motion.

Jumeau produced more mechanized dolls than any other

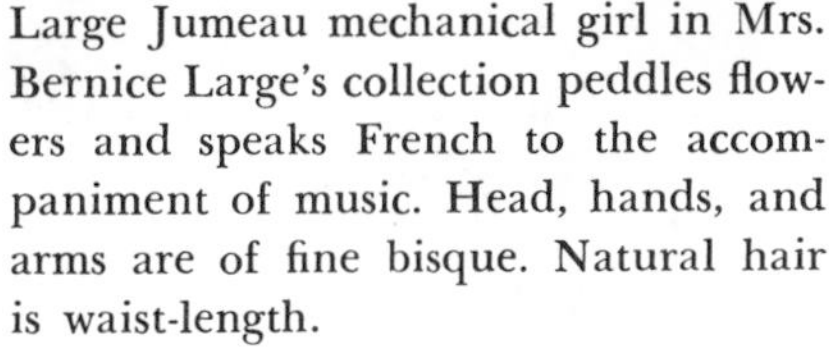

Large Jumeau mechanical girl in Mrs. Bernice Large's collection peddles flowers and speaks French to the accompaniment of music. Head, hands, and arms are of fine bisque. Natural hair is waist-length.

Wooden Joan of Arc marionette held by her owner, Mrs. Elizabeth S. Holloway. Hands are large in proportion to body, as is usual with marionettes.

manufacturer, although M. Bru took out a patent in 1869 for improvements in a mechanical doll he had first patented in 1867. This doll turned its head, and showed two facial expressions. Later, in 1872, Bru's wife made a "magical talking doll" which sang various songs.

In the collection of Mrs. Bernice Large, of Arcadia, California, is a 21-inch Jumeau mechanical doll mounted on a five-inch-high music box. This doll, typical of the Jumeaus of the 1880's or '90's, has long natural hair and a curiously made stuffed body of brown cloth. The arms and hands are fine bisque, matching the head. Metal rods built into the body run down into the music box. A flat metal key at the back of the box is wound, and the doll slowly raises her right hand, which holds a nosegay of ribbon flowers. On her left arm she carries a basketful of more of these flowers. Slowly she turns her head from side to side, and her chest moves, as if she were smelling the flowers. Her hand descends, and she speaks in a tiny, rapid voice. The French words are hard to understand, but may be the title of the musical selection being played by the music box. The doll moves and the music continues to play for a long time once the key is wound.

Even more elaborate is the 26-inch Jumeau called the Sorceress, which was sold by Kimport several years ago. It is made with works built on an irregular sequence. The doll lifts flower pot lids to reveal, in turn, a clown with a saucy, outthrust tongue, a little grinning ape, and a girl blowing kisses. A waving baton seems to direct the music box accompaniment.

An exhibit of antique mechanical dolls held recently in San Francisco's Sutro Museum—where there is a large permanent collection of old music boxes, player pianos, and automatic music-makers of the last century—included a number of mechanical dolls.

Among these was a beautiful Jumeau lady serving tea, a French maid ironing clothes, a lady acrobat balancing on one hand at the top of a ladder, a dancing tambourine player, and a papier-mâché peasant (made long ago in Stuttgart) out for a walk. Other dolls on display were knights and ladies, musicians and magicians, fortune-tellers, court ladies and gentlemen, clowns and peasants. Marked with an 1862 patent number was a mother wheeling her child. Musicians played bass viols, smokers blew rings, soloists sang, and an innkeeper attracted trade to his tavern by beating on a tin pan.

The New York World's Fair in 1964–65 had a vast number of dolls of all kinds entered by collectors, doll clubs, and various institutions, as well as several puppet shows. The Chrysler company, for example, ran a continuous puppet show in its large theater area; and a French revue, Les Poupées de Paris, starred caricatured figures of Frank Sinatra, Pearl Bailey, Elvis Presley, and many others.

Recognition of this kind always stimulates interest in dolls. In this fair, where mechanical dolls and figures played such a spectacular part, particularly in the Walt Disney creations, it was plain to see the fascination they had for men, as well as women and children, and why Disney has incorporated many of his animated figures in the settings he built at Disneyland.

The Tiki Hut at Disneyland is a mass assemblage of twentieth century mechanical figures, descendants of all the experiments and inventions of the past. In this one building, almost everything but the floor is made to move, speak, or sing. Even the flowers bow and break into arias, parts of the walls and woodwork suddenly become alive and start to sing, while costumed figures of people and animals move and speak. How the clockmakers of Strassburg would have loved it!

Collectors wishing to see the world's finest mechanical dolls—that is, a large number en masse—will discover that museums rather than private collections are the best places to find them. This is partly because a sizable collection of moving dolls requires far more space for display than an equal number of non-animated dolls. Mechanical dolls are also in the high-price category, and not every collector can afford to own more than two or three. It is also true that mechanical dolls more often appeal to men than women, and perhaps housewives find that large numbers of them are overwhelming.

It may be rewarding for collectors to inquire on this subject at neighborhood museums, because many museums have doll collections which are brought out only at certain times or seasons, or are shown only on special request. There are also multitudes of historical societies, particularly in New England and the eastern seaboard states, which can provide considerable information about mechanical, and other, dolls.

Puppets and marionettes, while seldom thought of as dolls that move, are in effect just that, except that they are animated by persons instead of mechanical gadgets. Puppets are commonly defined as figures which are moved by direct action of the human hand. Marionettes are figures manipulated by means of strings or wires strung through hooks or eyelets in doll-bodies, and attached to the hand of an operator who is concealed from the audience. Extremely lifelike effects can be created, and puppetry is one of the ancient arts which has never died.

Mrs. Elizabeth Holloway's unusual and lovely Joan of Arc is a true marionette. It is made of wood, with the face enameled.

The knees, shoulders, and elbows have extra metal plates which allow for flexibility. The hook on the top of the head and the metal eyelets which show on the hands were so placed in order to attach strings. More strings on other parts of the body assist in manipulating it, and the feet are weighted with lead in order to keep the figure in place on the stage. This is possibly a French marionette, but since it is not marked in any way this cannot be determined; nor is it possible to estimate its age, although the face resembles the French "fashion dolls" made of bisque or china.

Everyone who watches television is aware of the way dolls that move and speak can be used to sell soap, dog food, cereals and even automobiles; the future of animated dolls thus seems likely to be as long as the past.

13

FOLKLORE DOLLS

THE CLASSIFICATION of folklore dolls is a rather special one. A doll representing Johnny Appleseed, for instance, should be considered a *character* rather than a *folklore* doll, even though Johnny Appleseed's exploits are a subject of folk legend. True folklore dolls, whether derived from a specific character or not, may be said to have developed into *types,* in which individual traits are always subservient to a more general set of characteristics. But in this case, definition is probably most easily arrived at by example.

The hawkers and peddlers of eighteenth century London, who swarmed through the streets calling out their goods and services, were immortalized not only by the seller of hot cross buns, Little Tommy Tucker, Wee Willie Winkie, the muffin man who lived on Drury Lane and other characters of the Mother Goose rhymes, but also in the form of peddler dolls. (The British spelling of the word—pedlar—is often used, and Americanization of the word is a matter of choice.) Peddler dolls are fascinating, not only because they often seem more like real people than any other kind of doll, but also in as much as they provide a splendid means of preserving and displaying, in the form of wares, many of the odds and ends of doll collecting that accumulate over the years.

Originally, peddler dolls were usually owned by English women of the leisure class, and were kept under glass domes on the drawing-room mantelpiece where they could be admired, with additions to their wares being made from time to time. There was a great deal of rivalry among gentlewomen

Some of Mrs. Walter Wagner's fine peddler dolls of various materials. *Top, left to right:* China; wooden; leather; composition; leather; breadcrumbs; leather; cork; wax; wooden; breadcrumbs.

English peddler doll in Mrs. Hugh Dyer's collection was made about 1800.

Photo by Pinto Photo Service.

This modern peddler doll holding a doll was made by Dorothy Heizer.

who made these dolls between 1750 and 1850, and the hobby is becoming increasingly popular today. Peddler dolls were dressed and fitted out to represent many different types of traveling merchants, but the most popular have always been the "Notion Nannies"—perhaps because there are so many small items available for them to carry in their baskets or trays.

The basic style of peddler dolls was fairly constant, the 8- to 10-inch doll wearing a red cape, a black silk bonnet on top of a small lace cap, and carrying a flat tray or a basket filled with merchandise. The doll's head might be of wax, wood, china, papier-mâché, leather, cork, cloth, or whatever material happened to be currently popular. Sometimes china heads were covered with masks, to give a look of age that was most favored. Body, clothes, and some accessories were made by hand, with great care being given to each detail.

Every owner of a peddler doll tried to get the largest possible variety of items for her doll to carry, and as many as a hundred were not unusual. There would be laces, ribbons, buttons, piece goods, kitchen utensils, dishes, jewelry, miniature dolls and toys, all in correct scale. Whenever ready-made merchandise was lacking, the doll owner often made her own.

Mrs. Walter Wagner of Detroit has an amazing collection of peddler dolls, and in one group of them we find specimens of wood, china, leather, composition, bread crumbs, cork, and wax. One of the leather dolls is a man, but all the others are women. All carry flat baskets or trays spilling over with tiny objects useful to housewives. What fun it must have been to collect these trifles!

Another fine peddler doll belongs to Mrs. Hugh Dyer of Loudonville, New York. It is 12-inches high and dates from about 1800 or earlier. Both the doll and her wares are original. The toothless leather face and black glass eyes give her a remote, blank expression. Her auburn hair is most unusual and may have been cut from the locks of her first owner. She wears a sheer lace cap under her black taffeta bonnet, a hooded cloak of red wool, a white apron, and a brown print dress over a quilted pink chintz petticoat. Her underskirt is made with a money pocket, now holding a handkerchief. In her right hand she carries a box on which are printed the words: "From the Milton Emporium," and in the same hand, a tole lantern. As if this were not enough, a cord on her wrist is looped to a tiny fireplace bellows that is almost identical with that held by one of Mrs. Walter Wagner's peddlers. In her left hand, the doll holds a real little candle in a candlestick. The handle of her flat wicker basket swings from her left arm. This doll is in its original clothes and shows no signs of wear except for a little fading on the exposed parts of the dress and petticoat. Best of all, on the bottom of the base there is an oval label reading: "C. H. White, Melton, Portsmouth."

The Victoria and Albert Museum in London has a number of valuable peddler dolls. One pair is impossible to date exactly, but since the woman holds a copy of "The Reign of George IV," it cannot be older than 1830. The man's Napoleon-style hat is similar to that worn by the man in Mrs. Wagner's collection. Both heads are of kid, and the bodies are made of wood.

Another doll in the museum's collection of peddlers has a composition head and a wooden body, and is dated about 1836. She is dressed in an unusually elegant costume with a great many ribbons and frills, and stands in front of a table which holds her wares. These consist of dozens of pictures and trinkets, and a miniature copy of "Lithographed Views of Liverpool and Manchester Railway," which was opened in 1830. This table device is a good one for modern collectors to adopt when they want to make an effective display of a large assortment of small objects.

The idea of making one's own peddlers may be extended to the more ambitious one of a "bazaar," or an entire store, with both customers and salespeople represented by dolls, and the store shelves stocked with miniatures in correct scale. A famous assemblage of this kind was the Kendall Prize Bazaar, made about 1825 by Caroline Dodgson, mother of Lewis Carroll.

Marie C. Turner and her sister, Grace B. Turner of Brighton, Massachusetts, were so intrigued with the English peddler dolls which were the rage of London that they decided not only to make their own dolls, but also to write about them. You will find the titles of their books in the bibliography. One

Song seller peddler made by Marie and Grace Turner.

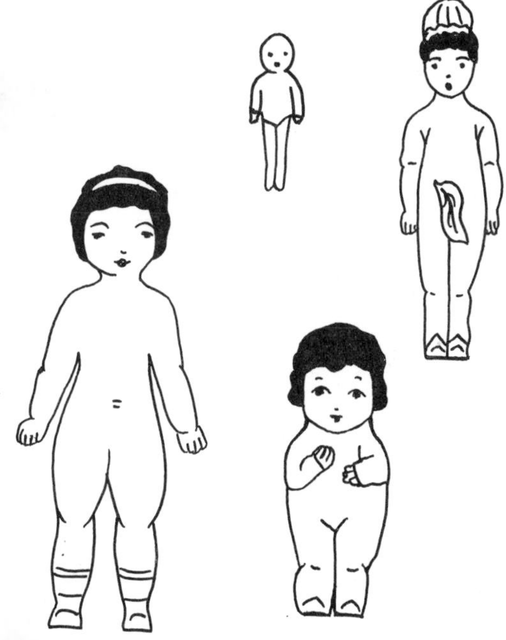

Frozen Charlotte dolls are found in sizes up to 12 inches and are made of different materials.

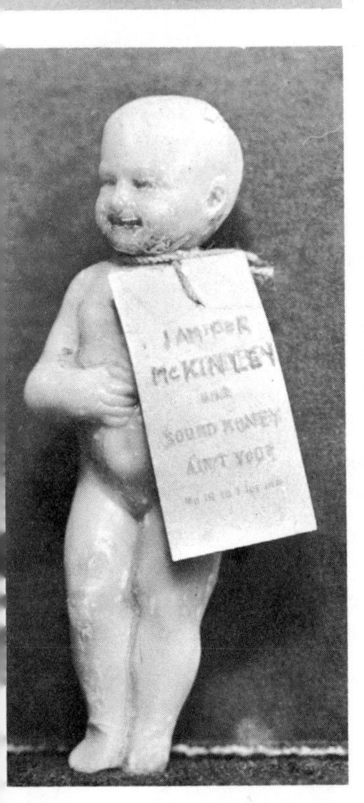

Frozen Charlotte soap doll made in about 1897 by Andrew Jergens & Co. for the McKinley Presidential campaign.

Courtesy, State Historical Society of Wisconsin (Trimpey Collection).

of the most rewarding extensions of their research has been the making of the merchants of early America, including the picturesque itinerant peddlers who once wandered through the countryside. The Turners' record of both the goods and the services sold on city streets and in rural America adds reality to the study of history and qualifies their dolls for use in schools, as supplements to lectures, and as an inspiration to collectors.

The Turner dolls average about 10-inches in height and are built on armatures of copper wire. The framework is built up and padded, then covered. It can be bent as desired, and the doll placed in all sorts of poses. The heads are made either of wood, ceramic material, or composition. It would be possible to use the apple heads described in the next chapter.

The dolls known as Frozen Charlottes also belong in the folklore division. The older names for these all-of-a-piece dolls are varied and often descriptive. They include: stiff, rigid, all-in-one, mummy, penny, cake, wedding cake, teacup, or pillar, depending on the part of country from which the doll comes. Actually, compact little dolls date back to the tomb figures and fetishes of antiquity, but for us, their history is comparatively modern and begins with the days when they could be bought for a penny apiece.

Although there are a few Negroes, Frozen Charlottes are almost always Caucasian. Some had clothes molded on, and a few wore hats or bonnets. Sometimes the doll was nude, or wore only shoes, and perhaps a bow in her hair. One tiny stone bisque in the author's collection is dressed in a fig leaf—or perhaps it is an apple leaf from the biblical tree. On her short yellow hair is a ruffled cap trimmed with pink and blue ribbons, and she wears high-topped boots, tinted pink. Across the back of her shoulders are incised the numbers 2155. For obvious reasons she has been named Prudence.

A more conventional penny doll is less than two inches long, of white glazed china, with black hair and tiny blue dots for eyes. The word Germany is cut into the body. She is in her original box, complete with a small mirror in a celluloid frame, a scrap of real sponge, and a cotton powder puff. The celluloid basin in the set could be either a large soap dish or an extremely small bathtub. This little doll was the kind so often used either inside or on top of the birthday cake, when penny dolls cost only a penny.

One of the Frozen Charlottes in the collection of the late Alice Kent Trimpey, who wrote *Becky, My First Love,* is the quaint little doll made of soap about 1897 by the Andrew Jergens Co. to publicize the presidential campaign of William McKinley. A tag around its neck reads: "I am for McKinley and Sound Money, ain't you? No. 18 to 1 for me." This doll is now in the museum of the State Historical Society of Wisconsin in Madison, Wisconsin.

The reason for the teacup name sometimes given these rigid dolls seems a bit farfetched, but the story goes that the little dolls were at one time used instead of spoons to stir the cup of tea, then taken home as mementoes of the tea party.

The largest of these one-piece dolls that we have seen was about 12-inches high, made of beautifully finished pink bisque. Although a few were 15 inches, this is a rare size. According to Kimport, all the large ones were boys. It is hard to see why a rigid doll should have been made so large, since most of the doll's appeal was in its tininess.

A true Frozen Charlotte does not have movable arms or legs. The arms should be close to the body, often with hands or forearms slightly extended, and the legs close together—made in such a way because they were easier to mold. This was the reason the dolls were solid; only a few of the better ones were made hollow.

From about 1840 to the turn of the century, the period when most Frozen Charlottes were produced, hairstyles varied widely, and this is reflected in the dolls. Most of them wore the shorter cuts, with bangs, colored head bands, luster or underglaze bows; a few wore wigs, but these were rare. Because they were made to be sold for only a penny, the painting and workmanship on penny dolls is crude.

The story of the way these dolls were named "Frozen Charlottes" is thoroughly American. The following verses of the Vermont ballad, as she had heard them sung, are those chanted by the grandmother of Mrs. Emily Stowell of Baldwin Park, California, and are considered to be as close to the original version as one is ever likely to hear. They also follow closely the words arranged and recorded by Alan Lomax, now to be found in the Archive of American Folk Song of the Library of Congress. A notation with the Lomax recording states that the words are to be sung in the key of D major, with harp-like accompaniment on guitar or banjo.

Depending on the place, the singer, and the word-accuracy of several generations of ballad singers, the verses have been known variously as Young Charlotte, Fair Charlotte, Charlotte, The Frozen Girl, and of both phonetic and semantic interest, The Song Ballet of Young Shollity.

There is supposed to have been an actual happening which inspired the ballad, in the way calypso singers make use of current happenings to tell a story in song. Phillips Barry, who has written a great deal about this New England legend, claims it was based on an actual event which took place on New Year's Eve, 1840, when a young Vermont girl froze to death on her way to a dance. A blind singer, William Lorenzo Carter, heard the story and turned it into a song. He wandered through the New England states and into the Midwest, singing ballads as he traveled, in the same way the minstrels of Provence sang as they went through the countryside, or the wandering harper of Scott's *Lay of The Last Minstrel* recited the traditional ballads of the Scottish Border. One of these "gleemen" is described by W. B. Yeats as a "poet, jester, and newsman of the people."

It was inevitable that because of individual human variance in accurately remembering words, as may be noted whenever a crowd sings the national anthem, the words of Carter's ballad have sometimes been changed, his lines reworded, and some verses either added or omitted. Since there was no single printed version, the result was confusing, but this is the way the song came to Mrs. Stowell:

YOUNG CHARLOTTE

Young Charlotte lived on a mountainside
In a wild and lonely spot,
No neighbors there for miles around
Except her father's cot.

And yet on many a winter's night
Young swains would gather there,
For her father kept a social board,
And she was young and fair.

It was New Year's Eve. The sun has set.
Why looks her anxious eye
So long from the frosted window forth
As the merry sleighs go by?

At the village inn fifteen miles off
There's a merry ball tonight.
But the piercing air is as cold as death,
Though hearts are warm and light.

But while she looks with longing eyes,
A well-known voice she hears,
And dashing to the cottage door
Young Charlie's sleigh appears.

"Oh, daughter dear," her mother says,
"This blanket round you fold,
For it's a dreadful night outside,
And you'll catch your death of cold."

"No, Mama, no," young Charlotte cried,
And she laughed like a gypsum (gypsy?) queen,
"For to ride in the blankets muffled up
I never can be seen."

"My silken coat is quite enough,
It's lined all through, you know,
Besides I have a silken scarf,
Which round my neck I'll throw."

With muffled face and silently—
The long cold miles were passed,
When Charlie, with these frozen words
The silence broke at last.

"Oh such a night I never saw,
My reins I scarce can hold."

And Lottie said in a trembling voice,
"I am exceeding cold."

He cracked his whip, urged on the team,
More swiftly than before,
Until another five long miles
In silence they passed o'er.

"How fast," said Charles, "the frozen ice
Is gathering on my brow."
Said Charlotte in a weaker voice,
"I'm growing warmer now."

"Why sit you like a monument
That has no power to stir?"
He asked her once, he asked her twice,
But she answered not a word.

Then quickly to the lighted hall
Her lifeless form he bore,
Fair Charlotte was a frozen corpse
That never could speak more.

He twined his arms around her neck,
He kissed her marble brow,
And his thoughts went back to when she said,
"I'm growing warmer now."

In other versions of the ballad, the moral issues of the event are stressed more heavily than in this one—the wild, vain daughter, defiantly wearing only a silken scarf to keep out the cold, and meeting a cruel end in the bitter night because of her disobedience.

Just as Mother Goose Rhymes and Charlotte's ballad have lived on, so will folklore and character dolls. There will also undoubtedly be "new" character dolls, emerging from new songs and ballads—or songs again made popular by the folk singers of today.

14

DOLLS FROM MANY LANDS

WHEN COLLECTING foreign dolls the greatest problem is not where to begin, but where to stop, since more and more of them are being made all the time. As world travel increases and doll collectors become more numerous, there are correspondingly more and more dolls from which to choose. Foreign dolls reveal many things about the people and countries of their origin, and thereby fulfill one of the principal requirements of most serious collectors: that dolls have definite meaning.

Our Mexican-made Casilda is an example of this. She arrived as a castoff, badly in need of repair. Her cloth-covered face was mashed; her body was dirty and faded and she lacked an arm. Her only garment was a print skirt; because it was obviously not from her native land, it was discarded at once. It looked as if her face might be restored by removing the cloth covering, building up the flattened features and saving the white, porcelain-looking eyes. Her hair was made of black yarn braided with strands of red and green thread, and had been fashioned on a basic cap of stiff black cloth. It was removed easily, all in one piece, and set aside to use again.

When the cloth was peeled from the face, its base proved to be a mask of coarse dark beeswax, two white beans serving as eyes. The teeth were five little white beads strung on a bit of wire bent at the ends and pushed into the corners of the mouth. The body of coarse cloth was stuffed with wild grass. The doll's history was clear. She had undoubtedly been made from the only materials available by someone in a village or rural district.

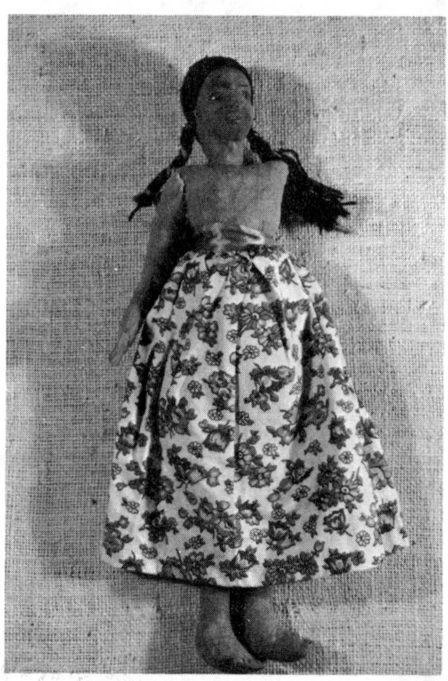

Casilda as she came to the author, with one arm, a flattened face, and a dirty, faded body.

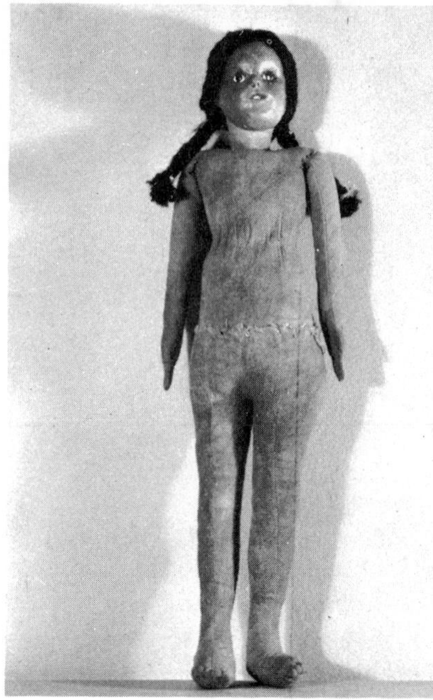

Casilda after she had been washed, received a new arm, and a new wax face, but before she was dressed in a gay and authentic Mexican costume.

This dollmaker was imaginative and ingenious, and yet one wonders whether she had ever seen a factory-made doll.

Mask-front heads like this are often used on foreign dolls and are fastened to the cloth head or half head; then the entire head is covered with stretchy cloth, like jersey or stocking material, and seamed at the back under the wig. This is a method home dollmakers may want to try.

In one collection, dolls made in eastern Poland and the Russian Zone of Germany have these mask-like faces made of papier-mâché and painted in natural colors. The dolls' hands are cut from red rubber, and the feet are shod in shoes of burlap or matting. The dolls' big sad eyes, and its clothes made from scraps of worn but beautifully woven wool and linen, eloquently tell a story of national heartbreak. Comparison between these Iron Curtain waifs and the crisp productions of modern West Germany is striking. Examples of each would be particularly revealing to future historians.

There are expensive foreign dolls, but the ones that most travelers buy are moderately priced and are chosen because of their regional or human interest. Perhaps it is wise to advise your traveling friends that your doll shelves are best suited to dolls about 8-inches high. Fortunately, almost all present-day foreign dolls are being made in this size, even in remote parts of Latin America. However, never reject a miniature doll, or a utensil you could use in furnishing a doll house or fitting out a peddler doll.

A doll collecting trip around the world might well begin in France, long the birthplace of beautiful dolls. French dolls like those described in Chapter 8, may form the nucleus of a varied group made in that country at different periods. There is room in such a collection for both the delicate bisque aristocrats and the humblest peasants of cloth, as well as beautiful modern plastics and synthetics. The dolls of Normandy and Brittany in their native costumes are favorites of travelers. So are the French dolls dressed in the habits of various Catholic orders. These can sometimes be found in already-assembled sets, but it is perhaps more meaningful to select them individually, or as souvenirs of particular cities or regions. The peasant types have always been among the most famous French dolls. They are still made and are frequently used as figures in Christmas nativity scenes.

There is a greater range of choice when German dolls are included in a collection of foreign dolls than with dolls of any other nation, because of Germany's long domination of the world doll market. World War I ruined that market, and before the country had a chance to rebuild its factories and reestablish its foreign trade, other countries had crowded in to take the lead. Then World War II destroyed what had been accomplished in the previous twenty-five years. It is easier to see the effect that war has had upon dollmaking in Germany than in any other country.

One of the best known modern German artists was a Bavarian, Bertha Hummel. Although her paintings and figurines

German celluloid boy (Muenchener) is dressed in the costume of old Munich, with leather pants, hand-made woolen socks that have no feet, and embroidered suspenders.

Like this British hussar, souvenirs of foreign travel combine well with doll collecting.

Dugald MacDonald, a china Scotsman made by the author.

A modern Tyrol child plastic made by Maria Reghini of Florence, Italy.

of children have been favorites for many years, she was already a recognized artist when, in 1934, at the age of twenty-five, she entered a Franciscan convent and took the name of Sister Innocentia. The convent sisters allowed her to continue with her painting until her death, twelve years later, in 1946.

Recognizing the success of her paintings and figurines, a Stuttgart company began to make Hummel dolls in 1951. Maintaining a quality of excellence that would have pleased the artist herself, they produced dolls made of durable, washable hard rubber—not china—dressed in the styles worn by Bavarian village children. Each one was clearly marked with a Hummel tag.

While no Hummel dolls of this kind are being imported today, Hummel figurines are being made in West Germany and sold in the United States. Although these figures are technically not dolls, many collectors do place them with their dolls.

With their delicate modeling and the soft colors of their fine bisque, the Hummel "Wanderbub" and other small-boy figures are particularly attractive. Japan has made many reproductions of Hummel figurines, but, if he is uncertain, it is easy for the buyer to determine from the label whether it is German-made or Japanese, since all are marked.

Many beautiful dolls formerly came to us from Hungary, and while the supply of them has ended, it is a good idea for collectors to watch for those which do frequently come onto the market from other sources. Hungarian bride dolls, with their elaborate and colorful costumes and fine workmanship, are outstanding.

Poland was also the home of brightly dressed costume dolls, and shared with Russia the creation of Matreshkas. These gaily enameled wooden dolls were hollow, made to come apart in the middle, one fitting inside another. A mother doll, for example, could be opened to remove a slightly smaller doll, which could be opened to reveal a still smaller one. As many as five or six dolls, all in entirely different costumes, were sometimes nested together this way.

Holland has always made good costume dolls, often of wood, with well made clothing, and of course, authentic little wooden shoes. They form a valuable record of the fast disappearing local and regional costumes of the country.

Liberty's of London exported beautiful dolls to the U. S. for many years, but now one must go to England to buy them. Collectors prize dolls with a Liberty label, whether they be picturesque Beefeaters, dressed in the medieval uniforms designed in the fifteenth century during the reign of Henry VII, or Buckingham Palace guards with their bearskin busbies, or the many other dolls of comparable quality. Great numbers of dolls were made in England at the time of the coronation of Elizabeth II, and their jeweled costumes are a special delight.

The author's own Scottish doll, Dugald MacDonald, was not made in Scotland, but he may be said to have originated there. His clan tartan is the one her ancestors wore, and his sandy hair and big-boned frame are family characteristics. Every part of his costume was authentically reproduced, from the cairngorm or brooch that holds his plaid on his shoulder, to the degree of overlap of his kilts. The sprig of white heather in his glengarry bonnet *did* come directly from Scotland.

There are other dolls from the British Isles: the Irish colleen with rosy cheeks, the quaint Welsh girl wearing a peaked black hat on top of a white linen cap or mutch, and the many men dolls in regimental uniforms.

Spain, Portugal, Luxemburg, Austria, Sweden, Denmark, Norway, Switzerland, Lapland, Greece and most of all, Italy produce numerous dolls. Italian dolls have helped build both the export and tourist trade of that country since World War II. The current catalog of one distributor alone shows dolls dressed in 85 different costumes of several European countries, as well as of each town and province of Italy.

One of the most prolific manufacturers in Italy is Maria Reghini, whose late husband, Ugo, operated a gift shop catering to tourists. She sells her dolls, and Florentine leatherwork, gilded wood, and mosaics from the factory of Alberto Orangi. Many dolls sold in American department stores are hers.

Admirers of Pinocchio can find many versions of him in Italy, and are likely to be particularly happy with the all-wooden ones produced by woodcarvers. The smaller figures are solid, but the large sizes are often made with jointed arms and legs. Both, however, show the long, pointed nose that made Pinocchio so famous. The same woodcarver who makes many of the Pinocchios also turns out gaily colored wooden Easter eggs and mushrooms, which open to reveal half-inch wooden peg dolls, similar to early woodens. Another Italian souvenir is the individual wooden doll-egg-cup owned by a friend. A tiny handknitted stocking cap goes with it, to keep the egg warm. Small items like this make ideal gifts for doll lovers and perfect selections for travelers, because they require so little packing space.

Russian tea-drinkers with their tall samovars certainly never needed the padded tea cozies so cherished by British tea-drinkers for keeping their tea hot, but for some reason, many of them have come from Russia. The cozies almost always represent placid, comfortably plump peasant women with full skirts and quilted petticoats wide enough to hide the fattest teapot. These dolls have cotton stockinette faces and arms, but of course no legs. The supply of these amiable characters is not as plentiful as it was at one time, but there are still many of them; they should not be ignored, for they have all the best qualities of character dolls, in addition to those of foreign ones.

South America is very doll conscious, and it is possible to collect dolls dressed in the local, regional, and national costumes of all Latin American countries. One unusual collection of little doll hats was brought back from Peru by an American mining engineer and his wife. The hats are only four or five inches in diameter, and represent the distinctive styles of different mountain villages in this country where hats form an important part of the native costume. The Peruvian woman who made them all specializes in this kind of doll millinery.

The capital and large cities and seaports of Ecuador, astride the equator, are predominately old-world. But Ecuador's tropical hinterlands are like no other place on earth; from many of the tribes of Indians, each with different customs and dress, come some of the most colorful dolls of the hemisphere. The best of them seem like real little people in structure and coloring. Whether barefooted and standing tall and straight, or bent under heavy burdens, most of these dolls wear handwoven cot-

These classic Peruvian dolls made of handwoven llama wool and rough linen are replicas of the people who live high up in the Andes.

A modern Mexican costume doll dressed in Tehuantepec fashion with characteristic lace headdress and blouse called a *huipil.*

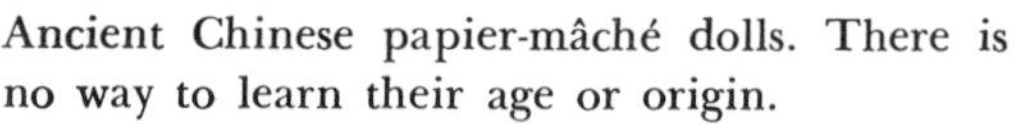

Ancient Chinese papier-mâché dolls. There is no way to learn their age or origin.

ton or llama-wool clothing similar to that worn by the natives. They often carry something on their heads or on their backs—wool for weaving, firewood, a musical instrument, or some article connected with their occupation, entertainment, or daily living.

Dolls represented as engaged in weaving are typical of Guatemala, where handloomed fabrics are so plentiful and exquisite, but there are also Guatemalan dolls depicted as busy with other crafts. It adds greater meaning to a collection if a definite connection between dolls and their country is kept in mind.

Lovers of miniatures always exclaim over the author's incredibly tiny Guatemalan bentwood box full of dolls. When a box is only 1½-inches long, imagine how small six dolls must be to fit inside. Each doll is different, made of yarn and wire, with every detail perfect, representing people you may see on their way to market.

Ever since American tourists discovered that they are living next door to a land of exotic bargains, every hotel, motel, and souvenir shop along the main highways and in the larger towns and cities of Mexico, is stocked with small dolls in native dress. Many of the doll-bodies are factory-made of plastic or celluloid, but their costumes are typical of individual parts of the country. For collectors who crave the truly unusual, and who can reach the areas where there are no paved highways, dolls can be found which might be called truly ethnic expressions of the people, and it is worthwhile looking for them in native markets and villages along the byroads. For Americans, these are probably the most easily accessible primitive dolls; but as civilization creeps out from the cities to the rural areas of Mexico, they will one day become impossible to find, although a serious effort is being made by the Mexican government to encourage craftsmen of the country to perpetuate techniques and designs, and to use in all their crafts the skills practiced by their ancestors. Tourists, however, eventually find what they demand; if they prefer gilded plaster Buddhas to crudely made Casildas, that is what the people will make. When tourists refuse to buy trash, they are helping the people, the country, and themselves.

Many modern dolls from the islands of the Pacific, including

Once plentiful, dolls like this from mainland China may never be made again.

our own Hawaii, are monstrosities; curios hardly worthy of attention except as souvenirs. Perhaps the most appalling are the ones made of coconut shells, seeds, rope, pods, and seashells, representing hula dancers. They are so obviously made to appeal to tourists that it must be assumed that people buy them.

For centuries, until the curtain fell between the Chinese mainland and the rest of the world, many beautiful dolls came to us from China. That vast country, with its treasures of incomparable arts, sumptuous silks, embroideries, brocades, jades and porcelains is now closed to us, of course.

To read over the sales lists of Chinese dolls published by Kimport in the early 1950's is as frustrating as glancing through an 1890 toy catalog to find dolls no longer being made, offered at less than today's cost of clothing them. For example, would you be interested in paying $2.15 for five and a half inch Chinese actor dolls with white and pink mask faces? Gorgeously arrayed in tinsel, vivid silk, braids, sequins, and cutout patterns of metallic paper, each doll is mounted on a base of black wood. At the same time you could buy sets of the traditional Eight Immortals, and Lao Tzu, founder of Taoism. These 5½ inch padded silk bas-reliefs are classified as paper dolls because of their paper backing, handpainted paper feet, and some paper accessories, but actually their cleverly overlapped garments are made of thinly padded silk, and their beards are real hair. These classic dolls were made in China for hundreds of years. Will there ever be any more? Their price in 1952 was $2.00 a set.

Equally budget-priced, the 12-inch Confucius doll with an enameled face and long white beard wearing elaborate ceremonial garments would be hard to resist. A haughty and resplendent Manchu emperor, also 12-inches tall, is robed in brilliant blue and tangerine, with pearls and a scepter, and trimmings of silver dragons. His empress is just as magnificent.

Perhaps the most famous of all Chinese dolls are the "doctor dolls" made of ivory, jade, carnelian, or transparent rhino tusk, and handed down from generation to generation as family heirlooms. For many centuries highborn Chinese ladies were allowed little contact with the world outside their own homes. The only men they were allowed to see before they were married were their own fathers and brothers. When a girl married, her mother gave her a recumbent female figurine, lying in such a way as to show her entire body. Thereafter, whenever the Chinese lady became ill, her maid took this figure to the doctor and pointed out the exact spot where her mistress was having distress and described her symptoms. The doctor could never personally examine his patient, but he then prescribed treatment. The owner of one particular "doctor doll" received the information about these "medicine ladies" directly from a Chinese woman who had been well acquainted with them all her life. Her own doll was supposed to be nearly three hundred years old, and clearly depicted a pregnant woman. While neither plentiful nor cheap, these dolls are still available.

It is when we come to the world of Japanese dolls, however, that we may be said to have reached the peak, the ultimate, in foreign dolls; historically, dollmaking has been considered to be one of the fine arts in Japan. An entire museum in Tokyo is devoted to dolls, and the modern Japanese make dolls just as earnestly as their ancestors made fine porcelains and paintings.

Although Japanese dollmaking has been a popular art for generations, the modern artistic types have developed largely since about 1927, when Takehisa Yumeji, a poet and painter, worked with his students to produce something more modern than had been attempted before. These new ideas prodded the old school of professionals to move away from their ideas of the past. Modern doll craftsmen formed a group and began to develop their own versions of artistic dolls; soon dollmaking became a national hobby, pursued by men and women alike.

The Tokyo Doll School was established in 1952, and it is now one of the largest of several doll schools in Japan. Teaching by mail, it has enrolled almost 30,000 students during the years, and these include many from North America and Europe, as well as Asia. The school publishes a monthly magazine (the English translation is *The Doll Monthly*), and the Japanese Dollmakers' Association, organized by graduates of the school, is active in training and recruiting new devotees.

Kits containing all the materials needed for making a Japanese doll are supplied by the doll schools, and in the U. S. there are many hobby and doll shops which carry them. Each kit contains a readymade mask for the face, made by pressing a mixture of paper and paste into a mold covered with Georgette crepe. There is a choice of ten or more masks to be used on a great variety of characters. Sometimes masks without eyes and mouth are sold, so the artist may have a chance to develop his ideas even more freely.

Other supplies furnished with the kit are the doll's cotton-stuffed body, arms, and legs. Wires project from the arms and legs so that they may be inserted in the body sections, and the doll placed in any position. The feet are made separately and also have built-in wires, to be pushed into the ankles. Pieces of patterned cloth for clothes are also in the kit, as well as a decorative piece of crepe (called a *tegara*) used in dressing the hair to make it look like a large flower. There are ornamental hairpins, or *kanzashi*, and traditional strings for adorning and tying the hair. Accessories include a differently patterned material for the *obi*, a hat, a parasol, a cord for fastening the hat to the head, and sometimes a bunch of wisteria, cherry, or peach blossoms. There is a small black lacquer stand in the kit, so that when the doll is completed, it may be fastened in the position desired for display. These dolls stand about two feet high; if carefully made and placed in lifelike poses, with their garments coaxed into graceful folds, they are decorative accents for a room, as well as a doll collection.

Less splendid, but perhaps more lovable, are the favorite little squatting men of Japan, weighted with lead so they cannot be overturned. This kind of doll is called Mr. Daruma, in honor of Daruma-San, an ancient Buddhist sage who traveled from India to Japan in the sixth century, A.D., and lost his legs as the result of remaining motionless for nine years squatting beside a wall, gazing at it perpetually as he meditated. Mr. Daruma is almost egg-shaped, and the legend is that you buy

Left and center: Modern wooden *kokeshi,* sold in all Japanese resorts. *Right:* doll sold in Japan in kits by doll schools is often obtainable in America.

him without eyes. If business is good, you paint in one eye; if it continues to improve, you paint in the other eye. If business is bad, he is left blind, as punishment. Other countries have similar toys, which are sometimes called roly-polys, or in China, *Pan-puh-too.*

The Japanese people love to travel about their country, and of course, take home souvenirs. Favorite items found in all Japanese resorts are gay wooden *kokeshi.* These folk dolls are made of turned wood and have a head and a body, but no arms or legs. They are painted with bands of two or three primary colors; flowers, perhaps chrysanthemums, adorn the front. Their simple shape and decoration follow the tradition of Japanese art, and although they were at first used as children's toys in the northeastern part of Japan, they are now almost exclusively sold to tourists.

There are countless other Japanese dolls, for although they are used as playthings, dolls have long symbolized friendship and goodwill among friends, and the complimentary gift of a doll from one person to another, as well as one country to another, has been a custom for many generations. Doll collectors of today who are old enough to recall the gay geisha dolls sold before World War I delight in the fact that they can find almost identical ones again, as well as the newer, finer products of the doll school artists. Sometimes, in fact, the once-scorned "Made in Japan" label even indicates an improved and quality product.

The Mark Farmer Company and Kimport Dolls both import dozens of foreign dolls and sell them by mail. Their catalogs are not only guides to buying, but are also full of general information about the dolls and the countries where they are made. In addition, such importers as these have access to markets travelers may never reach.

15

DOLLS CALLED "SECONDARIES"

THERE ARE MANY delightful dolls which are impossible to place in any conventional category. Many of them are by-passed by collectors who say they are only secondary items. Some day, however, they will be valued for their true charm, and those who own them will come into their own.

A material seldom mentioned in these days of synthetics is gutta-percha; yet in the last century it was a practical and often-used substance for making doll-heads and bodies. Caoutchouc is the name of the white gummy material produced by various trees in Malaya, and Central and South America, from which rubbers, balata and gutta-percha are derived. Contrary to popular opinion, different kinds of trees produce this substance—not rubber trees alone. Its use was understood long before our time. Until about 1851, when Charles Goodyear accidentally discovered the way to harden rubber, gutta-percha was used for dollmaking. It can be easily heated and shaped, and will retain its hardness, but it melts or loses shape if heated again. Mlle. Calixto Huret, a Parisian doll and costume maker, chose gutta-percha for making doll-bodies in 1850. On them she placed German porcelain heads, made so they would turn like the bisque dolls with swivel necks.

One little gutta-percha head owned by a collector friend was beautifully modeled and the material seemed as hard as metal. It had apparently been cast in a mold, for it was hollow and less than a quarter-inch thick. But at some time it must have been placed too close to a stove, for its little nose was flattened, and not from wear. The soft, lifelike colors of the head were very attractive and it must have been a beautiful doll before the accident.

It was Charles Goodyear who discovered that when rubber is mixed with sulfur and then subjected to heat, it will retain its elasticity but lose its stickiness and be unchanged in texture under all ordinary conditions. Due to this, he helped manufacturers of many articles, including dolls. Rubber dolls have long been popular, and the oldest memory many adults have of a doll is of one that squeaked by means of a small metal disk set into the rubber. Manufacturers made rubber dolls and doll-heads in all imaginable variations and styles. Unfortunately, many of them are not marked.

Collectors have always put rubber dolls in the secondary class, but perhaps this is a mistake, for the early ones, patented by Goodyear in 1854, are older than Greiner's papier-mâchés of 1858. Goodyear sold rights to his patent to different manufacturers, among them B. F. Lee, of New York, who held the rights for the rubber version of the Jenny Lind doll. Another Goodyear license went to the India Rubber Comb Company about 1851, and dolls imprinted with the initials "I.R.C.C." were made by them.

M. Bru, in Paris, took out rubber doll patents in 1876 and 1878; in 1875, two Americans, Ansil Monroe and Wesley Miller also patented rubber dolls. Monroe's patent covered the making of a swivel-neck, hard rubber head; Miller's was for a rubber doll built on a wire armature. If all claims made for these rubber dolls were true—they were said to be indestructible—there should still be many of them in existence.

Celluloid played a large part in the development of modern plastics, and has therefore been related to dollmaking. In fact, one of the earliest uses for celluloid was for the making of dolls.

In 1855, an Englishman named Parkes first made a substance called parkesine, to be used as a substitute for ivory. He mixed gum camphor and gun cotton pulp (a material made of cotton waste, nitric and sulfuric acids), put it under hydraulic pressure, then rolled it into sheets, ready to manufacture into many things. The same materials could also be mixed in liquid form, to be used as a coating on cotton, linen, or paper. It could be

Well-made European celluloid dolls with jointed arms. Probably not made for export because they are unmarked.

Doll from Ethiopia with a celluloid head and stuffed cloth.

Photo by E. R. Coburn.

One-of-a-kind dried apple dolls, "Mrs. 'arris" and "The Gossip," made in 1963 by Gwen C. Flather, show why apple dolls cannot be duplicated exactly, since drying produces different effects. Hair on these dolls is mohair.

colored, buffed to a high gloss, did not warp or discolor, and was not affected by moisture. Its chief disadvantage was its flammability. Apparently unaware of Parkes' invention, John W. Hyatt of Newark, New Jersey made the same substance about 1869, and gave it the name celluloid. By 1880 the Celluloid Manufacturing Company was operating in Newark. They began to make dolls under two patent numbers. As was often the case with manufacturing companies, dollmaking was only a sideline, a good way to use the scraps accumulated from the manufacture of celluloid collars, and other products.

Meanwhile, Germany put the new invention to immediate use in the fabrication of toys, and a company with an impressive name quickly dominated the industry. The Rheinische Gummi and Celluloid Fabrik Company of Mannheim-Neckar, Germany, not only sold their own line of dolls, but made dollheads and parts for other companies, and exported quantities of their goods to America. Their famous trademark was a small turtle or tortoise embossed on the neck or shoulders of the doll, or on an inconspicuous part of the arm or leg. Sometimes this was enclosed in a box or diamond-shaped frame. Often the words "Schutz Marke" (Protected Trademark) and a size number were added. Of course, after 1891, all dolls sent to the U. S. were also marked "Germany."

Many molds for bisques were also used to produce celluloid dolls in a large number of sizes. Some had painted eyes; others were of inset glass. Both molded hair and applied wigs were used. Even J. D. Kestner bought some of the best celluloid heads for his beautiful dolls. The Borgfeldt Company of New York sent special molds to Germany to be used for celluloid dolls. As we have noted, many Bye-Lo babies were made of bisque and cloth bodies; but the hands were often the tortoise-marked celluloid ones, exquisitely modeled with chubby widespread fingers. Some of the loveliest French dolls were also made of celluloid; in pre-World War II days, Poland also manufactured beautiful celluloid heads, often found in European dolls. Fine quality celluloid looks like ivory, and when painted in delicate natural colors it is entirely different from the overly-pink, roughly finished material we sometimes see.

In 1914, the Parsons-Jackson Celluloid Collar Company of

Cleveland, Ohio, made quality celluloid dolls of the scraps from their main line of products. The Parsons-Jackson doll was held together at all joints with metal springs. The trademark, a small stork, was embossed on the back of the head between the shoulders. These dolls are rare since celluloid collars soon went out of style and the factory closed.

From about the 1880's until World War I, doll house dolls were in great demand in both Europe and America, and some of the best of them were made of celluloid. Some of these small dolls had molded, painted hair; others had separate wigs, and were very attractive.

It is sad to see a doll that has been carefully made of some material entirely unsuited to dollmaking. There is no better example of this than the leather dolls manufactured by Franklin E. Darrow in Bristol, Connecticut soon after the Civil War. Why this ingenious man wasted his talent on a material that proved to be food for rats is hard to understand, except that his Yankee curiosity may have prompted him to see what he could do with something as cheap and plentiful as leather. His patent, issued May 1, 1866, described his process. He began with rawhide, cured in the usual way and cut into blanks of the desired size. In the words of the patent papers: "Boil two gallons of water containing one pound of lye and with the steam, saturate the leather. Then with die and press, stamp it in the desired shape." The doll-heads were made in two parts, glued together; then the features and hair were painted on. The customers supplied the bodies. Heads were from three to five inches high and had deep shoulders, with the Darrow label on the front. Mr. Darrow took a partner in 1867, and they went into the business of making rawhide belts for power machinery; but by 1877, the rats consumed their supplies, and they went bankrupt. The edibility of leather is the reason there are so few surviving Darrow dolls.

Metal dolls also enjoyed a brief popularity. That is, metal doll-heads, for few, if any, entire dolls were ever made of metal —unless one considers metal toy soldiers to be dolls. During the time when bisques were most popular, about 1890, there was a demand for unbreakable play dolls to be sold at a nominal price. Metal doll-heads of sheet metal riveted or soldered together were offered as an answer. They were first patented in America in 1887 by Joseph Schön of Germany.

The three best-known metal dolls are the Minerva, first marketed in 1894, the Juno made in 1900, and the German-made Diana. Although there were others, they were not marked and there is no way of knowing where they were made, or by whom. Minerva heads, which are probably the most famous of all, were registered in Germany by Buschow and Beck. In 1901 A. Vischer and Company registered a trademark consisting of the name and helmet of Minerva embossed on the doll's chest. Kimport Dolls has an original circular of Vischer's, which pictures and lists all the sizes and styles of the Minerva dolls. There were six sizes, from 11 to 18-inches high, with modeled, painted hair and closed mouth; eight sizes from 16 to 25-inches with painted hair and open lips showing teeth; and nine sizes having sewed-on curly wigs on both ball head and cut-out head types. Eyes were either painted or of glass. There were also a few socket heads made for jointed dolls. It was usual to import only the heads, and to attach them to sawdust-filled cloth or kid bodies in this country. The Juno doll-head was made in Germany by Carl Stanfus in 1900, and patented in the U. S. by George Borgfeldt in 1914. It was very much like the Minerva.

Some metal heads were made of tin; others were of brass or zinc which was enameled. Although they were advertised as "indestructible," able to withstand a child's rough play, the paint flaked off, the metal was easily dented, and of course the bodies did wear out.

Coming under the category of odd materials, or possibly *edible* materials, are the rice paste dolls of the Orient—delicate little figures that look like tinted wax or ivory. They are only a few inches high, but are fashioned with the most intricate details. The dolls are made on wooden pegs which fit into wooden or soapstone bases.

Ecuador's bread dolls are of much the same texture and color, but they are decorated with clear, bright vegetable colors. They are made of bread dough, lightly baked, then shaped into "pillar" doll form, with the arms close to the body. These dolls, called "Guaguas de pan," are made in Calderon, near Quito. Since they have a protective coating of varnish as a preservative, they are permanent. They are primarily made to be placed in cemeteries on All Souls' Day.

Other edible dolls are the gingerbread men we have today, whose ancestors were the elaborate gilded gingerbread figures of Europe in the Middle Ages. They were shaped in large wooden molds, carefully carved to represent persons in gala dress. The molds themselves are decorative in their own right, and it would be entirely proper to include them in a doll collection.

Depending on a collector's taste, and the space available, a collection can include many more edible and plant material dolls than we have space to itemize. A partial list includes dolls made of nuts, shells, cobs, acorns, lollipops, corks, beans, and pods.

Two kinds of folk dolls are worthy of a class name of their own—American primitives. These are the once scorned apple and cornhusk dolls of early rural America. As we said before, pioneer mothers contrived dolls from whatever was at hand, and the success of the doll depended entirely on the skill of the hands that made it. Yet with apple-head dolls, nature did most of the work, with only minimum assistance from hands.

Apple dolls are not made entirely of dried apples, but their heads are. If curiosity prompts you to make one, only a paring knife and an apple are needed. Johnathan apples, it is suggested, are the best variety to use. Select a large one to allow for shrinking. It is easier to work with the head, if a hole is first scooped halfway through the apple with an apple corer, and a wooden dowel or large skewer is then pushed firmly into the hole. When the drying is completed this stick becomes the framework of the doll's body.

First peel the apple and cut out deep hollows for the eyes. Do not attempt to smooth or sculpture the features, just block out the nose, mouth, and the flat planes of the face. Dry the head slowly, which will take some time, or speed up the drying by placing in the oven–on low heat, or it will turn into applesauce. Before it is quite dry, dab a tiny bit of rouge on each cheek and the lips—a mere trace of color. Two glass-headed pins stuck into the eye hollows will serve as eyes. Make a wig of fine white or grey yarn or embroidery cotton on a small piece

Dolls made entirely of dried cornhusks by the people of the Ozarks are marvels of ingenuity. Neither pins nor glue hold the husks in place; instead, narrow strips of the husks are tied where needed. Colors are from native fruits, and berries. Dried cornsilk is used for the hair.

of cloth, and glue it to the head. Make the doll's body of wire or pipe cleaners with narrow strips of cloth or stocking material wound around and around it. Or simply bury the wooden stick in a sort of pincushion made of cloth and fold a square of woolen material into a shawl to cover the body.

There is no more mystery about making dried apple dolls than there was in pioneer days, although modern methods probably vary as much as earlier ones. Some dollmakers insist that the heads must be dipped into a solution of alum and water to act as a preservative. One person uses a combination of sulfur and alum; another vouches for alum and lemon juice; others use nothing. The slow shrinkage of the heads will continue for years, but one way to retard it is to brush the head with clear varnish as soon as drying is well advanced. One apple-dollmaker discovered that when she used a quince instead of an apple, the shrinkage of a fruit four inches in diameter turned it into a head 1½-inches across.

Cornhusk dolls, American primitives, are still made by people in the Ozarks. Except for a bit of berry juice or food coloring, the dolls are made entirely of dried cornhusks. These are first soaked in water to make them pliable, then torn or cut and folded into shape. They are tied together with narrow strips of husks, but no glue is ever used. Horses and mules, also made entirely of cornhusks, are sometimes made to accompany the dolls.

Mention was made in an earlier chapter of the Negro or dark-skinned dolls made in Europe for sale in the colonies of France, Germany, and England. Both Bru and Jumeau made them, and they can be found also in the Simon and Halbig, and the Armand Marseille lines, as well as in a few others. A few Bye-Lo babies were also tinted brown. Most of these Negro dolls were made in the same molds as the others, but a few had distinctive features, and warm brown skin. Even earlier, Joel Ellis made a few Negroes by simply painting his basic dolls black.

There were also a few little Negro penny dolls, occasional black doll house people, and of course the printed Mammy dolls given as premiums with Aunt Jemima Pancake flour. These were soon followed by other members of Aunt Jemima's family—Uncle Mose and little Wade and Dinah. These all appeared later than the original Aunt Jemima, which was a paper doll, first offered about 1895. Cloth Aunt Jemimas and her family were given with advertising coupons from 1905–1923, then with a box top and ten cents in coin up to World War II. As far as can be learned, the company, which is now a part of the Quaker Oats Company, also made the dolls briefly after the war.

In 1950, Sarah Lee Creech designed a doll so authentically Negro that she hoped it would become an object of pride to her people. Mrs. Eleanor Roosevelt, as well as many artists and educators helped publicize her project. The dolls were produced by the Ideal Toy Corporation, and Life magazine gave it generous coverage.

Modern dollmakers, as will be shown in the next chapter, are increasingly designing lifelike and sympathetic colored children and old people, as well as creating new and unusual dolls.

Courtesy, Franks Doll Museum.

Three-faced bisque doll with sleeping face, crying face, and laughing face.

The modern advertising slogan, "What will they think of next!" has applied to dollmakers from the earliest times. Every device, material, and mechanical gadget seems to have been tried at one time or another. As an example, for several generations manufacturers have made dolls which have from two to five faces, instead of only oné. One of the earliest of this type is a primitive wooden head with four faces carved in the dark wood, supposed to have been make about 1800. As the head is turned, the doll laughs, cries, sleeps, and is placid.

A two-faced French doll of about 1850 was made with its head on a spring, but other early ones were rigid. The division between the faces was concealed by a bonnet or hood. Between 1860 and 1900, when there was the greatest rivalry among doll manufacturers, M. Bru of Paris took out three patents for multi-faced dolls, and in 1866, Domino Checkeni of Connecticut patented a four-faced doll of wax, the first American patent on record for such a doll. Fritz Bartenstein of Germany patented two dolls in 1881, one a composition under wax, and the other a two-faced wax doll. Mrs. Bernice Large of Arcadia, California, has a two-faced bisque baby marked with Barten-

The Armand Marseille Dream Baby was one of the best dolls made to compete with Bye-Lo Baby.

This Kiddie Joy, an Armand Marseille pillow baby which followed the Bye-Lo dolls, is in Mrs. Bernice Large's collection.

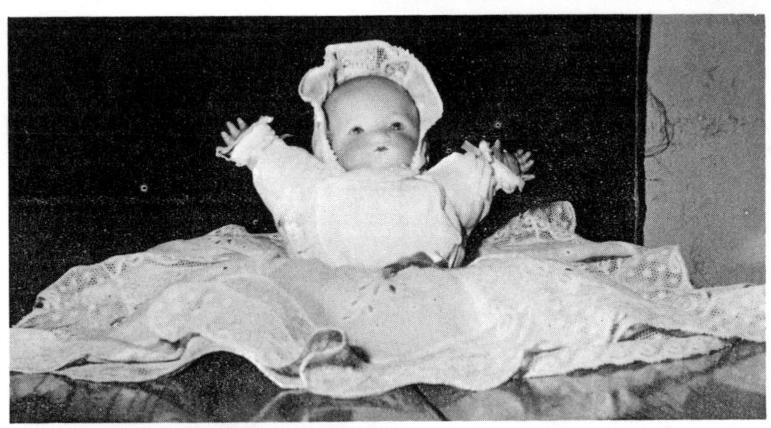

German-made half-dolls are often as fine as porcelain figurines. Many have natural hair, like two of these. Center doll shows how most of them were made, with holes for sewing to a cushion or framework base.

stein's 1881 patent number, although no mention is made in the Bartenstein records of such a bisque. One face of this doll is laughing, the other crying, and a cloth hood covers the joining.

Some of the earliest two-face dolls were operated by pulling a string, but it later became standard practice to turn the head in a socket by pulling on a metal ring at the top. There were so many variations of these devices that it is impossible to describe them all, or to identify many of them, because they were unmarked.

When examining multi-face dolls, notice whether the faces all seem to be of identical modeling and workmanship, or whether the smiling face is the standard type, and the reverse face is perhaps a little different in more ways than in the expression. This might indicate that the manufacturer used whatever molds he had for one face, and had new ones modeled only for the others. This would reduce the cost of production, but might also result in uneven quality.

Another type of doll which found favor with children, and which collectors now like to own, is the "topsy-turvy" rag doll. The two heads are sewed on opposite ends of the same body. The clothes cover one head, and can then be flipped over to disclose the other head. A white child on one end and a Negro baby at the other have always been favorites.

Some collectors restrict themselves entirely to baby dolls, and they have a great assortment of them to chose from. In spite of the fact that we have sometimes been told that no baby dolls were made before the middle of the nineteenth century, old prints and pictures as well as some of the dolls themselves, dating from as far back as the fourteenth century, prove this to be incorrect. This does not mean that dolls with grownup faces were never dressed in baby clothes, but that the natural affinity of little girls, dolls, and babies is too instinctive to have suddenly sprung to life in the times of Montanari, as has occasionally been claimed.

Baby dolls have been made of every material used for other dolls, but for some reason have seldom been as popular as children or adult figures. The Bye-Lo baby is a notable exception. Many baby dolls were made after the Bye-Lo success, and some of them were attractive but not distinctive. The Dream Baby of Armand Marseille is one of the best, and the Kiddie Joy and Nobbie Kid were also very fine. Almost all manufacturers tried to make a success in the baby doll market, and they continue to try, but the results are disappointing. In Chapter 21, which is devoted to the subject of commercial dolls being made today, there are pictures of some of the best modern baby dolls, but most of them seem to lack that particular spark of genius Grace Putnam put into her newborn Bye-Lo.

Another category of secondaries are the Bonnet dolls, which are always much more popular with adults than with children; their popularity with collectors grows as they discover what a large and complicated group this is. Perhaps the fact that the dolls' millinery is fastened to their heads accounts for the tepid reception children gave them. Children always enjoy the do-something features of a toy.

Bonnet dolls probably are not true antiques, although the definition of that word is controversial. The only way to determine when the oldest ones were made is through documented records and guesswork, based on the fashion of the dolls' headgear. There is a subtle sense of intuition, also, which most collectors acquire from experience in handling hundreds of dolls. This helps place the age and probable origin of dolls which are not marked in any way. Nevertheless, fine quality in both materials and coloring, rather than age, should be the collector's guide to buying Bonnet dolls.

Most Bonnet heads measure about 1½ to 6 inches, the most common being about 2 to 3-inches high. The heads were most often put on stuffed cotton bodies, with white bisque arms and legs. Fancy boots, shoes, and slippers were often molded or painted on the feet, and there was an infinitely varied amount of embroidery, ribbon, ruffles, pleating, and fanciful trimming on the hats or bonnets, for this was an age of feminine froth.

The different Bonnet styles fall into the categories of toques, caps, turbans, sailor hats, bonnets, and dozens of flower-shaped frills, as well as many which cannot be classified. A great number of series or groups bear fanciful names which delight collectors. The most common turban type is called "Cabochon

Turban." "Candle Wick," "Toboggan," "Pill Box," and "Thistle" trim are other popular names. The Flower series includes Bonnets made to look like flowers inverted on the doll-heads, such as Pansy, Rose, Buttercup, Hollyhock, Violet, May Blossom, Bluebell, Waterlilly, and Shamrock. Another smaller group represented insects such as "Junonia," (the butterfly), "Lantern Fly," and "Blue Bottle Moth." It is rare to find duplicates.

Kate Greenaway's paintings and illustrations of quaint Victorian children dressed in flowered bonnets, long filmy dresses, and flowing ribbons, will give the owners of Bonnet dolls many ideas for dressing them; both were in vogue in America at about the same time, 1871 to 1900. In fact, Greenaway drawings may have been used as models by German doll artists, because many of them were similar. There were Bonnet dolls a long time before Kate Greenaway began to paint, for there are early specimens with hats and bonnets modeled on their heads, some of papier-mâché, wood, and glazed and unglazed china.

By about 1870, most Bonnet dolls were made of white bisque with delicately painted features, and sometimes touches of luster. Often these bisques were the coarse, so-called stone bisque, but there were others of the finest Parian ware. Here again, perhaps figurine molds were sometimes used. It is necessary to constantly remind ourselves that bits of ceramic ware which we value so highly today were perhaps made in some German potter's spare time, since his income came from his work in a pottery and not as a dollmaker. If he chanced to sell a few doll-heads on the side, he would do it, but it is safe to say that entire factories were never devoted entirely to the making of Bonnet dolls. Few of them are marked, with the exception of Heubach, whose dolls are excellent. Mrs. Elizabeth Holloway's stone bisque Bonnet doll is typical of a favorite style of the 1800's and shows how easily a china head could have been converted into a Bonnet type by the dollmaker, simply by adding a bonnet to a conventional head and decorating it with ribbons and bows.

Finally, half-dolls, long ignored by collectors, now seem to be coming into their own. A half-doll is exactly what the name indicates, the top half of a human figure, designed to be fastened to a cloth base, which is then dressed as a doll. Many are made with a flange at the lower edge, often pierced with holes for sewing onto the body. Some of them are glued to the base.

It is debatable whether a half-doll is a doll or a figurine, but it is ordinarily classed as a doll. Some of the daintiest ladies (they are almost always women, instead of men, probably because of the greater possibilities of dressing in feminine styles) are posed like Dresden figurines. They often wear the same porcelain flowers and decorations, and may even have been made in figurine molds. The late 1920's brought a wave of popularity for half-dolls, and there were many white-wigged Colonial dames dressed in elaborate costumes of silk and lace which were transformed into telephone covers, non-functional pincushions, and boudoir lampshades.

Some half-dolls are very fine, made of bisque, china, Parian, and even wax, but more are made of plaster painted to resemble china. They are often worth collecting, and will probably some day be rare enough to have value as antiques. However, since half-dolls are still classed as minor secondaries, do not allow anyone to overcharge you for them.

16

DOLL ARTISTS OF AMERICA

A PREDICTION was once made by Grace Storey Putnam, creator of the Bye-Lo Baby, that some day the most distinguished artists would design and make dolls that were true works of art, and that the finest dolls in the world would then come from America. Her prophesy has come true, fulfilling her definition of quality as being not merely examples of novel or ingenious construction, but of mood and a sense of personality.

Today a modern group of professional doll artists is making dolls that qualify for recognition as beautiful artistic accomplishments, but which at the same time are unmistakably dolls.

It would be incorrect to say that there are only fifteen professional artists engaged in making dolls in the U. S., but we shall limit the artists in this résumé to that number. Others equally worthy, must be omitted.

These artists are the members of the National Institute of American Doll Artists, or NIADA, who united in 1962 with a common goal: the sponsoring of creative dollmaking.

Membership in the Institute is by election, and is determined by the excellence and originality of the applicants' work as judged by members. In addition to artists, a few doll collector patrons and long-time collectors are also elected to membership, and are entitled to certain priorities because of their efforts to further the activities of the Institute. Members sell their work independently, some through regular commercial channels, others directly to collectors; NIADA as an organization does no direct sales promotion work. Instead, it sponsors and protects the work of the doll artists.

The annual meeting of NIADA is held in August, the day before the opening of the convention of the United Federation of Doll Clubs. The Institute is compiling a program of colored slides of members' dolls, to be rented to doll clubs at a nominal fee. It is also planning to make a representative collection of members' dolls available to museums and large meetings in order to create further interest in dollmaking and collecting.

The artists of NIADA have individually been making dolls from eight to thirty-five years in the spirit Mrs. Putnam defined—as works of art. Many NIADA members received their first formal training in portrait painting before they discovered the wider possibilities of a three-dimensional medium. With only two possible exceptions, NIADA artists design dolls only for collectors, not as play dolls. They use all kinds of materials, including Parian, bisque, composition, cloth, wood, wax, and glazed china. The dolls are full of individuality and instead of being stereotype "pretty babies and ladies," the personality of each artist shines through.

HALLE BLAKELY

In listing members and describing their work, Halle Blakely comes first, alphabetically. She was a charter member of NIADA and began to make dolls in 1941. Her dolls were sold in stores until 1949, when she began to make them privately for doll collectors, and finally for museums. At first many of Mrs. Blakely's dolls were made with soft faces; later she began to use a harder material. There is a wide variety in her characters; she has made fashion ladies, presidents' wives, and portrait figures of famous people of all times. She likes to dress her dolls in dramatic costumes, and there are many brides, queens, and others in costumes full of fine detail.

In the early days of Mrs. Blakely's dollmaking, the curator of the Charles W. Bowers Memorial Museum in Santa Ana, California, helped her a great deal with her research, and each year Mrs. Blakely makes a madonna for the museum's annual madonna exhibit.

A lovely Dresden-like lady by Halle Blakely.

"Vie," a portrait doll by Muriel Bruyere, is of flesh-colored bisque.

A family group by Muriel Bruyere. *Left and center:* two Godey ladies; Mr. Gwilliam Ver Planck. *Right:* artist's mother at age thirty-five; artist's mother at age seventy-five.

MURIEL BRUYERE

When she prepared to become an illustrator and portrait painter, Muriel Bruyere could not have known the particular turn her talent would take—that she would eventually not only paint living people, but would receive recognition for her ability to make replicas of them. She graduated from the Woman's Art School at Cooper Union, New York City, in 1902, receiving two silver medals, and also studied at the Art Students' League in New York City. Then came an interval of being "just" a wife and mother. She emerged from this specialized occupation with added zest for her earlier training, and began to paint portraits professionally, sell small sculptures, and as a hobby, to create dolls. As with many other people, her hobby became a career; ever since 1932, Muriel Bruyere has been a professional dollmaker.

One of her greatest gifts is her ability to model appealing children. Her "Little Janet" was a portrait-in-the-round of Janet Johl's little daughter. Another child, 9-inch high "Vie," was made from a daguerreotype of six-year-old Viola Vernon, later the mother of Ruby Short McKim of Kimport Dolls. Only a few of these were made; some were sold dressed in polka dot dresses and lace-trimmed pantalets, while others, like the author's were left unclad, to be dressed at home. The flesh-colored bisque head and arms and the glazed legs are attached to stuffed-cotton bodies. Except for her first few dolls, all Bruyere creations are marked with the name BRUYERE incised in the soles of the feet. It is well to emphasize that except for the two Kimport dolls: Little Janet and Vie, and one set of White House ladies made for a California collector, all Bruyere dolls are entirely made and personally costumed by Mrs. Bruyere.

Mrs. Bruyere considers her "Famous Portraits" and "Famous People" dolls her best and most representative work.

Romney's "Miss Willoughby," Reynolds's "Strawberry Girl," and "Girl With Watering Pot," by Renoir, are all represented in Bruyere dolls. The artist has also made many dolls of children's storybook characters such as the Pied Piper and dancing children, and the fictional characters of Romeo and Juliet, Tom Sawyer, Orphan Annie, and many others. Most of Mrs. Bruy-

This Puritan family made by Helen Bullard shows three generations (*Left to right*). The dolls are carved from wood.

Dewees Cochrane's portrait dolls of the children of Mr. and Mrs. J. Grant O'Donnell of San Francisco.

Charlie Chaplin and the Kid are Strawberry Patch dolls by Gwen Flather.

ere's "Heirloom Portraits" are one-of-a-kind, made to order from photographs; they do full justice to her ability to achieve true likenesses. A family group shown here demonstrates the artists's skill with portraits in the modeling of her mother at the age of 35, and again at 75 so cleverly that one knows it is the same person at different ages.

HELEN BULLARD

Helen Bullard, 1963–64 president of NIADA, has been carving wooden dolls ever since 1948, when she headed a small company that made inexpensive wooden dolls which sold under the label, "Holly Dolls." Since 1954 she has been making dolls under her own name. For them she prefers to use horse chestnut wood, with clear lacquer as a finish. The wood mellows with time, but retains its original true skin-tone. The jointed wooden bodies are well made, insuring that Helen Bullard dolls will be intact and beautiful a hundred years from now.

Mrs. Bullard's projects include ingenious doll groups. Her "Three Rebels" is a group of three women, 1800, 1889, and 1928, each one holding a book which in the past strongly affected the status of women. Another project now under way represents nine generations of one family, costumed, as the artist describes them, to represent "prosperous little somebodies" of middle class station. These dolls are all made of buckeye wood.

The idea of costuming dolls according to a plan like this is worthy of study, for it gives them much greater significance. For example, the first generation of Mrs. Bullard's nine-generation project is represented by a man and his wife who were original Puritan immigrants to the Massachusetts Bay Colony in 1632. They wear the plain, unadorned dress prescribed by Puritan ordinance, avoiding worldly show, in contrast with the Cavaliers of the same period who wore lace, plumes, ribbons, and gold.

While still shunning vulgar display, the 1677 couple indicate greater prosperity and a slight lessening of austerity by wearing simplified versions of then-current fashions, rich materials, lace, and silver buttons. The third generation shows there had been a complete break with old restrictions; although the dress is still understated, it recognized the baroque fashions of the time with rose madder silk and satin. The man is very dignified in his "campaign wig," and his wife most elegant in her towering headdress called a "commode."

DEWEES COCHRANE

Dewees Cochrane, painter, sculptor, and designer, has had one of the most distinguished careers of any living doll artist, (and to avoid confusion, it should be pointed out that she has recently restored the final "e" to her last name; for years she spelled it Cochran). She is one of two NIADA artists with the longest records of commercial doll designing.

Mrs. Cochrane's years of preparation included early study at the School of Industrial Art (Philadelphia), the Pennsylvania Academy of Fine Arts, the University of Pennslyvania, and the International People's College in Elsinore, Denmark. Prior to making her first dolls, handmade Topsy, Turvy and their Mammy in 1934, she spent ten years in Germany, France, and Austria, in residence, study, and work. In 1938 she was named art director of St. David's School in Bermuda, and in 1942 became art director of the R. H. Donnelly Corporation in New York.

Soon after the opening of her own studios in New York City in 1935, she originated her Portrait Dolls. These were made on order from a good photograph and coloring information to look like anyone requested. Each doll, made of unbreakable composition, was a toy as well as an heirloom. Dolls were in sizes from 9 to 21 inches, according to age. Mrs. Cochrane was soon swamped with orders.

For three months in 1936, Mrs. Cochrane worked as a designer under contract to the Alexander Doll Company. In the same year she introduced her Look-alike Dolls, using six basic face shapes for American children, which she designed after studying hundreds of photographs and living models. Given an assignment, she could select a correct face form, and by matching colors and hair-do and using the corresponding body size, she could achieve a good resemblance at a lower cost than for an individually modeled portrait doll. It was also during 1936 that Mrs. Cochrane signed a three-year contract with Eff-An-Bee Doll Company for four of these Look-alike types, which were at first called America's Children.

The demand for her Portrait Dolls increased, and in 1939 she received a great deal of feature publicity, including a *Life* Magazine cover and feature article that attracted world interest of both manufacturers and retailers. But the beginning of World War II put an end to dollmaking when strategic materials were requisitioned by the government.

In 1946 a new and more detailed series of Look-alikes came from the Cochrane studios in Norwich, Vermont, and New York City. These were quality handmade dolls. In 1948 Marshall Field and Company invited Mrs. Cochrane to be their guest in Chicago for ten days when they launched their sales promotion of Look-alikes. Orders continued to come to Field's until Mrs. Cochrane closed her studio in 1959. This was Mrs. Cochrane's 25th year of dollmaking, and she now wanted to devote her time to doll designing, painting and writing.

Collectors who own a "Cindy" doll, made by Dewees Cochrane in 1947 and produced by Modern Plastics of New Jersey using their English patent, are especially fortunate. The patent covered "Kay-Sam," a method of quality latex casting evolved during World War II. These dolls were all marked on the left side of the torso with an embossed: "Dewees Cochran Dolls."

From the first, all Cochrane dolls have been made from the artist's own formula for an unbreakable latex compound, in sizes from 10 to 17 inches. They also feature wigs woven of fine human hair, which may be combed. The dolls are movable at hips and shoulders and have swivel necks. Both the dolls and their clothes are made with meticulous care, which will ensure them a long-time place in the doll world.

GWEN FLATHER

"Sculpturing with stitches" is the method Gwen Flather uses for creating her "Strawberry Patch" dolls—a name taken from the wild strawberries that surround her home, which is built to look toward the White Mountains and Lake Winnipesaukee, New Hampshire.

Inspired by reading Edith Flack Ackley's book, *Dolls to Make for Fun and Profit,* Mrs. Flather taught herself to make dolls. She also observed the dolls made by Bernard Ravca during World War II. These were fabric-covered, needle-modeled dolls, made by a method similar to the one Mrs. Flather adapted to her own use.

Every Strawberry Patch doll is built on an armature of copper wire wound with strips of cotton cloth. The heads are shaped from cotton, much as clay would be modeled, directly on the armature. Tiny stitches hold the cotton in place, then nylon stocking material is placed on top, as a kind of skin—again held by almost invisible stitches. Since it is practically impossible to duplicate dolls made this way, each doll is an individual creation.

Gwen Flather is adept at making both historical and character dolls, using real people, notable characters from fiction and theatrical personalities as models. Before she models the doll she carefully researches the background, activities, and personality of the individual she is going to portray. One of her latest creations is a lifelike portrait of Robert Frost at the John F. Kennedy inauguration; another recent doll shows the late President Kennedy in his rocking chair. An elderly artist at work on a painting is so unmistakably Grandma Moses that she needs no label. There is often a whimsical twist to these dolls, which reflects the pleasure the artist had in creating them.

The husbands of doll artists deserve honorable mention for their helpfulness. Mr. Flather, an architect, takes time out from his drawing board to make accessories—tiny pipes, tin bait cans with labels, buckets, books, slates, brushes, and even a telescope and violin—for his wife's dolls.

GERTRUDE FLORIAN

One of the first dolls made by Gertrude Florian was the grandmother doll in black silk and jet, with a little bonnet trimmed with violets. Called "The Widow Howland," it was a memory portrait of the artist's own grandmother. The doll

Robert Frost at Kennedy inauguration is one of Gwen Flather's Strawberry Patch dolls, now in collection of Magge Head Kane.

Photo by W. T. Rigby.

Gertrude Florian's "The Widow Howland" is a portrait of her grandmother. Beautiful modeling of face and hands is outstanding.

Ethan Allen, heroic figure of the American Revolution, as depicted by Gertrude Florian.

was made about 1940; Mrs. Florian's mother, Mrs. Grace Ridgway, worked with her, making the wig of her own white hair. This doll is now owned by Mrs. Charles Mills of Arlington Heights, Illinois, and has won many medals and blue ribbons. Mrs. Florian says that this makes her—the doll's creator—as happy as seeing a grown child do well in the outside world.

Another one of Gertrude Florian's fine dolls is Ethan Allen, dressed in the uniform of a Continental officer. This American hero never had his portrait painted, and as a leader of the Green Mountain Boys he wore a uniform of his own contrivance, not the regulation Continental uniform. This doll was not given his name at random, however. It was created only after the artist had studied many old records and felt that she really knew Ethan Allen. It is easy to believe that this is how he might have looked if he had worn authentic Continental dress.

In 1941 a large department store in Detroit asked Mrs. Florian to make seventy-five small dolls in English costumes and twenty dolls of different nationalities, 40-inches high, to be used in their Christmas display. The artist's own comment on this series is worthy of record. She writes:

> We made twenty all-different nationalities. We were lucky, because we lived then near a district called Old Corktown. It has since been demolished for area redevelopment, but was occupied then by Syrian, Mexican, Chinese, and Irish Americans. So many children to choose from, and I used live models. I used to go to bed at eight, and awake at 2 A.M.—no chance to work at all if I didn't, for everyone was so interested, and children were crowding in.

Since that time she has made many other dolls, including an entire series of nuns, several portrait dolls, historical characters, and more recently a group of Gibson Girl Heads—mature women. Her "Mother and Child in the Rocking Chair" is perhaps her best-known figure. She owns the original and has made only four copies.

Mrs. Florian makes her dolls of a bisque she has developed herself, which has an unusual living skin-tone. Every detail is modeled with extreme care, and she devotes particular attention to the doll's hands—perhaps the most difficult of all modeling. Mrs. Florian's mother worked with her until the time of her death in 1944, making all the wigs, while the artist designed, made, and dressed the dolls.

MAGGE HEAD

Magge Head's Adam and Ima Shyster are familiar to doll collectors, for Miss Head designed them and put them on the market in 1949, and they have been made ever since. The old people, 19-inches tall, were made with ceramic heads, arms and feet. A few were glazed; the rest were of bisque. Fifty of them were numbered consecutively. Magge Head's own token, a red cloth heart containing the history of the dolls, was sewed on their chests to avoid complete loss of identity of unmarked dolls. The Mark Farmer Company leased the copyright for Adam and Ima in 1954, and sold many of them. Later, rights of reproduction were sold to Pauline and Wayne Tharp of the Windy Acres Doll Museum, Carlos, Indiana.

Adam and Ima were not the first of Magge Head's dolls, for she began her career by making her Martha, in 1949. This was a 24-inch, one-of-a-kind doll with a high hair-do, a wood-putty head, and ceramic hands and feet. Trying to list all of Magge Head's creations and achievements is a hopeless task, for she seems to have been responsible for a wider variety of creative enterprises, in addition to dollmaking, than almost any other modern doll artist.

Her first untrained ceramic efforts included the digging of her own clay. She progressed to dollmaking, to the sculpture classes she holds in her studio in Modoc, Indiana, to writing a story about her ceramic pixies, and finally to a correspondence course in modeling. Many of her dolls are sold undressed or in kits, and many are reproduced either by lease or the purchase of reproduction rights. The presidential series—as well as that of Adam and Ima Shyster mentioned earlier—which begins with Martha and George Washington and is carried down the years to date, is produced by the Tharps of Windy Acres, Carlos, Indiana.

Group of Magge Head's portrait dolls make up this nativity scene. Her daughter and granddaughter were models.

Princess Elizabeth as a bride by Dorothy Heizer.

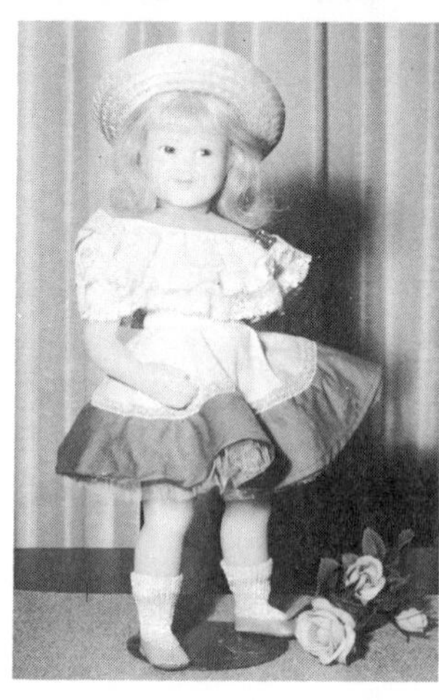

An enchanting wax doll by Gladys MacDowell.

Jane Seymour, wife of Henry VIII, is shown beside him in his portrait group by Grace Lathrop.

One of the finest Head dolls is her 21-inch Gypsy Mother and Nursing Babe, first produced in 1957. This doll won an award as the most outstanding entry in its class at the 1960 National Ceramic Show. Her Negro babies, children, and adults were pioneered in 1952 with the introduction of Aunt Abby, Uncle Plez, and later by Lil' Uke, Magnolia, Rosebud, and Peachblossom. All of these were first leased to Mary Farmer and then sold to the Tharps. Miss Head considers her best doll to be her Negro Mammy, Caldonia, first offered in 1957. Miss Head's skill as a sculptor is demonstrated in all her work, but never more effectively than in a Nativity scene, for which her daughter and granddaughter were the models. The faces and attitudes of the figures embody all the emotion of the Christmas season.

In 1960 Magge Head and an associate, Keith Kane, incorporated as Head and Kane, for the creation and reproduction of Head dolls. He took over the moldmaking and reproduction, while she continued her teaching and designing. They were married in 1962.

In 1964 the Hans Newdecker Company of Winchester, Indiana, put Head and Kane pixies and clowns into production as play dolls for children. These are being made now in vinyl. Head and Kane Inc. also produced a porcelain series of Famous Inventor dolls including Benjamin Franklin, Thomas Edison, George Washington Carver, Henry Ford, McCormick, Orville Wright, Wilbur Wright, Eli Whitney, and Alexander Graham Bell. Child dolls advertised under the name, "Kane's Rebels," made of porcelain in sizes from 5 to 14 inches, were introduced in 1963. Magge Head's 1963–64 venture was a correspondence course in ceramic dollmaking. Thousands of visitors and collectors admire the scenes which Magge Head painted for the Museum Dollorama in Cedar Rapids, Iowa. She previously modeled all the dolls used in them. There are twenty-two scenes, including Mother Goose Tales and dioramas from stories for children. Since May 1963 dolls designed by Magge Head have been marked on the back of the shoulders with date and name—Magge Head, M. H. Kane, or Magge Head Kane.

Magge Head's story shows what one woman can accomplish,

given talent and a driving ambition to overcome obstacles that would have discouraged others of perhaps equal skill.

DOROTHY HEIZER

Dorothy Heizer, now in her late 80's, is considered the dean of American doll artists, for she made her first doll in 1921—a flat-faced rag doll. Born in Philadelphia, she had a solid background of art education, attending the Pennsylvania Academy of Fine Arts, and studying under Cecelia Beaux, William Chase, and others. Her first dolls were made from great paintings and were elegantly dressed in brocades, velvets, and silk crepes, with accessories of seed pearls, cut glass jewels, tiny gold beads, ribbon, and veiling. Dorothy Heizer's dolls are made of layers of cloth built up on a copper armature, and padded with cotton. Fine cotton crepe is then stretched over the base, as a skin, and then delicately painted with opaque watercolor.

The first exhibit of Heizer dolls was held in 1924 at the Arts and Crafts Guild, Philadelphia. From then on she exhibited regularly, chiefly at Christmastime, in both Philadelphia and New York. In 1931 she was awarded the master craftsman's medal by the Arts and Crafts Guild.

The Depression affected these annual exhibitions; there were few people financially able to buy luxurious non-essentials like dolls. But the void was filled for Mrs. Heizer when Mrs. F. B. Noyes of Washington, D. C. ordered a group of English queens. These dolls are now in the Smithsonian Institution, and have probably been seen by more people than any one group of dolls anywhere.

Perhaps the most outstanding thing about Dorothy Heizer's dolls is her extreme attention to every detail. She has spent hours in researching each one, making sure that the features and coloring of historical characters are exactly right, that even the tiniest detail of costumes are authentic, and that all materials used are in keeping with the period. The artist even made the gold jewelry, bracelets and rings for her dolls using small seed pearls, gold-washed beads, and simulated gems. It is said to have taken Mrs. Heizer fifty hours to make a woman doll, and longer to make a man, depending, of course, on the amount of fine detail that was involved.

After 1936, the year of her husband's death, Mrs. Heizer devoted her entire time to what had previously been a part-time occupation—dollmaking. In 1940 she began to make dolls of a smaller size, which she sold through a New York shop; but since 1944, she has sold only directly to customers.

One of the highest points of Mrs. Heizer's career was the 1948 doll of Princess Elizabeth in her wedding gown, on which she sewed 45,000 pearls, rhinestones, and tiny beads. The strain of making this doll, together with the death of her daughter, forced her to reduce the number of hours she spent on her work; in 1961, failing eyesight compelled her to give up dollmaking entirely. For some years she had used magnifying clips on her glasses and a reading glass when she painted the faces of her minutely detailed dolls.

GRACE LATHROP

Grace Lathrop's dollmaking background began with years of free-lance art work in fashion illustrating, portrait painting, china painting, and several years spent in doing costume research for the old Metro-Goldwyn-Mayer studios in Culver City. In her own words:

> I make all of the dolls myself, in my own home, and try to keep the business on a hobby basis as much as possible. My dolls are included in many collections over the land. I have been making portrait and character dolls for many years, and have created more than forty doll characters, including many queens, famous American women, and pioneers. Some of the dolls have been dressed in keeping with their character, some have been sold undressed to collectors who wished to dress their own dolls.

Mrs. Lathrop's interest in historical figures is shared by almost all serious doll collectors, some of whom costume their own dolls, and others who become the customers of artists like Mrs. Lathrop and her associated NIADA members. It is probably natural for one-time portrait painters to be attracted to dolls as personalities, rather than as vague nonentities. Mrs. Lathrop's account of her dolls continues:

> Dressing the doll is part of the fun of owning it, I believe. The dolls I make now are all of porcelain, with sawdust-filled bodies, although in the past I have made dolls of other materials: cornhusks, dried apples, silk and cotton, and papier-mâché, also a special composition material. At the start of my doll making, the heads, hands, and feet of the dolls were hand-modeled from the composition material, and one of a kind made. But the doll business grew too big for that, so now I model a portrait likeness of the doll which is to represent the person intended. From the model I make a plaster mould. Duplicates can then be made, using porcelain slip, or liquid clay. But even then it takes a lot of work to create just one doll.

Mrs. Lathrop failed to mention that perhaps her best known doll is Clara Barton, which is in the Red Cross Museum in Washington, D. C.

GLADYS MACDOWELL

Gladys MacDowell's career, like that of many NIADA members, has taken a few unexpected turns. At its beginning in 1947 she was living in the Canal Zone, and wanted to add some Panamanian dolls to her already established doll collection, but was unable to find any she could use. After first experimenting with cloth, she turned to wax as her best medium, and completed the Panamanian group she wanted. After that first experience she went on to make many other dolls, specializing in portrait dolls of poured wax, with glass eyes, swivel necks, and embedded hair. Mrs. MacDowell has become so expert in the restoration of antique wax dolls that she spends most of her time on this highly exacting work.

LEWIS SORENSEN

The only man with the Institute, Lewis Sorensen, works with his own special wax formula, developed after years of

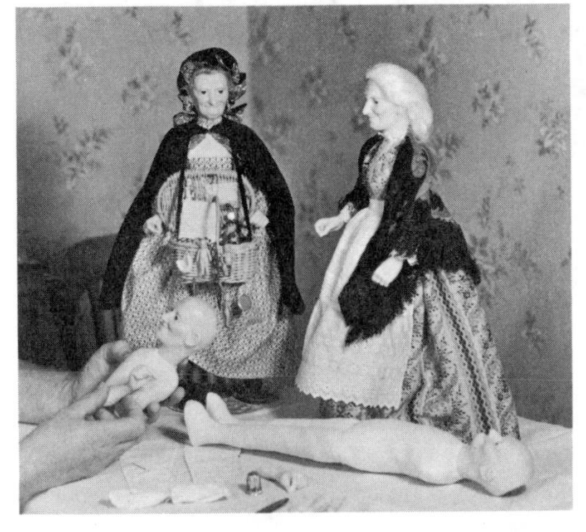

Lewis Sorensen at work on his little old ladies of wax gives an idea of his method of assembling the dolls.

Lewis Sorensen's perfect likeness of Queen Elizabeth II.

The Widow of Windsor, a lusty Tudor lady by Tamara Steinheil. It has all the vitality of the Good Wife of Bath.

experiment. He has perfected a material that will withstand both heat and extreme cold, and has such a natural-looking skin-tone that his life size wax figures seem to be alive.

For many years, Sorensen was a Hollywood dress designer; he then costumed dolls for collectors, and made and taught ceramics and painting. His doll characters range widely and include old people, lovely women, rugged men, and a few children. His Mormon Pioneers group is in the State Capitol Museum in Salt Lake City, and hundreds of his life size figures are in museums and wax museums all over North America. The Movieland Wax Museum near Disneyland in Southern California contains many examples of Sorensen's work.

TAMARA STEINHEIL

Baronness Tamara Steinheil was born in the Ukraine. Her father, Count L. deLilier, was a French engineer and art lover; her mother, a Russian, was a doctor of medicine and an accomplished pianist. She was raised in an atmosphere where both art and literature were a part of life, and dabbled with paints from early childhood. She attended schools in Russia, France, Germany, and Switzerland, and with her father wandered through countless museums.

Just before World War I, she married Baron George Steinheil. The war and the Russian Revolution took her husband and two of her brothers, and left her young, alone, and penniless. In 1923 she came to America. Her heritage of art appreciation gave her a good foundation for her new life in the United States; she tested several careers, including dress designing, lecturing, and hairdressing, but at the same time she always managed to continue with her painting. Another hobby she experimented with during this period was making masks and figurines from papier-mâché. Then, after seeing a doll exhibit in California, she was inspired to make dolls. All her knowledge of history and art served her well, and she could put into her dolls not only her interest in costume and style, but also the character of the times they represented. Perhaps some day Tamara Steinheil will make a group of dolls depicting all

Chaucer's Canterbury Pilgrims, for her Good Wife of Bath dolls which the artist calls her Widow of Windsor, certainly resemble the buxom lady in her ruff and stomacher.

MARTHA THOMPSON

Martha Thompson was one of the founders and charter members of NIADA, and sadly, the first one to be taken from the group by death, on January 26, 1964. She was another one of the artists to abandon portrait painting for dollmaking, and created many lovely bisque and Parian portrait dolls. Her talent for getting true likenesses was exceptional.

The largest group of her dolls was a series of nineteenth century men, women, and children, taken from tinted French and English steel engravings. Royalty, particularly the children of the British royal family, fascinated her, but she also made many doll portraits of other children. Her Betsy Sheffield, a little girl of 1907, and Betsy's "Little Brother," "The Laughing and Crying Babies," and the four "Little Women" were perhaps the most frequently reproduced of all her dolls.

In preparing this record of Martha Thompson and her dolls, we were delighted to have the cooperation of her son, Murray Thompson, Jr., as well as his permission to quote from his letter to us. Martha Thompson herself never sought public recognition, and was content to have her work known in the doll world. Whenever her dolls won some kind of honors at a National Federation convention, it was rarely because she had entered them herself. The following excerpts about Martha Thompson are from Mr. Thompson's letter:

> Mother took a long time in finding out what she liked to do best. From her early preoccupations like drawing fashion ads for the newspapers, before she was married, illustrating children's test pamphlets and textbooks for Houghton-Mifflin, doing some random pastel portraits of children, she turned gradually to work in three dimensions. She made a miniature fairy tale diorama, Mother Goose theme wall placques in plaster and oils, then a long stretch of making puppets and marionettes, including portrait models. By this time she had

Martha Thompson's group of dolls inspired by 1816–1820 French fashion plates are charming examples of her skill in both modeling and costuming.

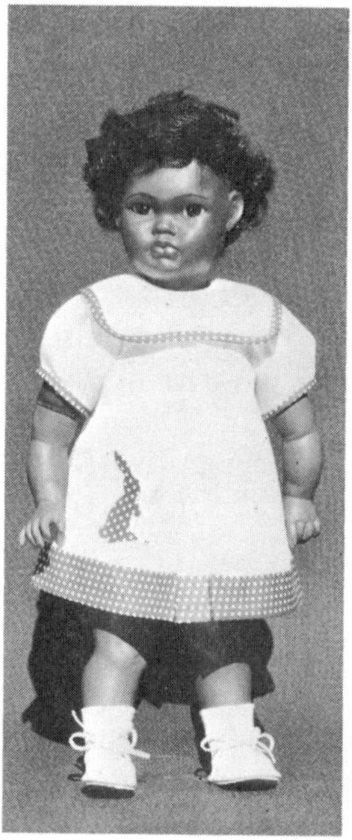

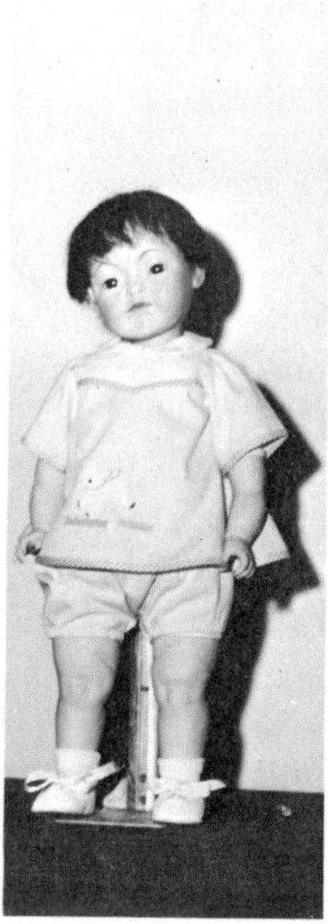

Pansy-Rose by Ellery Thorpe is one of the finest modeling projects of the times.

Harry, the bisque Japanese child made by Ellery Thorpe.

Mariel is a 13-inch blond doll with molded hair by Ellery Thorpe.

> gained enough skill with the sculpturing end of her craft to make it easier for her when she drifted into the doll enthusiasm.
>
> She yearned to make dolls in the same high-fired medium as the old German and French porcelain (bisque and Parian) but imagined the secret had died with them. However, she found out that Mrs. Emma Clear was putting out this kind of ceramics, so she took heart and set forth to learn to do likewise. . . . I am sure that one of the high spots of her career was when she took her first lot of heads out of that big kiln and felt the smooth, translucent luster that so approximates human skin in appearance—a far cry from the coarse texture of the pottery-clay she'd been confined to before.
>
> It was most gratifying to her to have people on her waiting list so patient with her when circumstances limited her output to a mere trickle, from time to time. Some waited three or four years for their dolls. Some never *did* get theirs.

Mrs. Thompson was often asked whether the British royal family ever received any of her many dolls representing its members. Mr. Thompson explains that British law limits those who may make presentations to the royal family, and continues:

> However, there is considerable doll collecting done in England and many of my mother's dolls found their way over, by one way or another. Someone in England recently reported seeing one of the dolls at a charity-benefit exhibition of paintings and objects d'art owned by the Queen Mother, so we have since then felt reasonably sure that at least one of the Martha Thompson Royal Family dolls had come to the attention of the family.

Among other dolls created by his mother, Mr. Thompson speaks of the French Fashion Plate dolls—Henry VIII and His Six Wives, with likenesses taken largely from Holbein paintings—and the Grace Kelly doll, in possession of the Princess of Monaco herself. It particularly pleased Mrs. Thompson that this doll, copies of which many collectors later obtained, brought a note of appreciation from Princess Grace. This doll is considered one of the best examples of the artist's skill with likenesses, in addition to being a beautiful doll in its own right.

ELLERY THORPE

"Gentle but strong" is the term used by a fellow member of NIADA to characterize the procelain child dolls made by Ellery Thorpe. The same words could be used to describe the artist herself. One feels that her dolls are loved children, and that if they were alive they would be just the kind of children this artist would have—natural, good, and unspoiled.

Her dolls all vary a little in size, but most of them are in the 13- to 18-inch range. They are made of delicately modeled, exquisitely colored bisque or Parian. Some have stuffed cloth bodies, firm but soft enough to feel lifelike. Many of them have wigs of real hair, made by Mrs. Thorpe and her hubsand Edwin; others have hair painted in mat colors. Her Negro dolls are not just colored dolls, but more like real Negro children with their own features and characteristics. All Thorpe dolls are dressed in handmade clothing, so perfectly made and detailed that they could well serve as child fashion dolls. Little Harry, whose picture is shown in Chapter 14, is one of Ellery Thorpe's more recent dolls. Her model was the small grandson of her Japanese gardener. She made many other children, but two of the most touching are the little boy and girl with big tears running down their cheeks.

In addition to her dolls, Mrs. Thorpe designs equally beautiful greeting cards, stationery, and paper dolls, almost all of which depict children.

FAWN ZELLER

Fawn Zeller is an outstanding portrait artist, specializing in infinitely small dolls with many miniature details. Her dolls are all made of high-fire porcelain and go into the kiln for at least four, and sometimes more firings. In order to carry out the finest details which are often painted with a brush of one hair, she does her sculpturing under a magnifying glass. The artist's enthusiasm and dedication are expressed best in her own words: "I enjoy minute work and the challenge of doing sculptured heads even small enough for lockets, and literally holding my

Clara Barton, founder of American Red Cross, as depicted by Fawn Zeller. It took eighteen hours to place individual strands of hair on the head. The doll, now owned by Martha Mills of Arlington Heights, Illinois, was based on a Matthew Brady photograph.

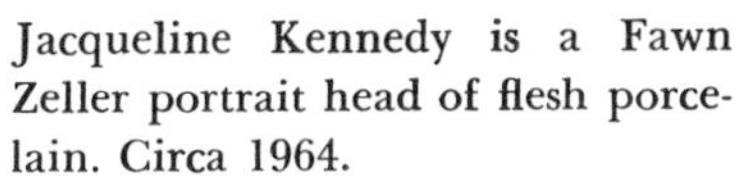

Jacqueline Kennedy is a Fawn Zeller portrait head of flesh porcelain. Circa 1964.

breath to steady my hand when applying the intricate detail in this small scale."

One of Mrs. Zeller's most outstanding dolls is her portrait doll of Clara Barton which was taken from a Matthew Brady photograph and made, primarily, because Mrs. Zeller wanted to make the clock in the background. The little kid gloves in Miss Barton's hands are about one inch long. One of the most recent Zeller dolls is her Jacqueline Kennedy head which can be made into a doll about 17-inches high. The likeness is splendid. It is available for collectors. So also is her "Angela," with curls and a garland of roses across the back of her head.

Mrs. Zeller is no longer making the smaller, complete dolls which she formerly made.

In her museum at Inverness, Florida, Mrs. Zeller's one-of-a-kind group of Famous People in Miniature includes a lovely 10½-inch Queen Victoria, made from a Winterhalter portrait of the queen at age twenty-five, as well as Franklin D. Roosevelt, Winston Churchill, Robert E. Lee, and Dwight D. Eisenhower. Another one of her outstanding portraits is the doll showing Elizabeth II in her coronation robes. This doll is only 9-inches tall, but the costume, copied exactly from photographs including the scepter, the orb and the crown, took an entire year to complete.

Mrs. Zeller made 250 souvenir dolls of "Miss Kentucky" for the Kentucky Blue Grass Doll Club, one of the many affiliates of the United Federation of Doll Clubs, when the organization held its second Miami convention several years ago. Fortunate owners of these dolls are to be congratulated, for Fawn Zeller's dolls will be prized by generations of artists as well as doll collectors.

17

DOLL REPAIR

FOR MAJOR REPAIRS valuable dolls should be turned over only to experts. There are many qualified professionals, and perhaps the easiest way to locate them is through a good doll hospital, of which there are many in all parts of the country. Sometimes the charges for repairs may seem high, but this is a skilled and specialized trade requiring training in a wide variety of processes, tools, and materials.

Humpty Dumpty, the most famous of all doll hospitals, owned and operated for many years by Mrs. Emma Clear, made fine reproductions of rare antique dolls; but it was Mrs. Clear's pioneering manufacture of reproduction *parts* for the repair of dolls, that must stand as her most enduring contribution to the field. Following in Mrs. Clear's path there are now a great many manufacturers and craftsmen engaged in making ceramic parts for repairing and restoring dolls. Several of them are listed in the Appendix.

There are many minor repairs quite within the capability of anyone who can sew or tinker. If you decide to try your hand at repairing, also check newspaper classified columns where such parts and services are sometimes advertised.

In addition to the manufacture of replacement arms and legs, these same mail-order houses specializing in doll repair almost always carry doll wigs, readymade cloth bodies, and even repair kits for restringing doll-bodies. It is satisfying to test your own skill, which sometimes can be turned to profit when you are able to work on the dolls of other collectors.

There are two opposing attitudes about doll repair and

restoration. One group insists that an antique doll should never be touched, regardless of its delapidated condition; the other is equally insistent that every doll in a collection must be complete and perfect, showing no signs of wear.

Most collectors take an in-between course, but tend to agree more with the first group than with the second, feeling, as a correspondent once said, that "a doll can be restored to ruination." These are the ones who ignore faded clothing and the mellowing of age, and take measures only when a doll is in danger of falling apart, or an arm or leg is missing. They will then sew up the rips and duplicate the missing limb as closely as possible, but leave the scuffed paint alone.

A cloth or kid body is often valuable in helping to date or identify a doll, and even if it is torn or ripped, it should be mended but not replaced. If too unsightly, make a kind of slip cover for it of new cloth, so that even if the original body is completely covered, it may be inspected to determine the age of the doll, or some detail of its making.

A doll's value is increased when it is dressed in its original clothes. Even when these are not in keeping with the rest of your collection, do not discard them. Rather, mark them carefully and pack them away in a safe place. If the doll ever goes to another collection, it is possible that these clothes will be called for, so don't throw them away.

A good example of the way museums handle the matter of repair is shown by the unrestored Queen Anne wooden doll in the Victoria and Albert Museum, mentioned in an earlier chapter. This doll wears a headdress to which a lacy veil or scarf is attached. It is a wispy ruin, like some of the lace on the doll's dress, but it has not been replaced.

However, it is often not simply a question of making minor repairs on a doll that is worn or faded, but of restoring missing parts, repairing nicks and cracks, or placing a head already owned on a new cloth body. Suggestions for solutions to each of these problems follow.

Many times a china-head, cloth-bodied doll is in perfect or acceptable condition except for a missing bisque or china arm or leg. Try to match the remaining one exactly. As suggested above, send for the catalog of one of the mail-order houses

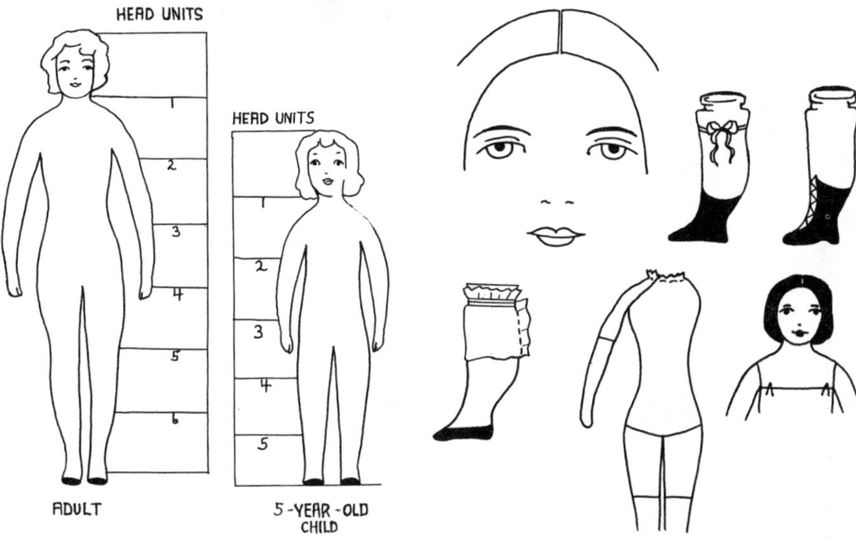

Scale of proportions for an adult as measured in head lengths, about six or seven units. Two or three units are used for an infant, increasing with the age of the child.

Top, left to right: Painted features of a traditional antique china doll; common type of china leg with painted boot and ribbon garters; common type of china leg with high-laced shoe. *Bottom, left to right:* Cloth section is fastened to china leg by winding thread in top groove before turning the cloth right side out; arm in its cloth section, is sewed to top of body; head is fastened to cloth body by sewing through the holes near the edge of shoulder.

offering a wide variety of styles and sizes, because there were really comparatively few types of arms and legs made to be used with the vast number of china or bisque heads. It is rather easy to find what you want.

There is a conventional method used by artists for determining the height of a person in "head" lengths. A head is the distance from the tip of the chin to the crown of the head. A man is 7 or 8 head lengths tall; a woman about 7 head lengths; an infant is from 2 to 3 head lengths. It was the failure of many home dollmakers to understand this scale of proportions that was responsible for the quaint elongated bodies of multitudes of papier-mâché and china dolls made in the nineteenth century.

Yet this is not the same measurement used in describing the size of a doll-head. Instead, the distance from the top of the head to the bottom of the shoulder is considered to be the height, and it is this measurement that must be used when ordering parts by mail. Most dealers' catalogs explain this clearly.

If you wish to order a new pair of doll legs, and not just duplicate those already on the doll, it is a good idea to make a diagram of your individual doll in order to determine the correct size to order. On a sheet of paper, make two pencil marks—one at the crown of the head, the other the number of inches your doll's crown is from its chin-tip. This distance is your unit of size for the entire doll. Now decide the approximate age your doll is to be—adult or child, and determine from the chart how many head units the doll should be. Make another pencil mark on your diagram to indicate where the soles of the feet should come. You now have a guide to follow in determining the height of the doll. The chart will also help you establish the proportionate length of the arms and legs and the placement of the waistline.

Many different methods have been used in the past for making doll-bodies, and for attaching arms, legs, and heads. If you are replacing a missing limb, be sure to use the same method that was used on the doll originally, so that all work will be as uniform as possible. One of the most common methods of making cloth doll-bodies is shown here.

Whenever it is necessary to replace the cloth section of an arm or leg, match the original material as nearly as possible. Use the same size of thread, same length of stitches, and the same amount of stuffing as was used on the original. Briefly, the idea is to duplicate as much as possible everything about the original so that the repair will be as inconspicuous as you can make it, even if the quality of the original material and workmanship falls below your own personal capability and taste.

Many old cloth doll-bodies were made of heavy muslin and often of cotton drilling. Sateen, longcloth, and white or pink percale also make satisfactory doll-bodies. The main requirement is that the cloth should be closely woven, and strong enough to hold tightly packed stuffing. Strong seams are also very important, and for this reason it is better to use a sewing machine than it is to sew them by hand. If hand stitching is necessary, however, use a backstitch and heavy thread. Seam allowances of 3/8 inch insure that the seams will not pull out during the process of stuffing.

Stuffing may be of cotton, kapok, or hair. Shredded foam rubber can also be used, but this material is cursed with a tendency to be lumpy. Sawdust, firmly packed into the cloth sections, is probably the best kind of stuffing; it is both durable and inexpensive. When in need of sawdust, visit your local lumber yard, taking along your own sack or container. You will be allowed to fill it with all the free sawdust you can use. The sawdust from white pine or some other light-colored wood is preferable to that of walnut or redwood. Sift it through a coarse sieve or colander to remove any chips and splinters; presumably it will be dry, but if you are in doubt, spread it in a shallow pan and leave it for several hours in an oven set at a very low heat.

The making of a complete cloth body is not difficult. Follow the diagram for making a pattern, and cut two pieces for each section. Stitch the two pieces of the body section together at both sides and the bottom edge, leaving the top open. Turn it right side out, stuff it firmly with sawdust and gather the top edges so that they just meet. In order to make the packing firm, push it into the casing with a smooth stick or the handle of a large wooden spoon.

Now sew the arm and leg sections together at the sides, but do not turn them right side out. Slip the china arms and legs into these casings, as shown on the next chart, allowing the cloth to extend only to the top of the china. Wind heavy sewing thread around the top in the groove of the china, several times over, then fasten securely. Now turn the cloth section right side out.

Stuff the leg sections up to the top of the cloth casing. Turn

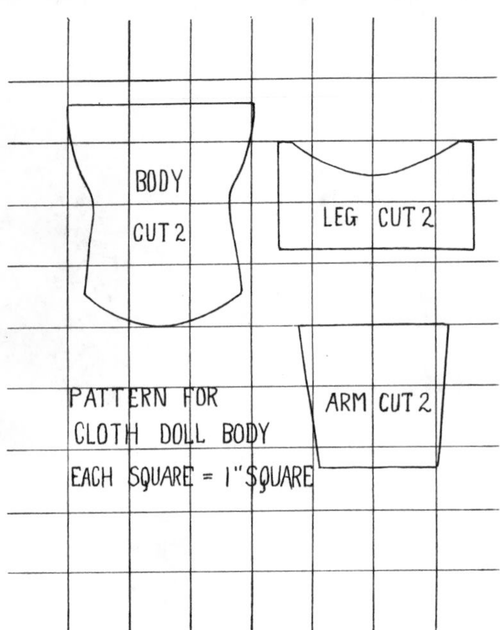

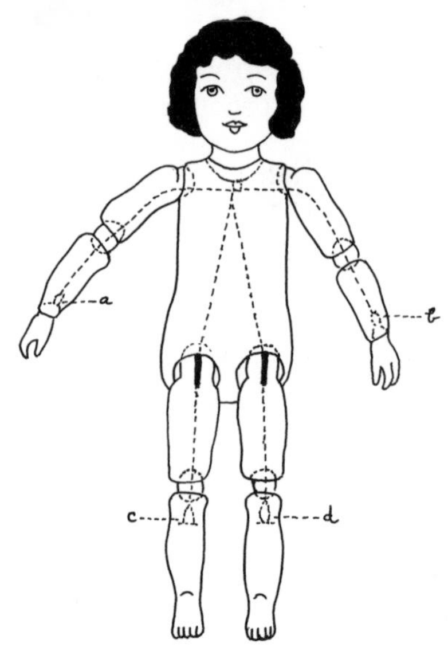

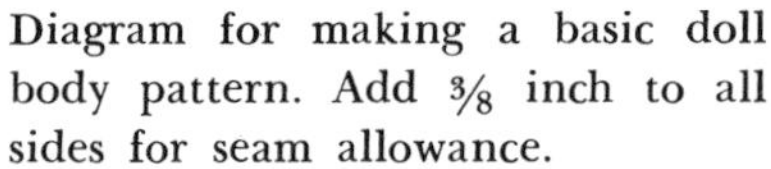

Diagram for making a basic doll body pattern. Add 3/8 inch to all sides for seam allowance.

Diagram for stringing a jointed doll shows how two pieces of elastic are to be used, one running from *a* to *b*, the other from *c* through the neck and then to *d*.

the upper edge under 1/8 inch, and baste together. With heavy thread, sew the top of the leg sections to the bottom of the body section.

Fill the arms only half full of stuffing. Sew them to the top of the body where the joining will be covered when the head is in place. Adjust the length of the arms at this time, checking to see that the tips of the fingers hang just to the bottom of the body section.

Now push the head down onto the body, working it into place until it fits snuggly. Sew the head to the body with a long darning needle and fine twine or heavy thread. To do this, push the needle through the hole in the bottom of the shoulder, then back into the body just below the hole corresponding to the hole in the back of the shoulder. Repeat this several times, then fasten the other shoulder in place the same way. Bury the end of the thread by running it into the stuffing for two or three inches before cutting it off.

In *Here Is Your Hobby, Ceramics,* we described the complete method of making china dolls, heads, arms, and legs. For collectors who enjoy experimenting with the making of dolls, it is fascinating to create modern and original models, or to make replica doll parts. Since temperatures must be brought far above the point that can be reached by a kitchen oven, it is necessary to either own or have access to a high-fire gas or electric kiln. The material needed is what potters call porcelain "slip" or liquid ceramic clay. Although it has been used, ordinary pottery clay is more coarse, and is not as well suited to taking on the fine details of a plaster mold. Many of the members of NIADA, it will be remembered, make porcelain dolls, using finely textured clay; there is no patent on techniques which are as old as the history of potters. The making of ceramic dolls also includes not only the actual modeling and firing of them, but also the glazing and painting. If a collector is to thoroughly appreciate dolls and be able to evaluate their quality, it is helpful to know a little about some of the fundamental rules for painting them.

The paint used on both glazed china and bisque is what ceramists call "overglaze" or china color and is the type long used for "china painting." It comes most often in powdered form and is mixed with an oily "medium" by means of a palette knife until it is smooth. The mixture is then thinned with turpentine and applied with a soft camelhair brush. In order to bind the colors permanently to the china, the piece must be fired in a kiln until the flux in the pigments melts and is bonded to the china or bisque. This process of painting and firing is often repeated several times until an exact effect is achieved.

In dollmaking, the finest, smallest brushes, preferably 000 or 00, are used to mark the eyebrows, edge of eyelid, and to outline the mouth. The faint blush-pink of the cheeks must be delicately blended at the edges. Instead of being painted a brilliant red, the mouth should be a soft, almost orange shade of red, and the delicate line of red often found above the eyes is this same pale shade. A tiny dot of the same red is often used at the inner corner of the eyes. The pupils of the eyes may be a delicate shade of blue or a medium brown, and the iris is black. Often a tiny bit of eye color is removed to give the effect of a highlight. Never, under any circumstances, should there be any indication of individual eyelashes in an antique doll, or even a line to indicate the lower eyelid. Occasionally, an old doll has faintly pink inner nostrils, or a delicate, curving pink line. This is a mere tint, if used at all.

The legs attached to many old china, bisque, and Parian dolls have painted blue garters, often with a bow and long curling ends. The bow is more often on the front of the leg, but is sometimes painted on the outside. The blue is a light Delft blue, rather than a forget-me-not shade. Slippers and shoes were sometimes painted on in a luster, but more often they were black. Flat-soled shoes, invariable before high heels became fashionable about 1860, were generally painted black with tan-colored soles. Sometimes these heelless boots or shoes were buttoned up the side, but more often they were laced. On other dolls, the shoes are a solid color, cut higher at the front and back than at the sides. Because so many old china and Parian heads were sold only as heads, to be attached at home to handmade bodies, more often than not an old doll's body also includes cloth hands and feet. This means that slippers or shoes must be purchased or made. The same styles of course apply to these as well as to the painted ones.

A minor fault of jointed dolls is their occasional need for restringing. This is an easy operation, for which you will need only round elastic and a long button or crochet hook. Round elastic may be obtained from department stores or sometimes from a furrier, as well as from doll hospitals. Before you start a restringing job, examine the doll to determine the size of elastic to use. Then measure from one wrist, along the arm, across the chest, and along the other arm to the other wrist. This will require one length of elastic. Another length is needed for the distance from one ankle, up the leg, through the body to the hook attached to the neck, down through the body and the other leg to the ankle.

The work of replacing the old elastic with new is actually

quite simple. Remove the old elastic and with the help of the long crochet hook, replace it with new. Follow the chart and tie where the old elastic was tied. Pull the elastic snug before making each tie so the body will be good and tight at the joints.

Another easily made minor repair is the replacement of a finger-tip or toe. First clean the exposed, broken surface—either china, papier-mâché, or composition. When completely dry, press a dab of plastic wood or of Durham's Water Putty down firmly on the broken surface. Let it dry for two or three days, then paint with a small brush dipped in household enamel or lacquer tinted to match the color of the doll's skin.

Sometimes an entire finger may have to be replaced. In this event, unless the doll is too small, drill a tiny hole in the hand and insert a piece of fine wire, or a piece of pipe cleaner, dipped in glue in the hole. When dry, cut the wire or pipe cleaner a trifle shorter than the finger is to be. Using this as a base, model a finger upon it of plastic wood or water putty, and paint it to match the hand.

The matter of paint has been happily solved for amateurs by model-making manufacturers. All craft, hobby, and paint stores display racks of small bottles of enamels in every imaginable color, made for painting model cars and airplanes. With one bottle each of white, blue, red, yellow, and black, you will have enough paint for many doll repairs.

As an example, suppose a missing finger has been replaced on a doll, and the plastic wood or putty has been thoroughly dried and smoothly sanded. The doll's body is covered with flesh-colored paint, and you wish now to paint the repaired finger in the same color. On a piece of glass or aluminum foil place a few drops of white enamel. Dip a toothpick in the bottle of red enamel, and mix it with the dab of white to get a pale pink shade, as close to the original body color as possible. Touch it with a speck of yellow. Continue to add more color until you have matched the original shade. If you decide the color should be a trifle more tan-colored, add a bit of blue. There should be very little difference in these colors after they dry, but if you wish to test the paint before you apply it, do so on a scrap of cardboard. Also, it is better to use two thin coats of paint, thoroughly drying the first before applying the second, than it is to use an excessively thick coat of paint. In using the enamel, use a fine brush and flow on the paint, blending it smoothly where it meets the old finish.

It is always important whenever making repairs to work carefully and painstakingly, never hurrying, and always allowing the paint to dry thoroughly as you proceed. It is also important to know when to stop. There's a temptation when you hold a paintbrush to touch up everything in sight—like setting out to paint a shelf and ending up repainting the entire kitchen.

It is easy to freshen the surface of wooden, wax, and papier-mâché dolls by simply wiping them carefully with a soft cloth moistened with liquid wax. This not only removes grime, but leaves a protective film.

Wax dolls are so valuable that it would be foolish for anyone but an expert to do more than this to them. Before trusting even a doll hospital with a wax doll, ask to see other wax dolls they have restored, for this is a highly specialized art. Experienced collectors have seen more than one lovely wax doll that has been ruined by clumsy re-waxing, so that it looked as if it had been dipped repeatedly in wax and all the fine modeling was lost.

One doll collector who makes her own repairs, uses ivory-colored wax candles from the dime store for the work, adding tiny pieces of red crayola to obtain flesh color. She tests the color by dipping little strips of white cardboard in the melted wax and letting it harden, since the color changes greatly when the wax is hard. She then applies the melted wax with a small brush to fill minor cracks, holes, and bare spots, not attempting to get a perfectly smooth surface until after the wax hardens. She then trims and levels it with a small knife, and rubs it gently with her fingers to smooth it and restore the gloss.

A dirty or touseled wig may be restored by carefully removing it from the doll's head and dipping it in and out of cleaning fluid. Hang it up to dry and air for a few days, then comb it carefully and glue it back on the head. If you wish to recurl the hair and have no curling iron, heat a small metal rod or an ice pick and wind strands of hair around it. Be sure the metal is not too hot and that the curl is not left wrapped around it too long.

The repair of composition dolls often consists of filling and painting cracks in the outer surface. These generally extend only through the exterior paint, so first remove all the loose, surrounding finish. Sand the surface of cracks to make it level. Brush with white shellac. Fill with plastic wood or water putty, and when dry, paint with enamel to match the body color. One of the grave faults of composition is its tendency to develop these long surface cracks, and it is often necessary, because of them, to completely repaint the doll. In this event, you will get a smoother surface if you use spray paint instead of a brush.

It is comparatively easy to rebuild a doll's broken shoulder by first building up the missing section from the inside to exactly match the other shoulder, leaving the broken edge exposed. Use modeling clay or florist's clay to do this. Then make a thick dough of Durham's Water Putty and butter the top of the clay with it to the level of the doll's shoulder. If there is to be a hole in the lower edge of the shoulder for sewing it to the body, make it with a match stick at this point, matching its size and location with the hole in the other shoulder.

Let the putty harden and dry, which will take several days. One advantage of this particular brand of putty is that it does not shrink as it hardens. No allowance has to be made for a difference in size while working with it. Carefully remove the modeling clay, and clean the under side of the putty replacement with cleaning solvent. Brush epoxy glue on a narrow strip of muslin and place it on the under side of the shoulder where the putty joins the china. Allow this to dry thoroughly, then sand the surface and give it a coat of white shellac. Enamel the new surface to match the china, as already described.

A repair of this kind can often be concealed when the doll is dressed, but only an experienced expert should attempt to repair a china doll whose face has been cracked or broken, since the best means of doing it may involve methods far too technical for amateurs. The same is true of many repairs on modern vinyl or plastic dolls, and in fact some of them are impossible to repair.

TIPS FOR MINOR HOME REPAIRS

It is easier to make small doll-bodies by hand than on the sewing machine. Take small backstitches, but use thread no finer than No. 50.

Sew small china heads to cloth bodies with heavy white crochet cotton instead of sewing thread.

Retouch small areas of glazed china with colorless nail polish.

Large, heavy china heads are often fastened to cloth bodies by inserting short pieces of woven cotton tape through the holes in the shoulders, and then sewing the tape to the body.

Several books listed in the bibliography are full of instructions and suggestions for repairing dolls. Among these are Clara Hallard Fawcett's *On Making, Mending, and Dressing Dolls,* and two efficient little books on doll repair by Ruth Davis Glover and Ruth Freeman. For anyone who wishes to turn professional, these are invaluable.

In conclusion, whenever you or someone else make repairs on a doll, jot down a little memorandum of the date and the work done, and fasten it to the doll's body or an inconspicuous part of its underwear. The amount and quality of the repair greatly affect the doll's value, and although you may think you will be the only person ever to own it, remember that dolls are often far more enduring than people.

18

FASHIONS FOR DOLLS

BECAUSE SO MANY dolls were made after 1850 we shall take that year as the starting point in discussing doll costuming. Europe in 1850 was not only the birth place of most dolls, but was also the source of much of the world's art. Culturally, Europe was the world, and thought of America as its naïve child, recently rebellious and too provincial to be taken seriously. Most Americans agreed with Europe. That is why Paris was able to dictate fashions for so many years, even after the two continents had grown further apart socially and economically. This attitude did not change until after World War I.

Does it seem a far cry from fashions to women's rights? Not at all, for fashion reveals much about ways of life, history and geography, to say nothing of wars and politics. Much of woman's social evolution involved her gradual discovery that she could choose the clothes she liked, instead of wearing what someone else decreed. It is significant that the first stirrings of liberation probably came from an American woman, Amelia Bloomer, a reformer born in New York in 1818. But Amelia Bloomer did not achieve fame because she was an early crusader for woman's suffrage and also wrote and lectured on the temperance question; she is remembered chiefly for her adoption of the "bloomer costume," originally devised and introduced by Mrs. Elizabeth Smith Miller.

As editor of *The Lily,* a paper dedicated to her causes, Mrs. Bloomer gave space to her ideas about unhygienic long skirts, high heels, restricting corsets, and tight clothing. Her costume took the form of Turkish trousers extending to the ankle in summer, and in winter tucked into high boot tops, worn with a scant skirt coming just below the knees. Other feminists who approved the costume were Mrs. Elizabeth Cady Stanton and Mrs. Lucy Stone (Blackwell), although all of them later returned to dress styles more in accordance with those of the day.

As early as 1857 a National Dress Association tried to influence styles and to encourage women to wear more hygienic clothing. These efforts had no immediate success, but probably, when added to later campaigns for a change in women's dress, did play an important part in bringing about improvements. A second National Dress Association was formed in Boston in 1874, at about the same time the Rational Dress Movement became active in England. Germany, however, was the only country of Europe where dress reform made any progress. In 1873 a series of lectures sponsored at the University of Munich by the Crown Princess of Saxony created some interest, but it was not until the participation of women in outdoor games that there was much enthusiasm anywhere for reform in dress.

Peterson's Magazine, published for a few years in Philadelphia beginning in 1856, showed some of the fashions that reformers were trying to abolish. It was *Godey's Lady's Book,* however, after Sarah Josepha Hale became its editor and used the magazine as an outlet for her ideas on women's rights as well as fashions, that probably had the most to do with the eventual change. Mrs. Hale never hesitated to publicize any cause she embraced, and her influence on the thinking of the country was impressive.

Godey fashions have always been beloved by doll dressmakers, who copy the fashion plates shown in Mrs. Hale's magazine. Here are the elaborate, lovely costumes with panniers, crinolines, pantalettes, leg-of-mutton sleeves, bell sleeves, bretelles, and fanciful little hats and bonnets trimmed with ribbons, feathers, and flowers. These are the fashions for the deep-shouldered china and papier-mâché dolls with serene foreheads, and hair dressed with loops over the ears or with long curls clustered at the back of their heads. These are the dolls that wear flat-soled slippers or shoes, lace mitts, and graceful fringed shawls.

In the middle of the nineteenth century Victoria was Queen of England; she and her Prince Consort were intent on increasing the British appreciation of Continental culture. Both the queen and her husband influenced fashions, as well as manners and morals, in both England and America. The visits of the royal family to the Queen's beloved Balmoral castle in Scotland brought Scottish tartans into popular favor and the red, black and white plaid of the Royal Stewart tartan appeared in all kinds of apparel from a small boy's kilts to his Mamma's fringed sash. Plaids other than the traditional ones were introduced, and there was a mad confusion of purples and pinks and oranges never seen in a Highland glen.

Meanwhile, in France the Empress Eugénie, married to Napoleon III, shed even more glamour on fashions. She was the essence of femininity, and her billowing skirts, laces, silks and garlands of flowers have always appealed to doll dressmakers. A tiny hat, worn tipped forward on the head, was given her name, and it again became the rage in the 1920's, for a time almost deposing the prosaic cloche. Dolls dressed in Empress Eugénie styles are not necessarily portraits, but these fashions do coincide with the dates when many fine Parians and bisques were being made. Eugénie reigned from 1853 to 1871.

The name of Jenny Lind is familiar to doll collectors, as we have seen, and perhaps there were actually some dolls made to resemble her. This Swedish singer, brought to America by the great P. T. Barnum, was born a few years before the Empress Eugénie and lived until 1887. The dolls commonly called Jenny Lind by collectors may also be dressed in Queen Victoria or Empress Eugénie styles.

Abraham Lincoln's wife, Mary Todd Lincoln, is also memorialized by doll collectors. Mrs. Lincoln loved beautiful clothes, and was often berated for extravagance by her husband's enemies. Although she was no longer young—nor beautiful—at the time her husband became President of the United States, she and the fashions of the 1860's live on in the doll world. It is doubtful whether a contemporary doll was made under her name, but many have been made since.

After the French Empire period, when high-waisted, narrow

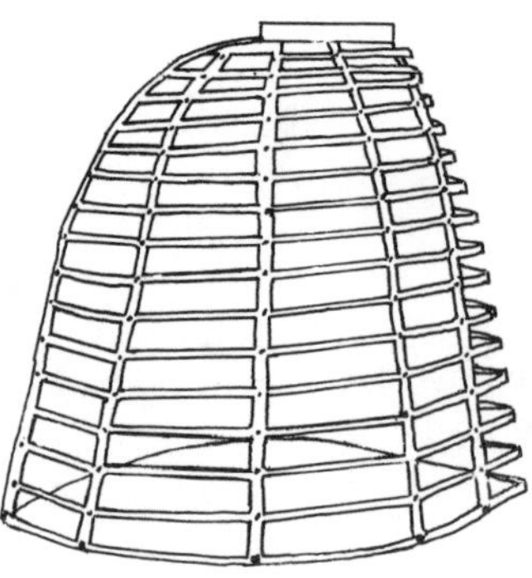

One type of hoop worn in the mid-1800's was a framework of tapes and steel springs fastened to a belt.

An 1874 doll, with kid body, porcelain head, and human hair wig, is dressed in a simplified replica of a Worth wedding gown of the period.

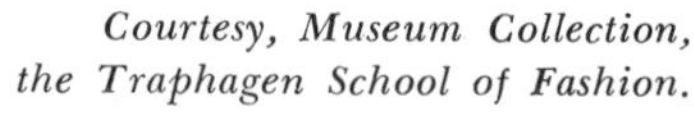

Courtesy, Museum Collection, the Traphagen School of Fashion.

China doll of the late 1880's wears striped silk "waist" with leg-of-mutton sleeves. Bonnet doll beside her is modern, made by the author from an old photograph.

This 1890 family was designed by author to live in a Victorian doll house. Details of dress and hairstyle are important when dressing period dolls.

skirts were fashionable, skirts became gradually wider and wider. In order to extend these skirts, women wore stiffly starched petticoats made with many flounces. Then it became popular to stiffen underskirts with whalebone, and eventually, about 1854, the hoopskirt, or "crinoline" as it was more commonly called, was introduced. The methods of making these steel-hooped frames which were worn under the dress varied, and were sometimes veritable cages; at other times some concession was made to comfort and the stiffening was less rigid. The hoopskirt remained in style for ten years or more, fluctuating in popularity as many other expedients were tried to take its place, but women persisted in wearing wide skirts that required some kind of stiff foundation.

The fashionable woman of the 1850's and '60's must have suffered actual pain when she was fully corseted and gowned. It is no wonder that Amelia Bloomer had her followers; or that Sarah Hale spoke out against the hourglass corset that crowded and distorted the body in order to cinch it into the 17- to 22-inch waist fashion ordained.

In addition to these hourglass corsets, respectable women wore many other unseen and uncomfortable garments. A chemise or vest was worn under the corset, and over it went a dainty beribboned, lacy "corset cover"; next came a pair of drawers, with an embroidered flounce below the knee. At least two petticoats came next. In winter, one of these was of embroidered wool flannel. The hoop or crinoline or other extending device went on top of these underskirts. After bustles became fashionable, one of them was placed over the crinoline. Over all this the woman of the time wore a dress made with lining and stays and fastened with dozens of tiny buttons. If she wanted to sit down to rest her feet—pinched into pointed-toe, high-heeled shoes several sizes too small—she must find a chair or sofa wide enough to accommodate all the wires and hoops.

If the idea of hoopskirts seems like an exaggeration, read what the fashion editor of an 1858 issue of *Peterson's Magazine* described under the heading, "Useful Novelties for The Month." The accompanying illustration shows a bee-hive-shaped cage made of ten vertical tapes fastened to a framework of sixteen circular metal strips, with a belt-device built in at the top of the front. The description follows:

> We take pleasure in presenting our readers with this new and useful article. It has, they will observe, many advantages. Among the most prominent of them is the shape, which is full of grace and beauty, a fact acknowledged by thousands of ladies and others who saw it at the late fair at the Crystal Palace, New York, and elsewhere. Another of these advantages is the manner of making it: the tapes being fastened to the springs by means of a clasp instead of being sewed, by which ripping is avoided. Moreover, as the skirt is made on a frame, each has the desired shape. In addition to this, the springs are made from the best watch-spring steel; are tempered by a new process; and are considered to be unequalled for elasticity and durability. . . . The sale of manufactured skirts is now enormous, and, we are glad to say that in getting them up, female labor is employed to a large extent.

It is not clear from the magazine drawing just how one got into this contraption. No price was quoted, but it was apparently considered to be of little importance since it was made to last a lifetime. Its function? To wear under a petticoat in place of hoops.

Hoops grew larger and larger until in 1870 it required from 20 to 25 yards of material to cover one. Something had to be done to change this, for the weight of so much cloth was giving the ladies serious back trouble. It was then that the bustle began to take the place of hoops, and skirts gradually became narrower. The bustle was an ugly device, but more humane than hoops, a weird contrivance of wire or stiffening designed to make a dress bulge out only in the back instead of all around. The front of the skirt looked normal, but Paris still fostered an exaggerated bunching of material at the back that was so extreme it was almost impossible for the wearer to sit down, forcing her to walk about in what was called the "Grecian bend,"—the unnatural leaning position resulting from carrying the whole mass of bustles, petticoats, and bunched fabrics of a back-heavy costume. It was almost as uncomfortable to wear a bustle as it had been to struggle with hoops.

Bustles gradually disappeared after 1885; but, although skirts became more tubular, excess fullness was still crowded at the back. In addition, the train now appeared, as if fashion were determined that a woman must be thoroughly uncomfortable in one way if not another.

But to the relief of dress reformers, who had for generations protested the discomforts and so-called dangers of tightly laced corsets, there was a gradual change in their design. By stressing the back of the wearer even more, corsets had to be reshaped to throw the bustline forward instead of compressing it. Also, it permitted the wearer to breathe more freely. It was not until the early 1900's, however, that "straight-front" corsets arrived, and the old hourglass effect went out.

During the balance of the nineteenth century, the actual construction of dresses became more and more complex, as if Paris couturiers were trying to discourage non-professionals from attempting to sew. In one lovely evening gown designed about 1885, Worth used five different textures: plain ivory taffeta for the bodice and train, ivory and gold velvet for the overskirt, ivory satin for the petticoat-front of the skirt, gold organdy ruching for neckline and sleeves, and wide gold fringe for the front hemline. This beautiful gown, owned by the Boston Museum of Fine Arts, and pictured in color in their Picture Book series, would be an enchanting one to use as a model when costuming a fine doll.

No woman of the nineteenth century dominated the setting of styles as much as the man who founded the great French House of Worth—Charles Frederick Worth. He was the world's first male dressmaker and the most outstanding of all Parisian designers from 1858 until his death in 1895. Everyone knew of his work after he won the approval of the Empress Eugénie, who gave him every chance to display his genius as a designer. Many of the costumes he designed are now in museums where doll dressmakers may see them and be inspired as they dress their finest nineteenth century ladies.

Victorian ladies adored jewelry, especially when it was made of jet. In the same issue of *Peterson's* magazine mentioned earlier, directions were given for making a crocheted jet bracelet, using one large curtain ring, two dozen smaller rings, and forty-four still smaller ones. These were covered with black silk twist, joined, and then covered with jet bugle beads. It was fastened with a jet clasp.

Other adornments in favor were the quantities of fancy buttons used on women's clothes before the coming of snap fasteners, hooks and eyes, and zippers. The collecting of buttons is of course one of the most popular hobbies of the twentieth century and is often appealing to doll collectors, who have no trouble finding ways to use tiny ornamental buttons which are just the right size for doll clothes.

The period from the 1880's to the end of the century is the one coinciding with the greatest popularity of bisque and Parian dolls, and they should be dressed in the styles then in favor. There are many places to carry on research of this kind, including fashion plates from bound copies of *Godey's Lady's Book,* Currier and Ives prints, reproductions of famous paintings, and the illustrations in histories and biographies.

In 1900 Paris was still the arbiter of fashion, but in other ways women were beginning to realize they could be more free to think, to speak, to choose. Perhaps the two-wheeled bicycle had much to do with this realization, for although a "lady" still rode sidesaddle on horseback, she could now put on wide knickerbockers and call them a cycling costume, not trousers. She could enjoy exercise in the sunshine and fresh air and at the same time preserve her Victorian modesty. Tennis was also a popular pastime, and of course demanded a specially designed costume. Even the gentle game of croquet, then so much in favor, could hardly be played in long trailing skirts and hourglass corsets. In fact, the bustle disappeared entirely, for who could ride a bicycle or play tennis or croquet while wearing such a device?

Queen Victoria died in 1901, and the first court of King Edward VII marked the beginning of a new age of fashion—elegant but simple. It was in 1902 that the final rebellion against corsets took place, with the acceptance of "straight-front" corsets. Now, instead of so much emphasis being placed on skirts, attention was centered on sleeves. In fact, a period of experimental sleeves followed; there were balloon sleeves lined with buckram, tight coat sleeves, the bishop sleeve, and combinations of types. The styles of necklines also varied. Daytime dresses almost always had high collars, often boned or lined.

The tailored suit made of woolen material was fashionable. Its many-gored skirt swept the street, and called for a facing of braid inside the hemline, or a dust ruffle. There were objectors who crusaded against the practice of wearing skirts that gathered filth, but, as always, there were slaves to whatever style happened to be in favor in Paris.

It was very fashionable to wear separate black woolen skirts with dressy tucked and shirred blouses, or "waists." The women drawn by Charles Dana Gibson and known as Gibson girls, almost all wear variations of this style.

For sheer feminine charm, the taffeta petticoat has had few rivals, and in the early 1900's it was almost mandatory for a woman to rustle when she walked. Many little girls must have longed to grow up so they could wear swishy silk, for those were the years when mothers and daughters dressed quite differently and never borrowed one another's clothes. That was the time when growing up meant that a girl was old enough to wear long skirts and put up her hair.

A typical woman of the first decade of the twentieth century may be described as wearing a wide, heavy hat, loaded with roses or ostrich plumes, on her pompadoured head. Her tucked chiffon blouse, lined with silk, was made with a high tight collar, wired to come up in points below the ears, and with full sleeves. For jewelry, she wore a string of gold beads and a wide gold bracelet. The watch on her bodice was fastened in place with a fleur-de-lis pin. She sometimes wore a silver "châtelaine" purse clipped to her belt, giving her a place to carry her handkerchief and smelling salts. Her blue serge suit was cut with a flaring skirt that completely hid her high-laced shoes and black lisle stockings. She had learned to gather a handful of skirt gracefully in her left hand to keep it from trailing in the mud or dust, for nobody had yet had the courage to cut skirts shorter, fearing that it would "rouse the animal nature" of men to see a lady's insteps.

Comfortable fashions were coming closer, although a few women still insisted on having a tiny waist that a husband could span with his two hands, and continued to loop their corset laces around a bedpost to create enough leverage to pull themselves into the desired number of inches. Shoes were often bought for size, rather than fit—size 2 being as large as many women would admit to wearing.

Finally, even Paris said that a normal waistline, bustline and hipline were permissible, but the shock of this change had not worn off when the glad word came in 1916 that hemlines must be raised as far as the anklebone. Again there were protests.

It was at this time, after this first experience with comfort, that feminine costume entered its modern phase. Women discovered it was better to breathe easily and move about with freedom, than it was to be "elegant." They began to suspect that no matter what Paris said, they had a right to choose what they wanted to wear. This feeling was not universal at first, but the minority grew to become the majority until, in the past fifty years, the basic changes in fashions have been quite superficial—mostly involving hemlines. Even the straight-hanging beaded dresses of 1927 could get by without comment in a modern crowd, provided the wearer's hairstyle was brought up to date and she changed her makeup.

As may be seen from the foregoing outline of fashions, there is a great deal for doll dressmakers to draw upon when costuming their dolls. Research is of the greatest importance, and it should come first, preferably based on the type and age of the particular doll to be dressed. In addition to the prints and drawings already mentioned, there are historical museums, references to costume design, family portraits and photographs, and many other sources and examples of authentic historical dress. It is better to copy the hoopskirted costume of a Winterhalter painting or the bicycling outfit of a Charles Dana Gibson girl, than it is to try to imitate the versions of them that someone else has created. In others words, go to original sources as much as possible. You will discover one of the pleasantest byways of doll collecting.

If you don't know how to sew, making doll clothes is a good way to learn. In fact, by means of a paper pattern you can make not only the clothes, but the doll itself. If you follow the directions on a commercial pattern, working carefully, you will learn every step in the approved way. Many girls have

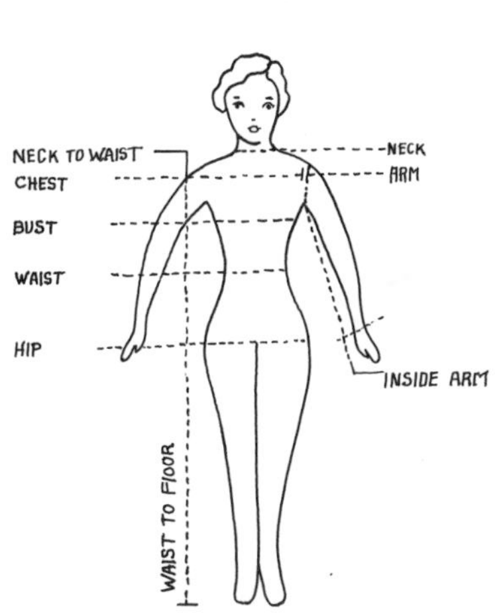

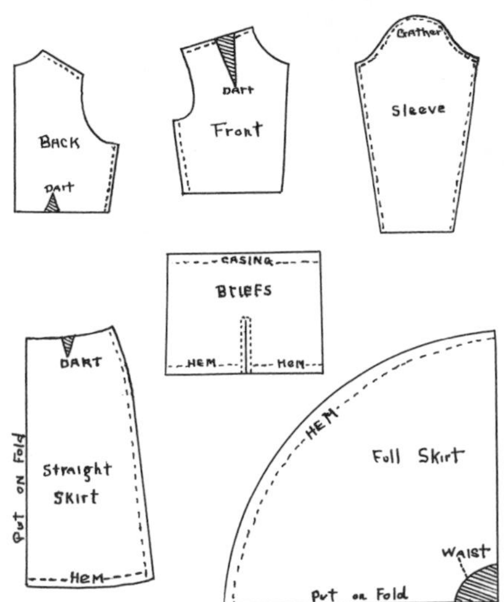

Measure a doll for clothes at each point indicated; then cut a pattern to fit. By following basic shapes given on pattern chart, one can make almost any style with only slight changes.

Cut basic pattern shapes based on measurements of individual doll. It is easy to modify or adapt them to many dress styles. This method overcomes problem of dressing dolls which have a variety of proportions.

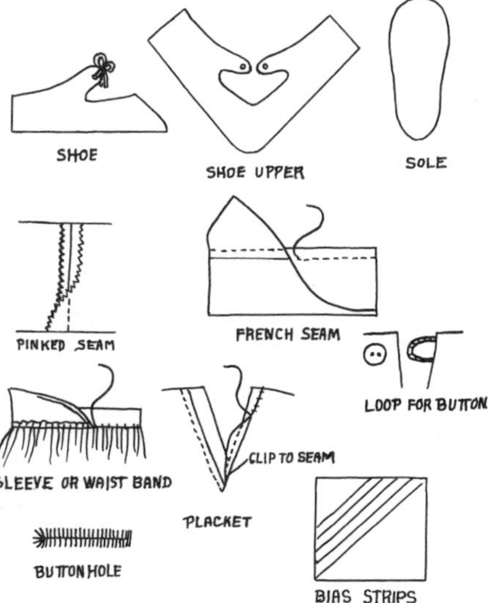

It is simple to make doll clothes. Here are a few basic methods to use.

learned how to sew by making doll clothes, and so have their mothers and grandmothers.

If you already know something about sewing, but hesitate to work without a pattern, there is a way to overcome the problem. Since there are only a few basic measurements needed, and rules to be followed, in making doll patterns, you will find it easy to fit whatever size doll you wish. All the embellishments and variations of a pattern are made on a basic shape that is cut from the following measurements: bust, waistline, hips at widest part, length of back from neck to waist, length of sleeve from shoulder to wrist or shoulder to elbow, and length of skirt. The chart shows these points.

Provided you have the doll you are about to dress, a pencil, tape measure, and a large sheet of paper, you can draft a pattern. It makes no difference whether the doll is large or small; the same rules apply. Follow the diagram for shaping the various pieces, using the measurements of your doll, and drawing them on the paper. Cut out the pattern, adding a seam allowance of 1/4 inch. Pin this trial pattern on the doll and make whatever corrections are needed until it fits. Now cut the permanent master pattern from this. Place it in an envelope carefully marked with identifying information and a sketch of the finished garment. Often you will be able to adapt a pattern already on file to make a different garment, without having to start at the beginning. It is easier to dress a large doll than it is a very small one, but on the other hand, there is more finishing needed on a larger garment than on a small one.

The material used for doll clothes is important; it should always be soft and fine, with tiny designs. Laces, trimmings, and buttons should be in scale. Wool should be soft and pliable and not tweedy. Use only the materials that were being made at the time the doll was made—an 1885 doll would wear one of the natural fibers, not a synthetic. The patterns of laces and other trimmings that were used so freely in the past are quite different from modern types, so if you have a chance to rip them from old garments, be sure to do so. It takes such a small amount of cloth to make a doll dress that you will be able to make use of extremely scanty amounts. Small beads, soutache braid, cut steel buttons, and all kinds of feathers should go into your dressmaking box. Don't even ignore bird feathers, picked up in the garden, or outdated costume jewelry that can be taken apart and used for trimming, or doll jewelry.

With your already fitted basic pattern, and a sketch of the garments you wish to make, assemble your materials. It is a good idea to make the underwear first, so the outer garments may be fitted over it. You may be tempted to skimp the details of the sewing on panties and petticoats, but that is a mistake. Watch the doll expert examine a doll and notice that she invariably looks first at the underwear, then for a mark at the back of the doll's head or shoulder. Outer clothing is always admired last.

Whatever the period of the doll, the same basic pattern may be used for either pantalettes or short panties. The only difference is in the length of the legs and the kind of trimming. Make a narrow casing at the top edge to hold a strip of elastic, and you will be able to avoid having to make a waistband and buttonhole. The panties should be cut just a trifle wider than the doll's hips and a little longer in the crotch.

Petticoats should be made with a waistband, and because it's a good idea to make all doll clothes so they may be removed for cleaning, fasten them with a tiny button and loop. In spite of the many petticoats worn by Victorian ladies, make only one for your doll. If you want a hoop skirt, stiffen the hem of the skirt with wire or buckram, but depend only on extra fullness to make a petticoat stand out. To do this, cut the petticoat much wider than the basic skirt, but add as much fanciness as you wish. Tucks, lace, ribbon, featherstitching, and insertion are all appropriate, for what woman has ever been able to resist frilly lingerie? Next, cut out the dress and fit it over the undergarments. It is really best to stitch all seams by hand, and to press them as you proceed. Only on materials that ravel easily is it necessary to make French, or felled, seams.

All fastenings used on doll clothes should be chosen according to the period represented. Thus, an antique doll would have buttons or ties only, while a twentieth century doll could have snap fasteners, hooks and eyes, as well as buttons or ties. Many contemporary dolls of course have zippers, in fact there are zippers made specifically for doll clothes, but they would be entirely out of place on dolls costumed in styles prior to World War II.

The study of hats is a hobby in itself, and more than one collector has made doll millinery her specialty, leaving the dressmaking to someone else. All the sources previously mentioned will furnish ideas for types of hats in vogue at different times. There are the towering headdresses of Colonial days with their plumes and cascades of flowers and ribbons, the scoop bonnets of the early 1800's with their flowing satin ties, the elaborately trimmed little wispy bonnets of the 1860's, the wide hats loaded with cabbage roses or ostrich plumes of the early 1900's, the revival of Empress Eugénie hats in the 1920's, and all the less dramatic head coverings which modern women wear. Many of the hats just mentioned can be built on a base of buckram or cardboard and covered with satin or taffeta, then trimmed with artificial flowers, feathers, ribbons, or lace.

Lace mitts, or long silk gloves are easy to make from sheer material or fine lacy material. Sometimes a doll is large enough to wear gloves made from readymade doll stockings. Shoes are easy to devise from scraps of thin leather or old kid gloves. Choose a style suitable for the period of the doll and whip the edges of the seams together with fine stitches and self-colored thread. Fasten with ribbon or cord ties, or a tiny button and loop.

Men dolls are amusing to dress, although small ones may be difficult. One solution, instead of trying to make an entire shirt, is to make a dickey, or false shirt front, with the collar attached. A narrow black satin ribbon becomes a realistic cravat, and a seed pearl a convincing stick pin. His trousers should be made of the softest houndstooth check woolen, or fine black felt. It is impossible to tailor a coat for an 8-inch doll much less to line it, so instead make it from black felt. You will not need to turn in the raw edges or even to make conventional seams—just overcast the inside edges together. A man's shoes may be made from pieces of an old patent leather, or leather, purse.

One of the happiest aspects of doll collecting is that it offers so many peripheral pleasures; and one of the most amusing of those pleasures is to walk through a variety store keeping your eyes open for objects and materials which can be made to seem like something else, and thus be transformed into doll clothing.

19

DOLL HOUSES

DOLL HOUSES have been popular in Europe for several hundred years, and in museums in France, Holland, Germany, and England there are many well preserved and completely furnished specimens which show that they were the delight of toymakers and craftsmen, and the treasures of men and women, in addition to being the playthings of children.

In referring to old records, we observe that houses for dolls were at first called "baby houses," and were often made in the form of single rooms set into shadow box frames. There were also houses of from two to four rooms, and sometimes giant mansions, scaled to hold large dolls. One common type of early doll house was built in the form of a cupboard, with hinged sides that could be closed and locked to prevent the loss of the gold and silver miniatures, silks, and rare trifles inside. A few doll houses had many rooms and attics, as well, filled with toy trunks bursting with what are now antique doll clothes, and bins and barrels packed with surplus furnishings, just as real houses might have stored them.

Perhaps the most famous antique doll house is the one owned by Queen Anne. Much later, but equally inspiring to lovers of doll houses, is the one which belonged to Queen Victoria. Much more recently, the doll house assembled by Queen Mary in the twentieth century, and exhibited at innumerable charitable events, carries on the tradition of royal interest in miniatures. All of these doll houses have inspired many of the magnificent specimens now in existence in England and on the continent. America has its own historical quota of doll houses, many of them in museums and in exhibits owned by numbers of historical societies all over the country.

A charming doll house now in the London Museum was made in 1740 in England. It is 4½-feet high and has four completely furnished rooms. The attic and basement areas are closed in, but the front is made in two sections with hinged doors. Each door is treated as the entire side of a room, with windows and draperies to complete the illusion. The kitchen is equipped with tiny copper kettles, a candle-box, jam pans, and flat-irons! A chambermaid doll waits beside the four-poster bed in the bedroom for her mistress, who is entertaining a guest in the downstairs drawing room. The dining room wall is papered with perfectly scaled handpainted wall paper, and forms the most distinctive feature of the house. The *gros point* carpet, Honiton lace cover on the dressing table, and thin cream-colored Leeds chinaware are only a few of the elegant furnishings.

This same 1740 doll house has several characteristics often found in others of the time. The outside is finished to resemble stone, with a double flight of stairs leading from the ground to a front door at the second story level of the house. Also like many doll houses of the time, the exterior is very simple.

After about 1800, more attention was paid to the exterior, and there were elaborations of inside flights of stairs. At first, staircases were built in short flights of from six to eight steps, a landing, then another flight. Stairways grew longer and more important architecturally, often with carved balustrades and railings. Some of them had delicate brass rungs and rails, fine enough to be actual architectural models, and there were even lovely elliptical stairs like the ones seen in the plantation houses of the American South. Most of these antique doll houses are now either in museums, or in the possession of the descendants of families who first owned them. There are seldom really old doll houses available to collectors, but anyone who wishes to study the subject in depth should consult Max von Boehn's *Dolls and Puppets,* Flora Gill Jacobs' *A History of Dolls' Houses,* or Vivien Greene's *English Dolls' Houses in the 18th and 19th Centuries.*

Because the age of dolls reached its peak during the reign

of Queen Victoria, 1837–1901, there are many surviving examples of houses for these dolls in existence in both England and America. There are also many doll collectors who have found that Victorian settings display their dolls to advantage.

Victorian décor was once looked upon with amusement, as being overly ornate and exemplifying the worst possible taste, as some of it surely is. But much American Victorian furniture was made of native woods: walnut, cherry, and butternut, by home cabinetmakers and village carpenters, and is simple and beautiful. In contrast, some of the factory-made furniture of the time was burdened with wooden gingerbread and nonfunctional knobs and curlicues. However, when this furniture is made in doll house size, it is often irresistible. It is also rather easy to find good specimens at still reasonable prices.

The size of a doll house is, of course, determined by the size of the dolls who live in it. The amount of room space the house will require is also important in deciding on its size. One collector who wished to make a Victorian doll house, dating from before World War I, and who owned a family of German-made doll house people, solved both problems. The bisque-headed gentleman is about 6 inches tall, and his wife is 5 inches. The blond nurse, dressed in the uniform of an English nurse and holding a tiny baby doll less than an inch long, is the same size as the wife. The scale of measurement of the dolls is therefore about one inch to one foot—an easy one to translate to the doll house itself.

In this instance, the only place in the collector's home where the doll house may be placed is rather small. However, there is an ideal location for it on the wall between two windows, where it will receive adequate light by day, and where a wall outlet will be useful for lighting it at night. A practical size, which will fit into the wall space, is 30 inches long and 12 inches deep. That will be adequate for four rooms and a bath, large enough to decorate easily. There will be a living room, kitchen and central hallway, with stairs leading to the second floor which will contain a nursery, bedroom and bath.

The house is constructed on a piece of ¾-inch plywood at least 3 or 4-inches larger than the house itself. If space permitted, another few inches could be added to the living room

Karl is fine doll house size. He has bisque head and hands, a stuffed cloth body, and is dressed in felt coat and trousers.

Pattern for making the Victorian doll house shows the size of the pieces required. House is in a scale of 1 inch to 1 foot to accommodate doll house dolls. It may be placed on a table or cabinet or hung on the wall by means of screw-eyes inserted in top edges of the back.

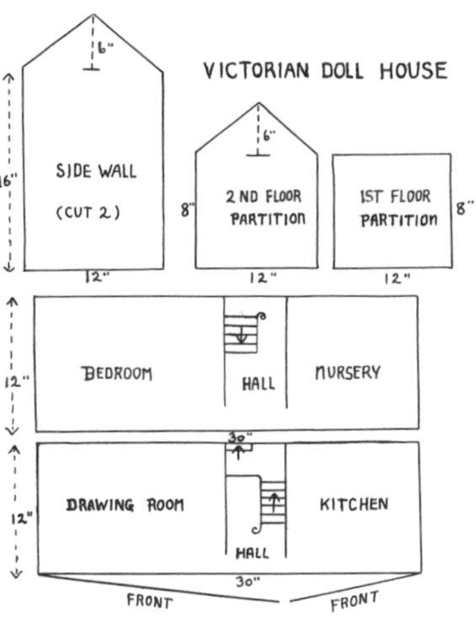

Victorian doll house may be opened to show the interior, then closed and its hinged door fastened with a metal catch. Doors and windows either are painted on the front or are cut out and the window spaces filled with glass or clear plastic. The front door may be made of wood and hinged to swing open.

end of the base, for either a conservatory filled with toy palms and plants, a miniature art gallery, or a veranda to hold porch or garden furniture.

The house is built of 1/4-inch fir or Philippine mahogany plywood. For this, a panel 4 by 8 feet will be needed, or scrap pieces of the same thickness. The only tools required are a handsaw, hammer, wood rasp, and a straight edge. Materials other than the wood are a few 3/4-inch wire nails, white glue or furniture glue, and fine sandpaper. Either paint or wood stain in small amounts, and wallpaper, if used, will be needed for finishing.

As shown on the diagram, cut two pieces, each 12-inches wide and 30-inches long; two pieces for the side walls, shaped as indicated; one piece for the second floor partition; one piece for the first floor partition. Make a two-piece front wall, so the sections will meet at the point where the partitions between the hall and the kitchen and nursery are placed. Hinge the outer edges of the door to the side wall of the doll house. The best way to fasten the pieces of plywood together is to brush the edges with glue, then drive several wire brads through both pieces, with the head on the under side of the base, or where it will not show.

Cut out the stair well of the second floor, and after making the stairs, glue them in place. The inner partitions will help hold the second floor in place, but it is necessary to also glue and nail them to the side walls. Cut two roof sections wide enough to overhang the side walls two or three inches, but flush with both the front and back of the house. The roof is shingled with scalloped strips of heavy cardboard, thin balsa wood or wood veneer. The ridge pole of the roof is ornamented with a strip of jigsaw gingerbread, painted to match the window casings. The chimneys are made of plywood, painted and marked to look like brick.

Inside the house, the entrance hall is a replica of one in an 1870 mansion, with stairs leading to a landing, then up to the second floor. The stairs are made of two stringers of plywood, notched to receive treads of 3/4 by 2 inches. These treads are glued to the top of the risers; then the whole stairway is glued in place in the house. The diagram of the modern doll house, which follows, shows this in detail. If desired, a realistic wooden or metal handrail may be added, and a carved newel post fastened to the end of the rail at the lower step.

The front door may be authentically set with tiny squares of colored glass—a typically Victorian touch. And don't forget to make a chandelier of crystal beads to hang in the hall by the front door. The two sections of the hinged front may be painted to indicate windows, or may be cut out and the spaces filled with glass or clear plastic. The two front pieces are fitted with a simple metal catch so that the house may be closed if desired. This is the framework of the house, all ready now for the decorator. It is easy to find ideas for decorating authentically in books and magazines devoted to architecture, decorating, and home building.

In a typical Victorian house the walls were papered, usually with all-over designs, or stripes, rather than with plain colors. Gift wrapping papers are ideal to use as wallpaper in the doll house, for they can often be found in just the desired colors and patterns and in the proper scale. Figured fabrics make good wallpaper substitutes, for many Victorian drawing rooms were hung with moire silk or damask panels framed with gilt molding.

The floors in a typical house of this period were carpeted, except for painted kitchen floors. Scraps of heavy woolen coating, velvet, or upholstery material may be used for carpeting. Deep reds, blues and greens are authentic colors. It is a good idea to make small rugs from pieces of felt, and add fringe at the ends. Ambitious women have for several generations made rugs or carpets of needlepoint. Whatever the material, be sure to keep both the weave and the pattern in scale with the rest of the furnishings.

Curtains, like the other furnishings, should conform to the period. Victorians were fond of lace glass curtains used with heavy plush, brocade, or satin swags and inside draperies, often looped up with cords and tassels.

The furniture of a doll house is often one of the main reasons for its existence, but it is impossible to give detailed plans for making it, or lists of pieces to use. Otherwise, all the spontaneous charm of originality would be lost, and the result would be as dull as a factory made and furnished doll house. In decorating, however, consider the use of mirrors—a decorator's trick for visually increasing the size of a room. Mirrors may be framed in small gilt picture frames or may be treated as built-in panels by outlining with very narrow matchsticks of wood.

Every Victorian kitchen had either a coal or woodburning cook stove, and of all the pieces of doll furniture, this is perhaps the most important. Such stoves are not always easy to find; and antique shops get fantastic prices for them. But if you are unable to locate an original stove, it is always possible to buy a reproduction. The doll supply establishments listed in the appendix carry a wide assortment of sizes. It may also be necessary to go to the same sources for a tiny Victorian footed bathtub and a cabinet washbasin. Other facilities were placed outside the house, at this time.

One reason Victorian interiors are so appealing is that they are filled with homey, sentimental things like melodeons, marble-topped tables, sewing cabinets, tapestry fire screens, whatnots, square pianos, and circular table covers edged with fringe that reached the floor. Favorite ornaments of Victorian times were silhouettes, waxed flowers and fruits, papier-mâché trays and boxes, lithographs, paperweights, bell-pulls, woolwork pictures, fine china, silver, and glass, both cut and pressed. Don't forget tiny charm bracelet objects when searching for hard-to-find furnishings.

A typical Victorian living or drawing room contained a pair of chairs with carved backs and seats upholstered in velvet or horsehair. The largest of the two chairs was called a "gentleman's" chair and the smaller one, a "lady's" chair. A matching sofa was always a part of the "suite." In addition, there would be a marble-topped table with carved legs to hold a large kerosene lamp with a flower-painted shade. On the mantlepiece there might be a pair of china figurines, or matching vases filled with feathers or wax flowers, a marble clock trimmed with gilt, and perhaps a glass dome covering a spray of shell or feather flowers. In more opulent mansions, oil portraits of ancestors were hung on the walls in heavy gold frames, and in less pretentious surroundings there might be realistic pictures of fruit, flowers, game, or perhaps landscapes. It was a major

Swedish modern doll house has an open plan for first floor, with no partitions. Kitchen end is divided by a cabinet, with range and refrigerator against outside wall. Fireplace in living end is made from a small spice can painted black; sofa is made with legs of plastic knobs and a top cut from a piece of synthetic sponge. Coffee table is an inverted chrome drawer pull. Armchair is made of balsa wood. Upstairs, bathroom has fixtures purchased in toy store. Bedroom rug and bedspread are made of Turkish toweling.

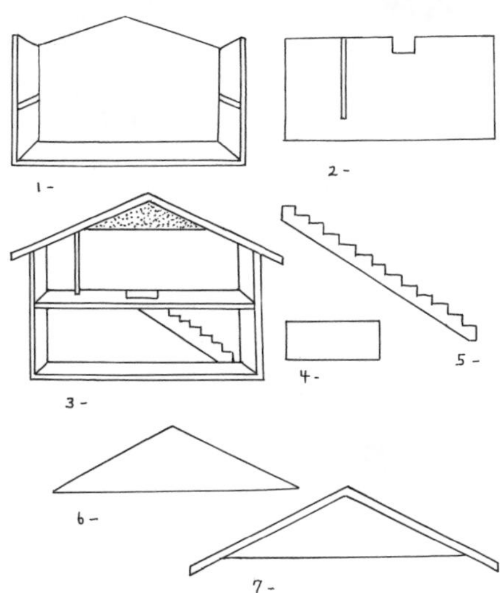

Construction details of Swedish modern doll house. (1) Floor, side walls and back, with strips at side to hold second floor. (2) Second floor, with partition between bedroom and bath. (3) Assembled house. (4) Pattern for stair tread. (5) Stringer for stairs, notched to receive individual treads. (6) One of the three roof trusses to which the two roof sections are nailed. (7) The front roof truss is finished with a fascia made of strips of wood.

Swedish design decorates the author's wooden cupboard of doll house size.

fear of the time that a room would look "too plain," so there are actually no limits to the amount of decorating or use of trinkets and fanciful ornaments that can be used in a Victorian doll house.

While the house just discussed is built and detailed in the style of the Victorian era, the same floor plan can be adapted to other types of architecture from New England Colonial to modern split-level western. The main changes would then consist of eliminating the gingerbread trimming, altering the type of shingles used, and of course using the furnishings characteristic of that time. Good models may be found in books and magazines devoted to home building, by observing actual houses, or studying model rooms in museums which have arranged historical furniture groupings.

If a collector wishes to break with the past and create an entirely modern house, a type of Swedish modern architecture is suggested. This will feature what is called "open planning" of the first floor, where no partitions separate the living area and the dining and kitchen sections.

The same materials that were suggested for the Victorian-style house may be used for this modern one; that is, fir or mahogany plywood. The methods of making it are the same as those described for the Victorian mansion except for the unique design of a trussed roof. This type of construction has the advantage of not requiring inside partitions to support the roof, as the entire roof is made separately and simply rests on the exterior walls. The illustration shows the shape and placing of the various pieces. It is a simple matter to make the house any size desired, preferably following the rule of 1 inch to 1 foot.

The painting and finishing of the modern house are different, too. For example, the outside is stained with a dark oil stain. The roof is covered with simulated aggregate roofing made by sprinkling pea-gravel, or the colored gravel used in aquariums, on the top of the roof which has first been brushed with glue.

The inside of the house may be stained or painted, or of course, papered. Floors, if not carpeted, may be covered with adhesive plastic paper, then treated in modern fashion by using area rugs. It is easy to make doll house furniture of balsa and

Working model of a European wooden clock stands beside a tiny rocking chair.

A modern doll house with all features for teenage fashion doll entertaining is fitted with a plastic cover and carrying handle.

© 1963 The Ideal Toy Corp.

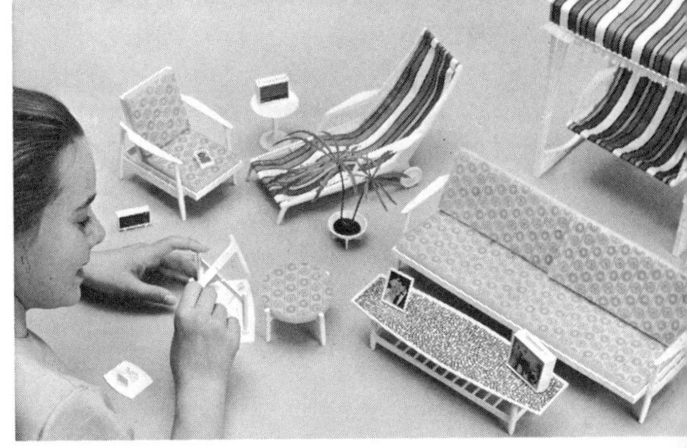

Contemporary doll house furniture is made in many attractive styles, in sizes to conform to regulation doll houses.

Courtesy, Mattel, Inc.

plywood. In fact, it is no more difficult than making model cars and airplanes, and if the doll collector does not wish to attempt it, perhaps some other member of the family will be intrigued with the idea.

In the author's collection is a Welsh cupboard painted in Swedish design which holds tiny china dishes copied from antiques, including a soup tureen, a blue Canton platter, and a Dresden latticework plate. Another collector owns a child's-size rocking chair large enough for a tiny doll, and a little wooden clock which really ticks. These pieces, shown together, are placed differently in the doll house; when the clock is on a table or mantel or hung on the wall, the two are in scale. This is an example of the way it is possible to create an illusion of reality by simply placing pieces of furniture in different locations.

Collectors who wish to buy readymade doll houses will find that toy departments offer several different styles. The little cottage made by the Ideal Toy Company, which may be supplemented with an outdoor play area and barbecue is only one example. Almost every toy manufacturer has his own version of a doll house. The Mattel Company, in addition to doll houses, also makes furniture which is the correct size for almost any other doll house. Many of these pieces are of plastic material, and so would not be suitable for doll houses representing a pre-plastic era.

A doll house is not a thing to be finished in a week or a month. Add to it only as you discover pieces of furniture or furnishings which are exactly right in size and truly authentic in style, making certain that they are worthy of a place in the heirloom doll house that it is hoped yours will become.

20

HOW TO DISPLAY AND EXHIBIT DOLLS

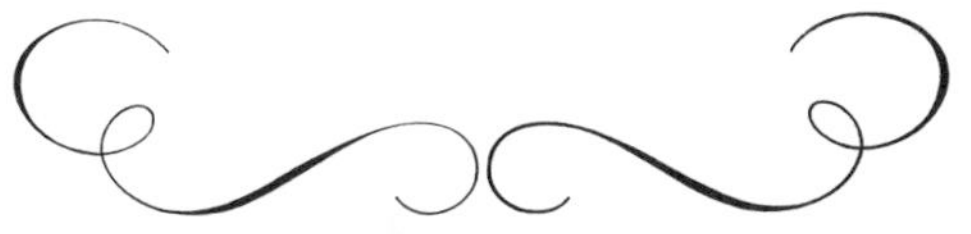

Most doll collectors enjoy sharing their dolls, either displaying them at home; lending them to churches, schools, libraries or museums; or using them, for instance, to illustrate lectures.

Home display is the first concern of most collectors, and while the housing of a doll collection may seem to be only a matter of converting an old china closet or bookcase into a place to store dolls, collections do grow, and soon dolls are scattered all through the house. More space must then be arranged, and eventually a den or another small room may have to be transformed into a doll center.

Sometimes suggestions for doll display that seem commonplace to one person are just what another has been looking for, and most collectors are constantly alert for ideas they can use. One friend, inspired by seeing a doll dressed in the style of an 1857 daguerreotype and placed in an enlarged replica of the original case, made her own adaptation of it. She dressed several family portrait dolls, matted them to represent the pages of an old photograph album, then framed them in a large single frame.

Another collector salvaged several large mahogany picture frames with gold liners, and converted them into doll cases by fastening narrow shelves at the back. The frame and glass were hinged so they could be opened without disturbing the dolls.

Picture frames have been used in many ways to create settings for dolls. It has been suggested that by placing separate doll-heads in a shadow box and draping the shoulders, the dolls will look like portraits; entire dolls can also be used. This is an effective way to treat an occasional antique that is puzzling to place. If a collector wishes to decorate a period room, paper dolls can be costumed in the fashions of the time and then posed against a velvet backing in a shadow box.

It is a simple matter for any home craftsman to convert a picture frame into a shadow box by building a shallow box, exactly the size of the frame opening, and nailing it to the frame. The back of the shadow box may be made separately and hinged to the top, or the frame (including the glass) may be hinged to the top of the box. Whichever side is made to open, it is important that a provision be made for placing or removing the exhibits inside.

One enthusiastic doll-lover has turned a small wall cabinet into a miniature display case for holding tiny dolls and their furniture—not *her* dolls and their furniture, but the dolls of her dolls. This idea could be extended, and the fantasy of building an entire dolls' doll house could be carried out. Sectional bookcases with glass doors are one of the favorite forms of display space. These may often be found in used furniture stores and refinished to match the furniture in the rest of the doll-display room. You may place a decorative background on the back and sides of the case, or create stage settings on the shelves for action groups of dolls. It is easy to add interior lighting of some kind, such as the fluorescent strips made for medicine cabinets, or even small spotlights. Old fashioned china cabinets are also usable, if you are lucky enough to find one. A mirror-back is an excellent feature of some of them, and gives you a chance to show both sides of a lovely doll.

A friend once wished to both protect and display an exceedingly old and valuable wooden peg-doll, so tiny it might be called sub-miniature. She found an antique gold watchcase —thick and rather large, and lined it with black velvet. She hung the case on an antique gold chain, and wore it as a locket. This calls, of course, for a case with the crystal intact, but the works removed.

"If you are descended from some well-defined racial strain,"

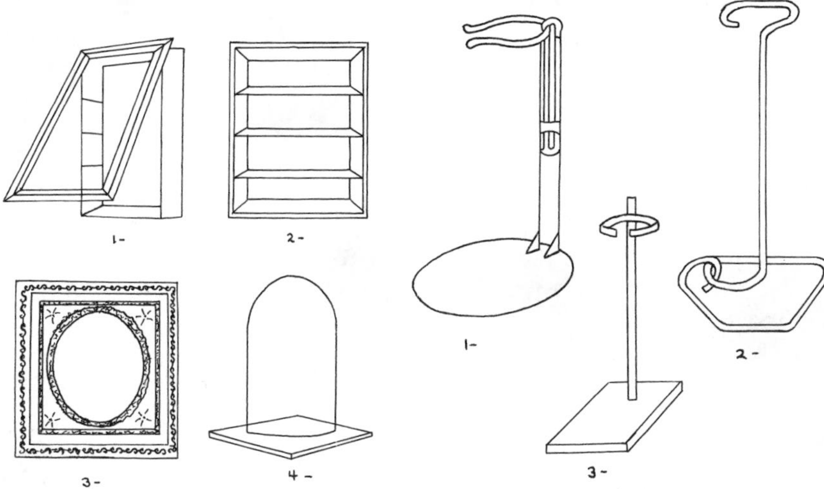

Cases for displaying dolls. (1) Shadow box with hinged lid is made from a large picture frame. (2) Simple shelves are best when they have glass fronts. (3) Copy of antique daguerreotype case is made of velvet, decorated with gilt, ideal for dolls of 1850–1880 period. (4) Clear glass or plastic dome resting on a flat base allows dolls to be seen from all sides, yet still be protected.

Stands to hold dolls upright. (1) The usual commercial stand, adjustable and made in various sizes. (2) Homemade stand of wood, with a metal strip for holding the doll. (3) Homemade stand made of coat hanger wire twisted to shape. Homemade stands should be painted a dark color like the commercial stand so they will be inconspicuous.

one collector suggests, "why not let that nationality predominate in the showing of pretty dolls—Italian, Polish, Welsh, any one of them could key a most colorful setting." An "All Nations Tree" was once described by a doll owner who had placed ornaments from more than forty countries, and dolls from many of them, on a tree used at a church tea. Another church's Antique Doll Tea made use of an easel-type board covered with a map of the world. Each foreign doll was thumbtacked to its native land and had a ribbon fastened to it. Red ribbons were used for Communist countries and white for Free World countries.

Doll displays have been used, and are still being made, to place in store windows. They help sell jewelry, books, clothes, toys, and even perfumes.

Many collectors believe that a file of all identifying data should be kept for each doll in a collection. This should include everything known about the doll—its origin, date, former owners, any repairs or replacements, and of course the doll's name, for every doll should have a name. Enter all data on 3x5-inch cards. Make labels for your dolls, numbered to correspond to the number on the card. These numbers should be fastened in an inconspicuous place to the doll's back or shoulder.

Some kind of stand is necessary to support dolls in an upright position. It is possible to make quite acceptable ones at home, using coat-hanger wire fastened to small circles, or rectangles, of wood. The loop of wire or strip of tin at the top of the upright is designed to fit around the doll's waist, while the clothes cover the entire stand completely. The Butler doll stands are old-time favorites, and all doll hospitals and supply houses carry them. They are made of heavy enameled steel with flat bases and wire holders tilted at just the right angle to hold a doll straight. The loop at the top spreads to fit either slender or chubby dolls, and may also be adjusted for dolls of different heights. The stands are painted brown, a good color because it blends into most backgrounds.

A background may consist of the various types mentioned earlier, or may be a variation of a screen, folded in thirds or halves, which can be placed in back of a doll when desired.

Another method of displaying dolls is to make them a part of a diorama. The difference between shadow boxes and dioramas is that a shadow box is most often made to be opened, while a diorama is usually sealed. Collectors of dolls should not neglect the possibilities of dioramas, for they offer not only the maximum amount of protection for dolls, but also a chance to place them in dramatic and realistic settings.

A few rules govern the making of dioramas, most of which involve the illusion of perspective, or a background with depth. One way to create the effect of distance is never to permit the bottom of the scene (the floor) to meet the backdrop directly. Camouflage this meeting point with shrubbery, a wall, the side of a building, or some other detail. Following the rule of artists, not only the size of an object diminishes with distance, but so do color, tones, clarity, and placement in relationship to the foreground.

The armed forces have for a long time made use of dioramas in their training programs, and during World War II developed several simple methods of making terrain models. Many of the same techniques can be used in building settings for dioramas used for doll display.

It is suggested that the first step in construction should be the creation of a firm base on which the scene may be built. This may be the plywood floor of the diorama case, which is covered with layers of cardboard or tightly wadded paper, then surfaced with a filler on which a final texturing material is placed.

Papier-mâché made of paper pulp and paste may be used for this filler, or an even more simple variation of it, which is both inexpensive and easy to handle. This is made by tearing, not cutting, newspapers or paper toweling into pieces about one or two inches square. Dip these pieces into liquid starch, then press them down on the foundation. Any number of layers may be used until the contour is satisfactory. Dry for several days before coloring.

The Navy devised a kind of dough for their dioramas, and the formula follows: "Take ¼ pint library paste mixed with enough water to make it the consistency of a thin batter. Add one pint plaster of Paris and 1 pint ordinary sawdust. Knead the mixture until it is like tough dough. Mold it in place directly on the foundation. The setting time is about fifteen minutes, so work rather quickly. Apply texturing material while the dough is still damp, and press into the surface. Sand, earth, coffee grounds, moss, excelsior, cinders, filings, or almost any substance may be used for texturing material."

As soon as the dough is thoroughly dry it may be painted. It is better to use tempera (poster paint), casein paint, or watercolors for this than to use an oil paint, for the former will dry with a dull surface and appear more natural. Tone the raw colors with a touch of raw umber to give the scenery a more realistic look. Also, remember that far-distant objects are less clear and often more gray than those closer by. As soon as the scene is dry, fasten the dolls in place and add whatever stage props are required to complete the effect.

The diagram shows a practical diorama case designed for the Visual Aids Department of schools in San Diego, California, whose use of dolls will be described more fully a little later. The cases are made of plywood, painted, and built with a handle on top. The backs are hinged, so the scenes may be changed or the dolls removed. A curved piece of clear plastic at

Interior of San Diego schools' storage and display case holds dolls upright on wooden slide-out bases. Full history of these Russian peasant dolls from Valcov, with descriptions of locality, its main industry, and origin of the costumes, is fastened inside lid.

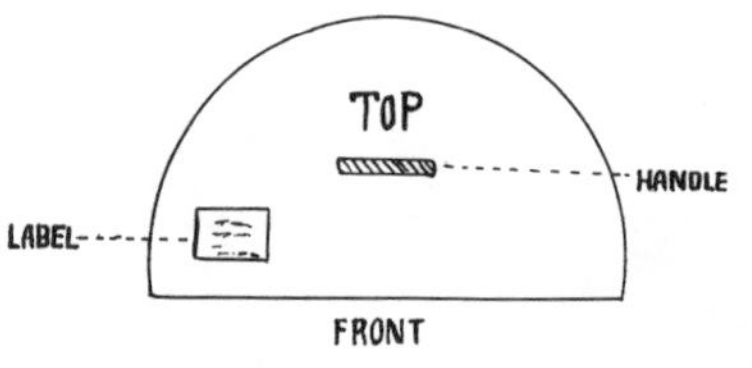

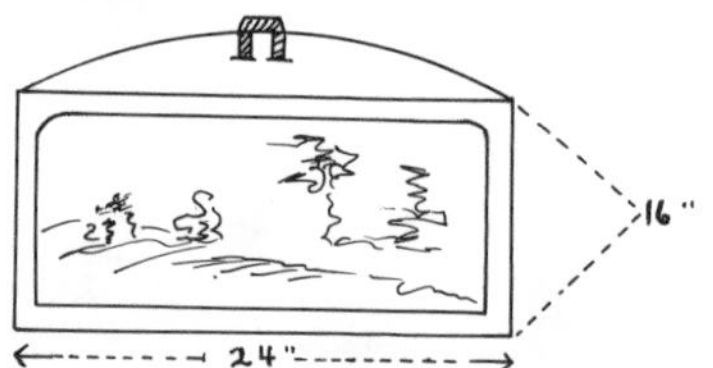

Portable diorama, designed by Sven Petersen, is used in Visual Aids Department of schools in San Diego. Case is plywood with handle and space for label on top and flexible plastic window in front.

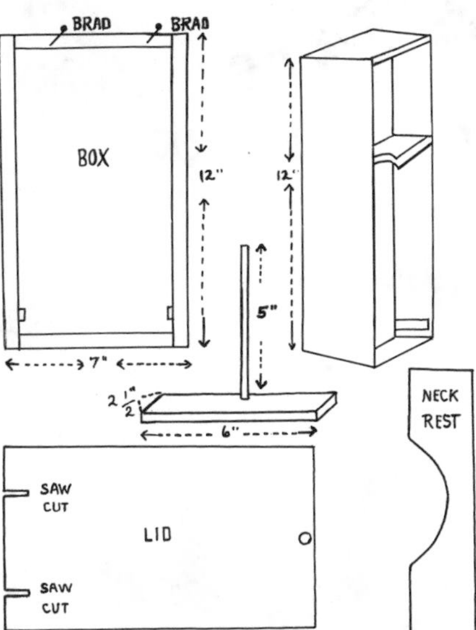

Hungarian bride doll in case, showing guide strips which hold the base in place. A lid with slots is held by the two brads on top front.

Construction details for making display case. Size is determined by height of dolls. Plywood is material used.

the front protects the contents. Such cases are well adapted to the display of small dolls, particularly for collectors, lecturers, and teachers who use traveling exhibits.

Another type of construction used by the San Diego schools which is of interest to doll collectors, is the wooden storage and display case which is used for an individual or group of dolls. It is so simple that almost any home carpenter would have no difficulty in duplicating it. The doll, standing erect, is supported by a wooden dowel fastened to a wooden base. This base slips under two guide strips near the bottom of a plywood case. A piece of plywood, cut in a curve, is glued inside the box where it will serve as a rest for the doll's neck. The lid in the top edge of which two slits are cut, is simply a flat piece of plywood. Two brads driven part way into the top

Homemade German "pyramid" is made of three wooden discs supported by columns and is bordered with candles. Large metal fin hung above it turns from the heat of the candles and causes pyramid to rotate. Dozens of small dolls can be displayed both on and around pyramid.

of the box fit into these slits and hold the lid in place. A flat hook fastener in the opposite end of the lid secures it. This arrangement is more effective than hinges would be, for it permits the complete removal of the lid, while the doll may either be left inside the case, or removed on its stand.

All information about the doll: age, origin, materials used in its construction, place of manufacture, former owners, unusual and pertinent facts about it, are entered on a card which is fastened inside the case. These same facts are entered on filing cards, which are used in the same way that library cards are used.

Special occasions and holidays offer endless opportunities for doll collectors to share and display their dolls. Christmas is perhaps the holiday most often associated with dolls. In Chapter 2 we described the use of Christmas crèches or nativity scenes, but there are other traditional ways to display dolls. A German friend, whose childhood was spent near the city of Chemnitz, in Saxony, has built what he translates as a "pyramid" which he brings out every year just before Christmas. This substitute for a Christmas tree is as nearly as possible like the one he remembers from his boyhood, and is of value to doll collectors, because so many small dolls are used on and around it—something hard to do effectively.

The pyramid itself is made of three plywood discs, supported by pieces of large wooden doweling. Metal candle holders are fastened to the outside edges of the two top discs. The entire pyramid is placed on a delicately balanced shaft so that it will turn at the slightest touch. The motive power comes when candles are placed in the holders and lighted. Their heat turns the fins of a metal fan suspended from the ceiling, and this makes the pyramid turn slowly. This of course is the same principle which operates the Swedish brass "angel chimes."

Small dolls and animal figures are grouped on and around the pyramid, and new ones are added each year, so that now there are dozens of them. There are miniature houses, trees, pieces of furniture, and tiny ornaments. The two shelves which hold the candles are devoted to the display of angels of wax, china, and bisque. Many of the wax angels are the small ornamental candles to be found in the stores at Christmas. There are so many dolls and ornaments, in fact, that it takes several days to unpack and arrange them each year.

The owner of the pyramid gets his greatest pleasure from sharing it with everyone in the small town where he lives, and when the word goes out that "the Georgi pyramid is up," children and grownups appear, the candles are lighted, and the tree begins to turn.

On a smaller scale by using the turntable of an old record player as a setting for small dolls dressed for special occasions a rotating table centerpiece could be made. Dolls may be used this way for birthdays, wedding anniversaries, Christmas, Easter, Thanksgiving, Columbus Day, Veterans' Day, and the Fourth of July. When set for a slow speed, and possibly connected with a music box or other musical device, displays of this kind always appeal to people who may never previously have been attracted to dolls.

Others countries have their traditional uses for dolls, and among the most famous are the Japanese observances of the

Doll Festival, *Ohina Matsuri.* Maretta Clough Wilcox, owner of the Doll and Toy Museum in Bergen, New York, describes the correct way to arrange dolls for this celebration, which is always held on the third day of the third month. (The Boys' Doll Festival is called *Tango-No-Sekku,* and takes place on the fifth day of the fifth month.) Mrs. Wilcox explains that the word "Festival" is applied not only to the day itself, but to the collection of dolls and furniture used. Although these Festivals may include ancient heirloom dolls, the dolls are mainly purchased by a family when its first daughter is born. Other dolls are added with the birth of each additional daughter.

An exact ritual is followed in the observance of the Doll Festival. A few days before March 3, a seven-tiered stand is placed in the family's best room, and is covered with a red cloth, symbolizing childhood. Each tier is decorated as a unit, according to tradition. On the highest shelf, a miniature gold-leaf screen, almost the width of the shelf, is placed. It forms a background for the two figures placed in front of it. These represent either the Emperor and Empress, or a pair of *dairi-bina* (exalted court personages). A tall handmade silk lantern stands at each end of the shelf, and between the two figures there is a low tea table with vases of cherry blossoms, a tea service, and a symbolic bowl of rice.

The next tier of the stand is occupied by three dolls representing ladies-in-waiting ready to serve her Royal Highness. Two of the dolls wear red kimonos, and the third, a white one. With them is their worktable with lacquered dishes and a brazier for cooking. The third shelf holds five little musicians or entertainers. At one end there is a young man; at the other is an old man. One carries weapons, the other a scroll, representing both military and civil authority. The fourth and fifth tiers display figures of servants and attendants and their furniture and implements. At the end of the fifth tier on the right, stands a small square pot holding a miniature blooming cherry tree two tiers high. A similar pot, holding a fruiting orange tree of the same size, is placed at the left end of the tier.

The two lowest tiers hold pieces of miniature furniture, and little tables covered with dishes of rice cakes, sweetened white sake, and food to be offered the exalted personages on the top shelf. Gifts brought by friends are also placed there, for guests of the family have been invited to come in and see the Festival. This is all considered to be a "virtue of the day" when mothers instruct their daughters of the shopping to be done, preparation and serving of the food, and the greeting of guests so that they may learn to be gracious hostesses.

The ceremony is carried on for three days. Each evening, grownups meet with the children and tell stories of the exploits of their ancestors, so they may learn them and in time pass them on to their own children. At the end of the three-day Doll Festival ceremony, the dolls are carefully packed in the individual little wooden boxes which fit into a larger box, and are put away until the next year.

While the Festival is primarily for children, adults participate almost equally. It is inevitable that students of folkways will compare certain features of the Doll Festival with the Hopi Indian kachina traditions, for both form ties between generations past and present in similar fashion, and help perpetuate, without written words, the most ancient customs of a race. Once again, we have proof that dolls can be more than toys.

Most of the foregoing information is related to displaying and creating settings for dolls which a collector wishes to keep in the home. There are people other than your friends, however, who can share in your hobby of doll collecting. By participating in community events, a collector can reach many of them. Local doll contests, often sponsored by clubs or church groups, which award prizes for different categories of dolls are certain to create interest. It is a good idea to stress the fact that there are many men who are also doll collectors, and not to limit attention solely to women and girls. In fact, if one award in the show were to be for toy soldiers or mechanical toys, little more would be needed to encourage masculine interest. Church organizations are favorite patrons of foreign dolls, and when members include people born in other countries, it is often possible to assemble an entire show within the church itself.

Many dolls collectors combine a natural or cultivated talent for public speaking with their hobby, and with some of their appealing dolls, are always in demand for public appearances before clubs. Girl Scouts, Campfire Girls and Y.W.C.A. chapters are only a few of the groups which welcome speakers on the subject. They are also often anxious to learn something of dollmaking as well as collecting, and anyone who can speak with authority on both subjects is doubly sought after.

While many doll collections are accompanied by the personal collector at public appearances, many times a collection is loaned—perhaps for a public display to public libraries, schools, and museums. These institutions have the opportunity of not only *filling* needs, but of *creating* them. Indeed, nothing that can be said about the advantages of displaying dolls, cannot also be said about their public appearance. To what better use can a doll be put than to entice non-readers, visually-minded students, or museum browsers to become conscious of the fascination of the past and present.

Almost every library has at some time been given a collection of valuable dolls. When there is a shortage of display space the dolls must be stored, and sometimes they are almost forgotten. It is worthwhile for a collector to ask at the desk about the existence of such stored collections, for they often include rare dolls one may wish to examine. However, libraries do often display dolls to advantage in connection with books. Children's departments often show entire or partial collections of dolls, and there is no reason why adult sections should not do the same. Biographies, histories, plays, novels, may all be frequently displayed in the company of appropriate dolls.

"Seeing, hearing, looking, and listening are major ways and means by which human beings learn. Helps to looking and listening make the whole world a real audience for events occurring in all corners of the globe." These words are in the audio-visual handbook written by Wittich and Schuller, and used by the Instructional Aids Department of the San Diego, California city schools. This school system is only one of the many throughout the nation to establish such departments, and to bring its own audio-visual aid exhibits into history, social studies, and geography classes.

The San Diego Visual Aids Department occupies a large part of the city Educational Center, and from it, over 140,000 students, attending more than 150 primary and secondary schools, are supplied with the use of almost 11,000 items. These include educational motion picture films, 35mm film strips, 78, 45, and 33⅓ recordings, study and art prints, and nearly a thousand exhibits, models, and dioramas. It is these exhibits and dioramas which particularly appeal to doll collectors, for they consist of many outstanding and beautiful dolls of all nations which have been presented to the department, and whose display can be adapted to private collections.

When not in use, the cases containing the dolls and the dioramas owned by the department are stored on shelves. When a teacher requests the use of a specific doll or diorama, the case is removed, its index card is marked, and delivery is made to the school by a Center truck which makes regular deliveries and pickups each week. A teacher's request for the use of a doll or diorama is an indication that her class is studying a country, a region, or an event. There are dolls from all countries—many of them from countries like China and the European satellites, now closed to trade with the western world. There are dioramas which show pre-Revolutionary families in their homes, pioneers building log cabins, Gutenberg engaged in printing a book, even cavemen fighting sabre-tooth tigers. Many of the diorama figures are small dolls and of course, most of them *could* be dolls.

The educational value of exhibits like these is obvious, for it is much easier to see, than it is to imagine, the way people dressed or how they lived. Also it is true that the thorough research involved in creating a genuinely worthwhile diorama is of benefit to its builder as well as its audience. It is impossible to build a scene authentically without studying all the elements involved. A diorama should therefore only be attempted by someone who enjoys prolonged research and who has the patience to execute minute details.

The habitat groups found in museums are actually life size forms of the portable dioramas we have been discussing. Museums also have made use of adaptations of the diorama idea for a great number of years, so we have all been exposed to visual education, perhaps without recognizing it.

The connection between teaching, museums, and dolls, is

illustrated in the operations of New York City's Traphagen School of Fashion, founded in 1923 by Ethel Traphagen. Her philosophy was that the more a student knows about the history of fashion, and the more he or she absorbs the actual fashions of the past, the better qualified that student will be to design today's clothes—the primary purpose of the school.

The school owns about 1000 of the most carefully costumed dolls, used for costume research and as inspiration for modern design. All of these dolls are dressed in costumes in proper scale, entirely authentic in every detail. The three-dimensional figures are considered by the school to be preferable to pictures, as teaching aids. Traphagen's Museum also includes actual costumes, covering period fashions of the eighteenth, nineteenth, and twentieth centuries; regional costumes from around the world; and accessories such as jewels, fans, shawls, hats, shoes, lingerie. It is noteworthy that some of the full-size costumes in the collection and the miniature dresses of the dolls are almost identical.

Traphagen owns a graphic traveling exhibit of fashion, which it loans free to teachers, schools, libraries, colleges, and museums. It also holds numerous exhibits of dolls and fashions. One of these was the group of eighty dolls sent to the New York World's Fair in 1964–5 and displayed in the Doll Collections Museum Theatre. The group was in three divisions: pairs of male and female peasant dolls in regional costumes from around the world, authentic in every detail; small boys and girls of 1775 to 1932 who might have stepped out of the paintings of Gainsborough, Romney, and Raeburn, and famous novels of the past; and, thirdly, famous actresses—Lily Langtry, Sarah Bernhardt, Anna Held, Elsie Janis, Eva Le Gallienne, Katharine Cornell, and many others.

In addition to other activities appealing to doll collectors, Traphagen publishes a biannual magazine full of accurate and varied articles and pictures related to dolls and fashions, and often containing ideas for displaying the dolls in private collections.

As mentioned in detail in earlier chapters, almost all museums throughout the country have doll collections, which have often been helpful to doll collectors in their search for information. This suggests a question: "What shall I do with my doll collection when I am through with it?" Our best advice is to enjoy your dolls always, and make sure that when you are gone they will pass to a museum, or some other collector, who will enjoy them. Storage in a museum basement is better than throwing your dolls in a trash can. Sending them to a salvage shop may make a scavenger happy, but it is hardly fair to serious collectors.

21

DOLLS OF TODAY

ALMOST EVERY doll collector is like the well known man who could have bought the corner of First and Main Streets thirty years ago for a dollar a front foot—but didn't. "If she'd only known," the collector says, "Grandma could have bought a dozen Parians just as good as *that* one, for less than a dollar!" Or, "Why didn't someone make me take care of that homely baby doll I had when I was six? I loved it, and it was a Bye-Lo baby."

Perhaps the collector didn't realize thirty years ago that there would ever be doll collectors, but is well aware *now* of some of the things all collectors should remember. Once the habit of collecting is established, for example, there is no excuse for permitting good things to escape. One should look around today and decide what is so good that it will be even better in twenty, thirty, or forty years. A first edition Raggedy Ann doll would be fifty years old today, but she would have greater value in both sentiment and dollar terms than identical ones that can be bought in a modern department store.

It's been several generations since manufacturers went about the business of making dolls in a relaxed way. For a long time they have been asking themselves, "What's new? What's different? How can I meet competition?" It's been some time since a little girl simply asked for "a doll," and not a "Lambie Love," a "Minka Marie," or a complete wardrobe for a Barbie's Caribbean cruise.

What has happened? Where are the little girls who dressed their dolls in homemade clothes that were kept in an old shoe box? They have grown up to become doll collectors, and their daughters and granddaughters live in a world full of plastic dolls with real-life wardrobes. These twentieth century fashion dolls mark a new trend in dollmaking, and demonstrate the effectiveness of mass production and modern advertising; but they also prove that dolls have a universal appeal, which is anything but modern.

Of all the American dollmakers struggling in a fiercely competitive market, the number one company is Mattel, Inc., of California. The company is a whole new world away from the toymakers of Nuremberg or the tinkering Yankees of Vermont. Every operation of Mattel's research and development department, directed by Jack Ryan, a former missile engineer, is carried on behind locked doors. Visitors are carefully screened, and it is virtually impossible for anyone not directly concerned with the section to obtain entrance. Everything Mattel does is on the same scale—the biggest, the newest, the fastest. It is, therefore, hardly strange that Mattel's Barbie doll is the largest-selling doll in the history of the industry, with total sales amounting to millions.

Barbie is a long-legged teenage doll, 11½-inches high, with jointed neck, shoulders and hips. She is made of hard plastic and her rooted Saran hair is made in a choice of blond, ash blond, platinum, brunet, and red. The doll was designed by Ruth Handler, one of Mattel's founders, who is the company's vice president. Her husband, Elliott, is president.

Barbie was created about a dozen years ago for Mrs. Handler's daughter, who liked to pretend that her dolls were teenagers and to make clothes for them. After much research by Mattel, Barbie went into production. In order to meet the competition of cheap plastic dolls made in Japan, and in a way joining her opposition, Barbie was originally made, and continues to be produced in Japan. The difference in production costs between Japanese and American labor is large enough to make the difference between profit and loss.

Barbie's boy friend, Ken, was introduced in 1961 as a doll "first"—a male fashion doll. More than a million were made the first year. Barbie's girl friend Midge was the next to join the group. Her clothes and Barbie's are interchangeable.

Barbie's little sister Skipper, a pre-teenager, and Ken's buddie Allen were added to the line in 1964. Another version of Barbie, with three separate and glamorous wigs, came out the same year. She was called the Fashion Queen Barbie. The wigs were a reflection of the craze for wearing wigs. Since a popular trend of that kind is often short-lived, this doll might be a good one for collectors to acquire. In a few years, after the fashion wanes, a doll with changeable wigs would be of greater significance in a doll collection than an ordinary doll would be.

The device really responsible for Barbie's financial boom has been the sale of costumes and accessories for these dolls. It is said that Mattel produces more articles of apparel for dolls than any of the nation's clothing manufacturers make for people. It would be wearisome to list the dozens of dresses,

The Million Dollar Family. *Left to right:* Skipper, Barbie, Allen, Barbie, Ken and Midge.

Courtesy, Mattel, Inc.

ensembles, "fashions paks," theater costumes, travel costumes, sport costumes, and assortments of accessories (including everything from sunglasses to roller skates) that are made for these dolls. A recent addition to Barbie items, is her miniature plush poodle whose accessories are listed as: a velvet and corduroy jacket, net tutu, hat, mask, ear muffs, collar and chain, dog food bowl, and a bone.

Fashions change, and with them doll fashions, but in addition to clothes, Barbie has other possessions. There are sets of furniture for her "Dream House"—inside, and on the patio. There is a little theater which folds into a compact carrying case, and is designed to give Barbie, Ken, Skipper, Allen, and Midge, and future members of the family, a place to stage plays and wear their theater costumes. The set includes a booklet with the scripts of seven different plays, and all the props and scenery needed for them. Barbie not only has her "Dream House," but also a fashion shop where she can hang still more dresses. The establishment has a modeling stage, a waiting room for customers, and a mannequin with movable arms.

New sets of furniture for the "Dream House" were put on the market in time for the 1965–66 season, as was Barbie's Dream Kitchen-Dinette, Skipper's Dream Room, Barbie's Campus (and campus wardrobe), in addition to a deluge of new costumes and accessories. Barbie games, *Keys to Fame*, and *Queen of the Prom*, are designed to be played by two to six children in the six to twelve age group. By simply turning a crank, anyone can play Barbie's "Ge-Tar" which is fitted with a patented musical unit, has nylon strings, and an adjustable carrying cord.

Many of these products are made by companies franchised by Mattel. There are books, a book club whose membership receives a new Barbie book each month, a magazine (subscription 25 cents a copy to members of the official National Barbie Fan Club, which encourages members to mail in fan letters). The makers of McCall patterns hold a franchise for the patterns of Barbie clothes so that anyone who wishes to sew may make the garments at home. Needlework magazines often print patterns and instructions for making Barbie clothes, particularly knitted ones.

The Mattel identifying wrist tag is attached to each doll. From a collectors point of view, this is not good, for a paper label is easily lost. If you purchase a Barbie doll for your collection, be sure not to remove the label, for as we have mentioned before, a doll without a mark is generally less valuable than one with its original label.

No one knows how well the plastic material used for these dolls will withstand time and use. Will it crack or fade? Will it soften and disintegrate? Not even laboratory tests can answer these questions. As far as construction is concerned, the jointed heads and arms prove to be well designed. In fact, rough handling by a three-year-old of our acquaintance has failed to damage her Barbie—even the hair is intact, after a year's tousling.

Another Mattel innovation was Chatty Cathy, introduced in 1960. Her voice mechanism was designed by Jack Ryan. Instead of speaking only a single word, as dolls have been doing for a great many years, Chatty is able to say eighteen different things at random—and without batteries. She is 20-inches high and has a movable head, arms, and legs. She also is provided with costumes galore, and her rooted Saran hair can be brushed and combed.

Shrinkin' Violette was the 1964 introduction to the Mattel talking doll family. She is 12-inches tall, and has a soft body and yellow yarn hair. At first she appears to be just another rag doll, but she is more than that—when her speaking ring is pulled, her mouth actually moves and her eyelids flutter. She speaks eleven different phrases, and will sit alone.

Baby Pattaburp is another recent introduction. She is 16-inches high and has rooted synthetic hair. She has her own special feeding bottle; the milk disappears when she is fed, then magically reappears. Placed over your shoulder and patted, she burps realistically, not once but twice.

Charmin' Chatty is Mattel's "educated doll," certainly a triumph of mechanization, for she comes with five records of ten sides, containing a total of 120 different sayings. The records are inserted in a slot in the doll's left side. This 24-inch doll is made like most of the other Mattel dolls, with movable head, arms, and legs. Her hair, either blond or brunet, can be

Chatty Cathy, the popular talking doll, appears here in her nursery school dress.

Courtesy, Mattel, Inc.

Vogue Dolls offers a full line of quality Negro dolls in three sizes.

Courtesy, Vogue Dolls, Inc.

brushed and combed. Her eyes open and close, and she wears little plastic eyeglasses which give her a studious look. There are other play and costume sets available for her, and one set of costumes of different foreign lands is accompanied by records which speak in French, German, Italian, Spanish, Russian, Japanese, and English—and a British accent, too.

Chatty Baby can babytalk, cry and laugh. When her speaking ring is pulled she is able to make eighteen different expressions at random. There are no batteries. She is 18-inches tall and has a typical baby face.

Tiny Chatty Baby and Tiny Chatty Brother are 15 inches, similar in materials to the larger Chatty Baby, except that Tiny Chatty is also made as a Negro baby. She speaks as fluently as her larger sister.

Completing this overpowering array of accomplished dolls, Mattel's singin', swingin' Scooba-Doo may have some future historical value for collectors and language students. Her vocabulary consists of far-out remarks like, "Play it cool—Don't be a square," and "Hey, doll—like you're way out." She is 23-inches high, has a soft, stuffed body, and wears a denim shift.

In addition to all these plastic and cloth-bodied dolls, Mattel's make paper dolls. Chatty Cathy, for example, is about 9-inches high and is printed in color on stiff cardboard. There are forty-five costumes and accessories printed in color on thinner paper, ready to cut out. The entire kit is packaged in a sturdy cardboard tote bag—a practical feature, making it easy to store. Because paper dolls are more expendable than plastic ones, it is safe to say that in a few years these currently inexpensive printed paper dolls will be more valuable than some of the others.

This story of the Mattel company shows why many other doll manufacturers offer a teenage doll to challenge Barbie, a preteenager to compete with Skipper, and at the same time introduce their own novelties.

Vogue Dolls, Inc., is one example of modern dollmaking. Incorporated in Malden, Massachusetts, the company has been making dolls and dolls' clothing for more than fifty years. The history of the company is largely the story of Mrs. Jennie H. Graves. She began by making doll clothes as a hobby, first for

Jan is another of the popular teenage fashion dolls with interchangeable wardrobe.

Courtesy, Vogue Dolls, Inc.

Baby Dear has set-in eyes and soft, flexible body.

Courtesy, Vogue Dolls, Inc.

friends and neighbors, then for church and charity bazaars, and finally for a Boston department store. When her first large order came, she went out and solicited the help of her neighbors to cut and sew the clothes. From these few helpers came the force of more than 700 New England women who make the doll clothes today.

'Jama Baby is a doll combining several functions—pajama holder, sleepytime companion, and bed decoration.

Courtesy, Vogue Dolls, Inc.

Madame Alexander baby doll has set-in eyes and blond hair and is modeled in beautifully colored plastic.

Courtesy, Alexander Doll Co., Inc.

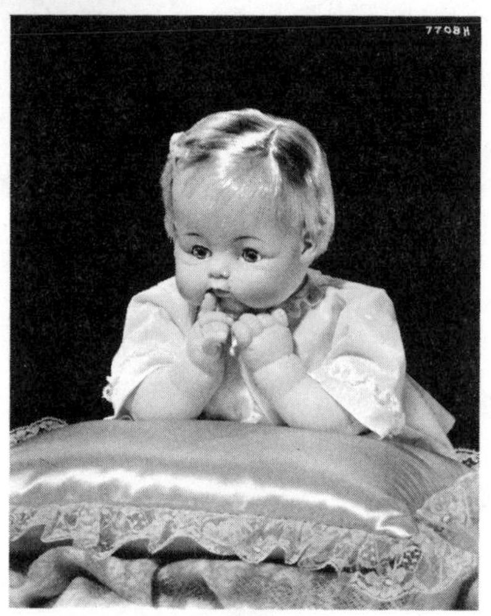

With the coming of World War II, Mrs. Graves was no longer able to import the dolls she dressed from Germany, so she began to buy from the American manufacturers who were just beginning to do this kind of work. It was shortly after the war, in the 1940's, that she struck upon the idea of designing her own dolls and sub-contracting their production to American doll manufacturers. The first of these was little Ginny, the pre-teenage doll named for Mrs. Graves' oldest daughter, Mrs. Virginia Carlson, who had by that time finished her study in a school of designing, and was creating doll clothes, as she does today.

Vogue Dolls has one of the few, if not the only complete lines of quality Negro dolls: drink-and-wet infant Ginnette, pre-teenage Li'l Imp, toddler-age Ginny Baby. Ginnette is made only in the 8-inch size; Li'l Imp in only the 11-inch, while Ginny Baby is in 8-inch, 12-inch, 16-inch, and 18-inch sizes. These Negro dolls are the same in every way, except coloring, as Vogue's regular line and bear the same names.

Another doll made by Vogue is the company's answer to Barbie—teenage Jan. The same clothes, in fact, may be worn by either doll. She has sleeping eyes and rooted hair. Baby Dear is an attractive soft-bodied baby doll with the floppy limbs that children like. This doll also has sleeping eyes and rooted hair as do the other soft-bodied dolls, Li'l Dear, Bunny Hug, and 'Jama Baby. This latter doll is a combination of a cuddly bedtime toy and pajama holder, which can also be used as a daytime bed decoration. Vogue's 1964 introduction was Posie Pixie, unusual because its body is made of flexible molded foam which is soft, yet may be placed in any position. This doll demonstrates the fact that there is still a demand for soft-bodied dolls. In fact, the difference between a homemade rag doll and Posie Pixie is only superficial.

One of America's most outstanding doll artists and manufacturers is best known as Madame Alexander. For more than forty years she has headed a firm that employs 600 people in a White Plains, New York plant and a New York City office.

Madame Alexander has created such name dolls as Brenda Starr, the Dionne Quintuplets, the Sonja Henie skating doll, Margaret O'Brien, Judy Garland, and Jane Withers motion picture dolls. The theater and opera have played a large part in Madame Alexander's designs, and she made a group of famous actresses, gowned in the roles of their greatest successes. Doris Keane in "Romance" and Geraldine Farrar in "Carmen" are only two of them.

Possibly Madame Alexander's favorite group of dolls is the one requested by the British government on the occasion of George VI and Queen Elizabeth's visit to South Africa. The three dolls represented Queen Elizabeth, Princess Elizabeth, and Princess Margaret, and they were dressed in silks, satins, and laces trimmed with seed pearls and rhinestones.

A later royal group, which depicts the coronation of Elizabeth II of England, is historically correct to the smallest detail. Madame Alexander's group, valued at more than $25,000, was first exhibited at the Abraham and Straus store in Brooklyn during Coronation Week in May 1953. Then the entire group, consisting of thirty-six figures, was given by Madame Alexander to the Brooklyn Children's Museum, where they are on permanent display. Collectors who wish to see this glittering pageant will find many things to inspire them.

Madame Alexander's baby dolls are distinguished by fine modeling, and lifelike feeling. She will probably be long remembered for her glorification of the American baby and the little girl in pigtails and pinafore.

Among the most popular Alexander child dolls have been her "Little Women," or Meg, Jo, Beth, and Amy, and their mother Marmee, inspired by the famous family in Louisa May

The four girls of *Little Women* and their mother have long been favorites with dollmakers, and these are by Madame Alexander.

Courtesy, Alexander Doll Co., Inc.

Alcott's book. One of the latest additions to the Alexander doll line is the Trapp family group from *The Sound of Music.*

American Character, Inc. has answered the Barbie competition in a slightly different way than any other company. Instead of trying to sell more clothes and ensembles, their doll, Tressy, is directed to appeal to the girl who not only wishes to dress her teenager as her own elder sister dresses, but to style the doll's hair as she would like to wear her own. An advertising slogan used by the company reads: "Then came Tressy, a teen model doll with a lifelike figure, high fashion clothes—and hair that really grows."

Tressy, who was first introduced in 1963, is the same size as Barbie, 11½ inches, and can wear not only her own outfits, but also clothes which fit any other doll of that size. The attraction of the doll therefore is centered on the hairstyling kit, makeup kit, and hair dryer more than on the costumes. The hairstyling kit includes doll-size rollers and curlers, lotion, applicator bottle, atomizer with spray, pins, brush, comb, haircare booklet, and a carryall case. Tressy's own hair-glamour magazine shows special styles created for her by leading American hair stylists. American Character also offers a portable beauty salon for Tressy. In 1965 the body of the doll was changed to give her knees that bend.

Tressy's little sister, 9-inch Cricket, also has hair that grows. These can wear the pre-teenage costumes made for Skipper and the other dolls her size.

Tressy's feminine concern with hairstyle promises her a place in the future. Since curlers, rollers and lotions are replaced to suit changing hairstyles, collectors looking for dolls which will be of historic value, should not ignore Tressy. American Character has made dolls and toys since 1919. In addition to Tressy and her sister, American Character's recent catalog lists 17-inch Tiny Tears—"a kissable, washable, bathable baby doll," that cries real tears, has individual outfits of clothes, and packaged shampoo and soap kits; Teeny Tiny Tears, a 12-inch doll with more clothes, kits, shampoos, and soaps; and Teenie Weenie Tiny Tears, only 9-inches tall, who has a six-way wordrobe, each piece packaged with individual soap tissues and a "Magic" sponge.

Teeny Tiny Tears drinks and wets and can be bathed.

Courtesy, American Character Doll Co.

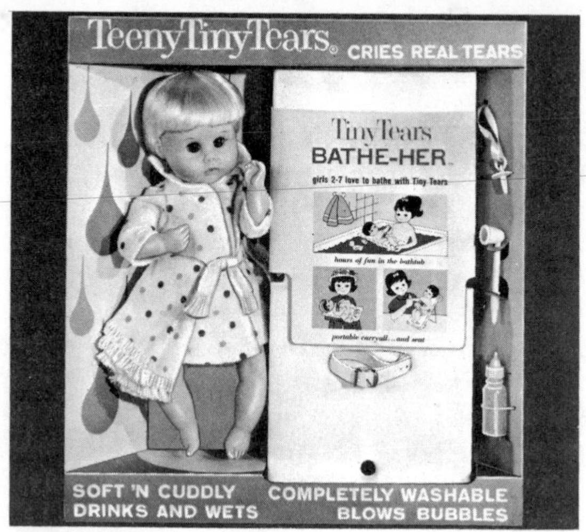

Pepper is Tammy's freckled, snub-nosed nine-year-old sister.

© 1964 The Ideal Toy Corp.

Tammy is regular teenage size, but her figure and appearance give her a younger look.

© 1964 Ideal Toy Corporation.

American Character is doing something of far more importance to collectors, however, by importing top quality lines of European dolls to the United States through its international division. These dolls, beautifully detailed and handcrafted and attractively dressed, are protected by international copyrights in both Europe and America. They look like adorable modern children, and are worthy of comparison with the best pre-war French and German bisques. They are far superior in design and quality to most of the American-made dolls, and while it is impossible to list them all, collectors who are buying with an eye on the future should examine them. Like all imports, these dolls are carefully marked with the name of the manufacturer and the country of origin, but with the possible exception of one or two from Germany, wear costumes and hair styles similar to those of other modern dolls and are not dressed in traditional "foreign costumes."

American Character imports dolls made by three different Italian manufacturers. The first in Italo Cremona, plastic girls made in 16, 17, and 18-inch sizes, with synthetic wigs and moving eyes. It is hard to select a favorite, for they all have wistful childish faces and excellent skin-tones. The second manufacturer from Italy is Ratti and Valenzasca, selling under the firm name of Ratti. These dolls also have synthetic hair and moving eyes, and come in sizes from 13 to 18-inches. The third firm whose dolls are imported by American Character is Luigi Furga and Company under the trade name of Furga, which sends an even larger number to this country. Their dolls include one little blond boy, Feliciano, in a long-sleeved blouse and Continental dress-up style blue velvet trousers and silk cummerbund. He and his sister, Angelica, who has an assortment of clothes of fashionable modern cut, are only 11-inches tall. Other dolls by Furga are from 13½ to 21-inches tall.

In addition to these Italian dolls, American Character also imports a line of French-made dolls. These are sold under the name Poupées Bella. Several are 10 to 13-inch infants; others are modern little girls with plastic bodies and moving eyes, some of them as large as 18 inches.

The dolls of Rheinische Gummi und Celluloid Fabrik are the only German-made dolls imported by American Character.

They are beautifully crafted in a dozen styles. Like the other European dolls just mentioned, most of them are dressed as modern children. However, there are two or three which might be called character types, including a 12-inch tall aged sailor playing a concertina, and Hansel and Gretel in traditional peasant clothes.

Tammy, the teenager, and Pepper, her pre-teen sister, are the Ideal Toy Corporation's additions to the modern fashion doll aggregation. Both have plastic bodies, washable Saran hair, and varied wardrobes appropriate for everything from cheerleading to weddings. Tammy is advertised as the "best dressed doll in the world," and because she is the same size as other teenage dolls, about 12 inches, she can wear the clothes made for any of the others. Pepper is a freckled, snub-nosed little 8-inch doll with sparkle and charm. Her clothes, and she has many, are for the nine-year-old.

It is possible that collectors may wish to concentrate on the various pre-teen dolls rather than on the Barbie age bracket. They are equally well equipped with wardrobes and accessories, and have the advantage of being the size many collectors prefer —8 to 9 inches. Perhaps it is only an illusion, but it sometimes seems as though they have a little more individuality than the doll teenagers.

Tammy's father and mother and brother Ted were brought into the family, and Ideal's slogan for them is, "the best dressed family of dolls in America." This emphasis on dress is of course uppermost in the advertising of almost all teenage dollmakers, for one well-made doll can wear many, many costumes, and when styles change, can be sold an entirely new wardrobe.

Ideal Toy Corporation makes far too many other dolls to list here, but their infant, Tiny Thumbelina, has been an extremely popular doll. This proves that there is still a market for a typical "play doll" with a good plastic body. The newer, "Crying Thumbelina" is made in both 17- and 20-inch sizes; when it is picked up and held upright, its key-wound crying and wriggling will stop.

Based on "The Flintstones," the Ideal Toy Corporation's television network show in 1964, the firm introduced Tiny

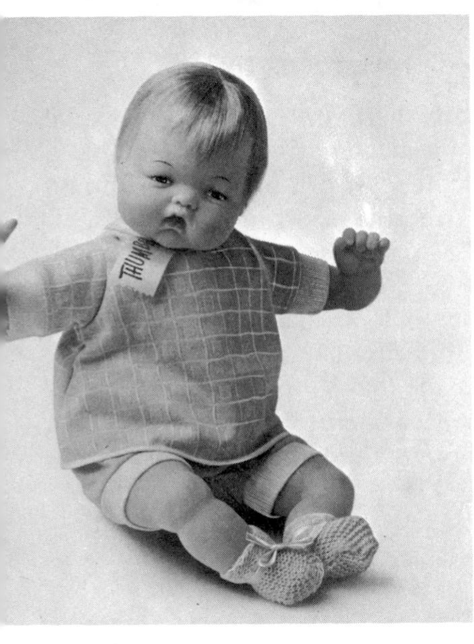

"Crying Thumbelina" is a favorite baby type, with plastic body and Saran hair.

© 1963 Ideal Toy Corp.

Mary Poppins was sculpted to resemble Julie Andrews, star of the Walt Disney film. It is a foot-tall vinyl doll with rooted hair and a wardrobe that includes her wondrous umbrella.

Courtesy, Horsman Dolls, Inc.

Bam-Bam and Tiny Pebbles, with their three-dimensional cave house, a log cradle, and a domesticated dinosaur used as a stroller. These dolls, in spite of their far out names, are among the most natural looking and attractive of all modern dolls.

The Raggedy Ann and Andy dolls, discussed in Chapter 3, are manufactured by the Knickerbocker Toy Company, and are still, after fifty years, made to look exactly like the first ones. Some of them are also being fitted with imported music boxes. Both types are now also made in a 39-inch size with bands on the feet which may be slipped on a child's feet, so the child and the doll may dance together to the sound of music from the doll's built-in music box. The Knickerbocker Company is also making a real old-fashioned 18-inch rag doll with yellow yarn braids and a sweet painted face. There is a larger size as well, fitted with foot-bands like those of the Raggedys so that it may dance with a child.

Certain to become a doll immortal is Horsman Dolls' Mary Poppins. The original Mary Poppins stories, written by P. L. Travers, and first copyrighted in 1934, related the doings of the most beloved nanny in children's literature. The stories as retold by Nancy Fenno, were copyrighted and published in book form for Walt Disney under the title, *The Magic of Mary Poppins.* The Horsman Mary Poppins doll was timed for simultaneous release with the publication of the book and the opening of the Walt Disney motion picture, which starred Julie Andrews as Mary Poppins.

The doll is a 12-inch plastic, sculptured to resemble Miss Andrews. Her rooted hair is fashioned in a bun, and she is dressed like her prototype, from her prim little hat to her high black shoes. Her outfit includes a doll-sized umbrella like the wondrous one described in the story, a magic carpetbag, a lace-trimmed party dress with hat to match, gloves, stockings, and a work dress and apron for every day. Horsman has made a great many other kinds of dolls of outstanding quality through the years, but in making collectors' choices, we nominate this one as our favorite. She not only looks like a doll, but also like a real person. To quote the song—she's "supercalifragilisticexpialidocious!"

There are a great many collectible dolls being made today;

far too many to enumerate in a limited space. It has been possible to suggest only a few of those considered particularly adaptable to the use of collectors. A much larger assortment of beautiful, well made and, probably, equally excellent dolls manufactured by notable firms, have had to be omitted.

There is a final category which may appeal to some collectors. It could be called the "is it or isn't it a doll" group. One example would be the Trolls—plastic figures with large buggy eyes and a shock of hair, which are used as lucky talismen. They are of Scandinavian origin and are made in a variety of styles, dressed in many different kinds of costumes. They may or may not prove to be of more than passing value to collectors of oddities.

At the time of the 1964 national election, Remco Industries, Inc. of Harrison, New Jersey, placed on the market plastic portrait figures representing both candidates for the presidency: Lyndon Johnson and Barry Goldwater. They had movable heads and arms and were designed to stand on any flat surface or the dashboards of automobiles. Their paper packaging carried all the familiar campaign slogans of each candidate, and the figures wore campaign buttons. They are worth collecting for their future historical interest.

These may be the figures which we heard it suggested be treated by the ancient ritual of sticking pins into the candidate one wished to have defeated—a practice inherited from the shadowy side of human history.

Other borderline figures in this category of "is or isn't" are the Cowboy Pete series, also made by Remco. These are sold in sets, together with plastic backgrounds and settings. At about the same time, the Gilbert Manufacturing Co. offered a set of James Bond figures, inspired by the famous spy stories, motion picture, and television characters. These are the kind of topical figures which may some day be classified as rarities.

Other figures of interest are Johnny Hero and G. I. Joe. It is hard to know where to place them, as the manufacturers do not wish to have them called dolls. In at least one mail order catalog for 1965, the year of their introduction, the figures were shown in the section devoted to miniature trains, trucks, and airplanes—far removed from all doll advertising.

Since toy soldiers have been longtime favorites of men and boys all over the western world, as related in Chapter 2—and these come close to being the same thing, on a larger scale—we suggest that doll collectors open a special section of displays made up exclusively of military and sports figures.

Johnny Hero is the All-American Athlete. His uniforms are made in perfect miniature detail to represent all teams and leagues of all American sports.

G. I. Joe is the Action Soldier, Sailor, Marine, parachutist, pilot, deep-sea diver, frogman, etc., which is made by Hassenfeld Bros., Inc., of Pawtucket, R. I. under the trade name, Hasbro. The figures are made in the U. S. of durable plastic and are beautifully crafted, with jointed bodies which can be made to assume and keep the most lifelike positions. Complete uniforms and equipment for all branches of service are available, as well as the materials and instruction for making various settings for displaying the figures. These figures are so sturdy and so accurately clothed and equipped that they are certain to have great historical value, beside their current appeal.

Of the many and varied dolls manufactured today, it is too soon to know which will become the treasures of future collectors, rather than the fads of today. But a look at the history of dolls would indicate that it is the dolls with the rare qualities of warmth and charm that have lasted and become truly great dolls. There have been Raggedy Ann and Andy with their I LOVE YOU hearts; the Bye-Lo Baby, made by a mother who loved babies so much she felt compelled to evoke the emotion in other people; the blue-winged Kewpies who spent their time getting people out of, and not into trouble; Shirley Temple dolls, which looked exactly like the real-life little girl with curly hair and dimples whom no one could resist. But it is the doll that somehow touches the heart that survives the fads and fashions to become a collector's treasure.

BIBLIOGRAPHY

Ackley, Edith Flack, *Dolls to Make for Fun and Profit.* Philadelphia-New York: J. B. Lippincott Co., 1938.

———, *Paper Dolls: Their History and How to Make Them.* New York: J. B. Lippincott Co., 1939.

Baldet, Marcel, *Lead Soldiers and Figurines.* New York: Crown Publishers, 1961.

Bard, Bob, *Making and Collecting Military Miniatures.* New York: Rolton House, 1957.

Blackham, Olive, *Shadow Puppets.* New York: Harper & Brothers, 1960.

Carroll, Lewis, *Alice in Wonderland,* published in *Complete Works of Lewis Carroll.* New York: Random House Inc., 1937.

Christopher, Catherine, *Complete Book of Doll Making and Collecting.* New York: Greystone Press, 1949.

Colton, Harold S., *Hopi Kachina Dolls.* Albuquerque, New Mexico: University of New Mexico Press, rev. ed. 1959.

Costain, Thomas B., *The Three Edwards.* Garden City, N. Y.: Doubleday & Co., Inc., 1958.

Early, Alice K., *English Dolls, Effigies, and Puppets.* London: B. T. Batsford, Ltd., 1955.

Eldridge, Charlotte Blakely, *Godey Lady Doll.* New York: Hastings House, 1953.

Fawcett, Clara Hallard, *A Guide for Collectors.* New York: H. L. Lindquist Pub., 1947.

———, *On Making, Mending and Dressing Dolls.* New York: H. L. Lindquist Pub., 1949.

———, *Paper Dolls: A Guide to Costume.* New York: H. L. Lindquist Pub., 1951.

Fenno, Nancy, *The Magic of Mary Poppins.* Racine, Wisc.: Whitman Publishing Co., 1964.

Field, Eugene, *Poems of Childhood.* New York: Charles Scribner's Sons, 1897.

Fraser, Antonia, *Dolls, Pleasures and Treasures.* New York: G. P. Putnam's Sons, 1963.

Freeman, Ruth, *American Dolls.* Watkins Glen, N. Y.: Century House, 1952.

———, *How to Mend and Dress Old Dolls.* Watkins Glen, N. Y.: Century House, 1960.

Gordon, Lesley, *A Pageant of Dolls.* New York: A. A. Wyn, Inc., 1949.

———, *Peepshow into Paradise.* London: George G. Harrap & Co., Ltd., 1952.

Greene, Vivien, *English Dolls' Houses of the 18th and 19th Centuries.* London: B. T. Batsford, Ltd., 1955.

Hall, Carrie A., *From Hoopskirts to Nudity*. Caldwell, Idaho: The Caxton Printers, Ltd., 1938.

Harris, Henry, *Model Soldiers, Pleasures and Treasures*. New York: G. P. Putnam's Sons, 1962.

Jacobs, Flora Gill, *A History of Dolls' Houses*. New York: Charles Scribner's Sons, 1966.

Johl, Janet Pagter, *Your Dolls and Mine*. New York: H. L. Lindquist Pub., 1952.

Jordan, Nina R., *American Costume Dolls*. New York: Harcourt, Brace & Co., 1941.

———, *Homemade Dolls in Foreign Dress*. New York: Harcourt, Brace & Co., 1939.

Leloir, Maurice, *Dictionnaire du Costume*. Paris: Librairie Gründ, 1951.

McClintock, Inez and Marshall, *Toys in America*. Washington, D. C., Public Affairs Press, 1961.

Ozawa, Satako, *Dolls of Japan*. Tokyo, Japan: Toto Shuppan Co., Ltd., 1957.

Peters, Harry, *Currier and Ives*. Garden City, New York: Doubleday & Co., Inc., 1942.

Roberts, Catherine, *The Real Book About Making Dolls and Doll Clothes*. Garden City, New York: Garden City Books, 1951.

Roe, F. Gordon, *Victorian Furniture*. London: Phoenix House, Ltd., 1952.

St. George, Eleanor, *Old Dolls*. New York: M. Barrows & Co., Inc., 1950.

———, *The Dolls of Yesterday*. New York: Charles Scribner's Sons, 1948.

———, *Dolls of Three Centuries*. New York: Charles Scribner's Sons, 1951.

Travers, P. L., *Mary Poppins*. New York: Harcourt, Brace & World, Inc., 1963.

Trimpey, Alice Kent, *Becky, My First Love*. Baraboo, Wisc., Remington House, 1946.

von Boehn, Max, *Dolls and Puppets*. Boston: Charles T. Branford, Co., 1956.

White, Gwen, *Dolls of the World*. Newton Centre, Mass.: Charles T. Branford Co., 1963.

———, *European and American Dolls*. New York: G. P. Putnam's Sons, 1966.

Young, Helen, *Here Is Your Hobby, Ceramics*. New York: G. P. Putnam's Sons, 1962.

———, *Here Is Your Hobby, Doll Collecting*. New York: G. P. Putnam's Sons, 1964.

Books and Pamphlets
PRIVATELY PUBLISHED

Boston Museum of Fine Arts, *Great Costumes, 1550–1950*. Boston, 1963.

Bullard, Helen, *The American Doll Artist*. Ozone, Tenn., 1965.

Coleman, Elizabeth, *Dolls, Makers and Marks*. 4315 Van Ness St., Washington, D. C., 1965.

Davies, Nina S., *The Jumeau Doll Story*. Translation of book by J. Cusset, printed in Paris in 1885. Published by Nina S. Davies, 1957.

Gerken, Jo Elizabeth, *Wonderful Dolls of Wax*. 1965.

Glover, Ruth Davis, *Repair Dolls*. Cleveland, Ohio, 1960.

Hart, Luella, *Directory of British Dolls*. 145 Monte Cresta Ave., Oakland, Calif., 1964.

———, *Directory of the French Doll, 1801–1964*. 1965.

———, *Directory of German Dolls*. 1964.

———, *Dolls Tell the Story of Brittany*. 1965.

Turner, Marie C. and Grace B., *Peddler Dolls*. Brighton, Mass., 1962.

——— *More Peddler Dolls*. 1964

Wilcox, Maretta Clough, *Dolls, Books and Toys*. 16 Lake St., Bergen, N. Y., 1964.

Wright, Barton, and Evelyn Roat, *This Is a Hopi Kachina*. Museum of Northern Arizona, Flagstaff, Ariz., 1962.

Yearbooks of Doll Collectors of America are obtainable from Kimport Dolls, Independence, Mo.

Stories About Dolls

Bianco, Margery Williams, *The Little Wooden Doll*. New York: The Macmillan Co., 1925.

Burnett, Frances Hodgson, *Racketty Packetty House*. New York: Charles Scribner's Sons, 1961.

Cox, Palmer, *The Brownies: Their Book*. New York: Dover Publications, reprint 1966.

Gates, J. S., *Book of Live Dolls*. Indianapolis: The Bobbs-Merrill Co., Inc., 1945.

Gruelle, Johnny, *Raggedy Ann Stories*. Indianapolis: The Bobbs-Merrill Co., Inc., 1947.

Parrish, Anne, *Floating Island*. New York: Harper & Bros., 1930.

Upton, Florence and Bertha, *Two Dutch Dolls and a Golliwog*. New York: Longmans, 1910.

Publications for Doll Collectors

Antiques, 601 Fifth Ave., New York City.

Doll News, official publication of United Federation of Doll Clubs, Inc.

Doll Talk, Kimport Dolls, Independence, Mo.

Doll World, official publication of International Doll Collectors Clubs, Inc.

Fashion Digest, Traphagen School of Fashion, New York City.

Hobbies, 1006 S. Michigan Ave., Chicago, Ill.

News of Dolls, Doll Questers, 169 Giralda Ave., Coral Gables, Fla.

Spinning Wheel, Hanover, Pa.

The Toy Trader, 2112 Middlefield St., Middletown, Conn.

Incorporated Doll Clubs

National Doll and Toy Collectors Club, Inc.
Gertrude Reinhardt, 1421 Omega St., Elmont, New York.

United Federation of Doll Clubs, Inc.
Mrs. Jean E. Bath, 514 E. Mitchell Ave., Cincinnati, Ohio.

Dolls and Doll Books

Mark Farmer Co., El Cerrito, Calif.
Kimport Dolls, Independence, Mo.
Paul A. Ruddell, Doll Books & Books on Costume.
461 Ben Franklin Station, Washington 4, D. C.
F. A. O. Schwarz
745 Fifth Ave. at 58th St., New York City.

Doll Hospitals and Repair

Clara's Doll Hospital
5911 McClain Lane, Paradise, Calif.
Doll Clinic
769 East St., Dedham, Mass.
Flatbush Doll Shop & Doll Hospital
2247 Church Ave., Brooklyn, N. Y.
Mills Doll Hospital
1623 Avalon Blvd., Wilmington, Calif.

Doll Repair Supplies

Doll Hospital Supplies
(Bessie F. Magee) RFD West St., Middlefield, Conn.
Doll Repair Parts, Inc.
9918 Lorain, Cleveland, Ohio.
Jack's Fixit Service
4235 E. 10th Lane, Hialeah, Fla.
Jack D. Wolfe Co., Inc., ceramic materials, 724 Meeker St., Brooklyn, N. Y.

Doll School

Tokyo Doll School
No. 53, 1- chome, Yoyogi, Shibuya-ku, Tokyo, Japan

INDEX

INDEX

Numerals in italics indicate pages on which illustrations occur.

NOTES

NOTES

NOTES

NOTES

NOTES

NOTES

NOTES

NOTES